THE PLACE IN THE FOREST

R.D. Lawrence's account of life in the Ontario wilderness

The Place in the Forest

R.D. Lawrence's account of life in the Ontario wilderness

R.D. Lawrence

Natural Heritage / Natural History Inc.

The Place in the Forest
by R.D. Lawrence

Published 1998 by Natural Heritage / Natural History Inc.
P.O. Box 95, Station "O", Toronto, Ontario M4A 2M8

Design by Molly Brass
Printed and bound in Canada by Hignell Printing Limited, Winnipeg, Manitoba.

Canadian Cataloguing in Publication Data

Lawrence, R.D. (Ronald Douglas), 1921—
The Place in the Forest

Includes index.
ISBN 1-896219-29-2

1. Zoology – Ontario. 2. Animal behavior. I. Title.
QL791.L3 1997 591.9713 C97-931071-7

Natural Heritage / Natural History Inc. acknowledges the support received for its publishing program from the Canada Council Block Grant Program. We also acknowledge with gratitude the assistance of the Association for the Export of Canadian Books, Ottawa.

Contents

FOREWORD

IN 1954, SOON AFTER MY ARRIVAL in Canada from Europe, I took up a homestead in Ontario's Lake of the Woods, at the time a region where the forests were dense and mammals and birds were plentiful. There, I learned a good deal about the wildlife of the region, but it was not until I found "The Place" in April of 1960 that I became totally committed to the study of Canada's wild ones, as well as to the study of their forestal habitats and of the streams that gave life to all.

Today, reminiscing over the three years during which I studied the fauna and flora of that area, I realize that although I have learned a great deal about the living things that accepted my presence in their domain, I will never be able to learn all that there is to know about the wild ones that inhabit this great, sprawling country that is Canada.

Nevertheless, looking back on "The Place in the Forest", which is the second of twenty-seven books that I have written—all of which deal with wildlife—I find myself somewhat surprised that, by and large, I managed to produce a narrative that did at least some justice to the mammals, the birds, the insects and, unquestionably, the forest that still today exists, although it has been reduced in size by logging during the twenty years since my departure. Although much has changed in my life and in the world since I wrote about The Place, my beloved Joan has passed away and I have lived in other parts of Canada, the richness of this wilderness experience remains intact. Thus the text being presented here remains in original form.

Despite the fact that it was coincidental, it pleased me when "The Place in the Forest" was published in conjunction with Canada's 100th birthday. Today, if my health continues as it has been doing for the past seventy-five years, I will be delighted to see the book enter the 21st century.

R.D. Lawrence
1998

ONE

THERE IS A QUIET IN THE WOODS that comes only once each season. The trees stand naked, waiting. Below their swaying tops the soil weeps for the brown curled objects that are reminders of the fury of last season; of the bite of the frost that sank invisible fangs deep into the crust of the earth. Leaves and grass, shrub and bush, they all died then and now they lie among the skeletal shapes of others like them, relics of past years that still remain, visible, but eroded or rotten, forms of jelly or beautiful shapes wrought by a million microscopic things that used tiny teeth to work a fretwork design on the bodies of the dead.

Some of the life in the woodland, the warm, pulsing life that defies each bitter winter, moves slowly under the trees; birds perch expectantly on branches, waiting. And under the earth in burrows and caves and under rocks, and even packed unconscious between layers of cold soil, other things wait too, and the wind, as though unable to decide on a new role, puffs gently; not cold, not warm, but a hesitant element that feels its way through the labyrinth of timber and twigs and stone and earth. And above all these things the rose fingers of early sunlight thrust upwards over the rim of the land, tinted shafts that promise gentle warmth this day, and the land and all that is in it know this, for there have been many signs during the last week. Slowly the soft snows melted during short sun-days and crusted again at night when the cold returned. But after each day the ice layers became thinner and more shiny and at last only a few stubborn patches of white remained to mark the passing of winter.

This is the first day of spring which is about to happen in the forest. Every year it comes, softly, almost unnoticed during its first hours of life, then, as the sun rises higher into the sky, a new warmth filters downwards and the earth responds to its energy. Almost by magic the small green plants begin to thrust upwards and the sap, the blood of the trees, begins moving in veins that are concealed in branches and trunks and the creatures of the forest feel this awakening and they respond to it, silent and expectant at first, knowing, but waiting for the right moment in which to voice their pleasure.

In a small open place between a red maple and a towering white pine a few shreds of yellow-green grass are risking a look at their awakening world. Nestling between them, parts of it resting on the jaded discards of autumn, there is a small white shape, conspicuous against its sober background; a blade of grass is rising through a cavity that is punched through the blanched object. The cavity once held a round brown eye, and there was flesh and skin and sinew and fur clothing the white thing last year. But now all that remains of the snowshoe hare is the bleached skull, the sites of its nose and eyes and mouth and ears marked by smooth-edged holes; fine dark lines criss-cross the cranium, showing the intricacies of design which Creation worked into the head of the humble forest creature. Looking at these lines one may wonder at the cunning of the power that drew them. See how each section of bone fits perfectly one into the other? Each combines to form a strong case for the brain that lived inside during the lifetime of the hare. And yet, this is but a minor creation of nature. Look again at the small skull and see what is happening around it...the blade of grass growing through it is greener than those which are farther away. Why is this so? And why is it also taller than the other stems? And why, if we look really close, do we see that in this place, immediately around the white bone, there are many tips of green already showing under the cover of the dead leaves and grasses?

It is the secret of life we see happening here, and there are places just like this one all over the forest. Special places, prepared last year by a thousand different things much as a farmer prepared his land for the harvest, and though each worker of the wilderness performed its task in its own way, each had the same purpose, each helped to rebuild the world in which it lives, unconscious one of the other, unaware of its reasons for doing its share, yet co-operating perfectly with its neighbours and combining to form what the scientists call the Ecosystem, that strange partnership of living and non-living things which ensures the survival of the land through death—for even non-living things can die—so that decaying bodies will put new vitality into the soil.

The earth, which is the mother of all things, must be fed. Late one evening last autumn a red fox vixen, alone now that her cubs had grown and left the den, was walking stealthily through the forest. She was hungry. The hare left its form almost at the same time as the fox, for it too was hungry. Hopping away from the rotting stump that had concealed its shape during the hours of light, the hare began to eat. The fox, because she had to first catch her food, went hungry for some time after leaving her den. She stopped often, sniffing at old hare trails, visiting many forms, those places in which the snowshoes take their rest, inspecting each carefully before she went on, patient and silent, her red coat blending perfectly with the dim, sun-splashed light, her back legs nearly invisible against the lower shadows of the woods.

The hare had no need to wander far. It nibbled at grasses and small shrubs, now and then picking at a young fiddle-head fern for the extra moisture these plants contain in their stems, and stopping often to prick up its long ears to listen for the approach of one of its many enemies. But the hare failed to hear the stealthy fox and just as it lowered its head to eat after one of its pauses, the vixen sprang. Death came quickly and easily to the hare. A lightning snap, the lifting of the fox's head, a sudden jerk and the dangling hare was dead, its neck broken. The vixen ate of the hare, sating her hunger, then, pausing only to lick clean her face and paws, she padded away, heading for a nearby stream in search for water.

Much of the hare was eaten by the fox, but there was some of it left; shreds of skin and flesh, pieces of bone that contained calcium and marrow, and the fluid of the body, the blood, which soaked into the ground and began at once to replenish the earth.

Hour by hour, day by day, the life of the forest came and fed off the remains of the hare. Birds flew down and found substance to pick, and rodents, and insects, and the grass and the small wild flowers, and some of the tree roots; all these had a share of the scraps that were left by the fox, until only the bleached skull remained, a marker which showed that here was a replenished piece of soil, that the body of the hare had fed a multitude of creatures and had even managed to give nourishment to the seemingly-lifeless earth.

Strange, shapeless life first began on earth some one billion years ago, a span of time too vast for any of us to imagine; but since its first primitive beginnings in the ooze of a primeval swamp to this very day and year, the unexplained spark of vitality that exists in all things has used amounts of food so vast that if they could be added together they would make the planet earth look like a small melon. And yet matter—the soil, the trees, the water, the plants, the animals and even man—is neither created nor destroyed. Instead it has existed on earth since the beginning of time and it has been used over and over again, year after year, century after century. When the earth was created, matter developed, completed its growth and formed life; since then, the same matter that formed when this planet was born is still in use today. It comes from the earth, goes through many stages of development, rising always higher during each of its many existences and, finally, in a different form, returns to the earth from which it came, there to be recreated and slowly returned to the surface. The process is tireless and as sure as eternity. Yet it is not just one thing that is happening at one time, but many things, happening all the time. And while it continues, the earth shall live. If it ever stops true death will come and there will be nothing, for our planet receives little usable matter from other parts of the universe and it loses hardly any at all into the vastness of space.

χ

I first saw The Place on a warm day in autumn. It was one of those Indian Summer afternoons that are the prelude to cold weather which come, after a taste of frost, both as a warning of what lies ahead and as a promise of what will be when winter is again spent. We had been driving slowly along a country highway in eastern Ontario looking for a piece of property to buy, and we saw the 'for sale' sign, drunken and almost illegible, clinging to a poplar tree by one rusted nail. We stopped to explore and were immediately charmed by an old logging trail that wound gently through heavy stands of mixed timber, its floor littered with russet and brown leaves. At the end of it was a multitude of granite rocks and the beaver lake.

A mass of water lilies, some of them still showing their yellow or white blooms, littered the water. In the centre of the lake was a small rock island and on the island an untidy mound of sticks and mud told of the beaver lodge, a big one. A few late mallard ducks winged up from the water as we appeared and a blue heron *cra-aa-ad* at us at it lifted its ungainly, stilt-like legs and spread its enormous wings. The mallards and the heron flew out of sight and we stood admiring this little piece of wilderness. We looked at one another and we smiled and we both more or less spoke at once. We would buy this land, if we could possibly manage it.

At first The Place represented only an escape from the bustle of city life. It was to be a weekend retreat, a base from which we could take our canoe and go fishing, exploring the meandering Head River and stopping now and then to dip in some of its deep holes, hoping that bass or pike would take our lures. For some time we had no name for our land. Indeed, it has never really been named for its present title just grew. When talking about it my wife, Joan, and I simply referred to it as 'the place', using lower-case inflections to the title and it was not until a friend asked what we called our property that we even thought about naming it. For a time we cast about in our minds for a suitable appellation and then we gave up and continued identifying it vaguely as 'the place'. One day I noticed that both of us were stressing the first letter of each word and The Place it became.

As one weekend followed another and we got to know our property, as the dying leaves of autumn became first dusted and then smothered by snow and as one by one the migrating birds rose to take the skywards south, The Place began to exert a compelling influence upon both of us and its trees and rocks and plants took on almost magical proportions. Not that The Place is much to look at to the uninitiated. To them it is just another piece of forest land, a tangle of evergreens and hardwoods, of shrub and grass; an inanimate part of Canada, which has within its geographic boundaries a million other sections of forest seemingly just like this one. But such a view is held only by those who do not know. We who are aware see The Place with different eyes. There is nothing inanimate here! To be sure, death is a frequent visitor, but so is life, and even during its bleakest times, when obese grey clouds frown upon the area and the wind moans and drives the snow before it, the elements of living are still present, omnipotent and powerful enough to reach out and make themselves felt.

Coming from the teeming egotism of city dwelling a sensitive person must immediately be made aware of influences exerted by this piece of land, though initially it is only a vague sensory awakening that creeps into the bemused mind and nags at the conscious, jogging gently at instincts that have been long buried by the veneer that is civilization. The air is clear and there is a quiet that is not quiet, but which, by its very softness instills a sense of peace and well-being. A small bird sings, invisible in a hazel bush. Somewhere high in a pine a red squirrel scolds the intruder; the aspens whisper, rustling their heart-shaped leaves, murmuring, as they have been doing since the beginning. Above this busy medley the heavy sighs of the pines make sounds that seem to echo the contented yawn of creation. And contrasting with this robust sonata the delicate whirr of a dragon's wings impinges upon the auricular range as the brightly-hued mosquito hunter passes swiftly on wings of lace. Sitting on a downed log a person soon gets to dreaming here. The mind is calm and there is rest in the body of the person who abandons the senses to the peace of this setting.

From the first, The Place puts its mark on those who visit it, but if a person wishes to become close to this land, to become attuned to its vibrations and changes, time and patience and, above all, understanding are needed. The mind must be opened to the moods of the land; there must be kindness in the heart, appreciation in the soul. Fear and the superstitious beliefs that have grown within the framework of civilisation must be cast aside. Days of wandering through the cloistered denseness of The Place must be followed by nights shared with the trees and the living things while the green stars and the moon and the changed sounds of darkness soak deeply into the mind. And these nights, at first, are the hardest to endure, for man has ever feared the darkness and the unknown. Yet without experiencing the night here one cannot know the whole of The Place, for the mood changes with sunset and there are things and quirks of character that are only noticeable during the hours between the two lights.

The wilderness closes in at night. A commonplace spot in daytime becomes a mysterious, aesthetic Eden after dark. Immensity shrinks as vision is lost and sound is magnified so that the organs of sight become secondary senses. A lone man strains to hear in the bush night and his nose, atrophied by centuries of misuse, begins to probe the odours around him. Somewhere close, but beyond the power of sight, a raccoon waddles slowly through the underbrush. At first only the sound of the creature's passage alerts man to the presence of another being, and the sound alone cannot supply recognition. Fear comes then to those unaccustomed to the ways of the wilderness. The old, superstitious fear that has stalked man ever since his intellect exerted itself and began probing for understanding, rushes in and the imagination escapes in panic and the harmless plodding of a small raccoon assumes sinister proportions. Then, instinctively, the nostrils begin to twitch as forgotten senses urge upon the mind the need to decipher the sounds of the night. The pines come first to the mind through the olfactory channels; then, slight at first, a cloying, musky odour travels up the nostrils. It is too strong to be overlooked, now that the nostrils are probing again, too weak to originate from any of the large predators of the bush. The eyes are still useless, but now the mind has something other than sound to classify and soon calm descends upon the neophyte human in the wilderness night.

Following closely upon this calm is interest. The originator of that at first terrifying noise has been identified. There is nothing to fear, and curiosity, man's most helpful ally, takes over. How large is this creature? Where is it going? What will it do? Oblivious now of the imagined phantoms lurking within the underbrush, the mind whirs upon a new tangent. This is a challenge. Man must again prove his superiority. He must pit his intelligence against that of the night prowler; it must be stalked, watched, catalogued, so that its habits will never again be a fearsome mystery.

Thus passes the first night on The Place and in the morning, awakening within the canvas walls of his tent, a person discovers that he is a little richer for the experiences of night. And a little smaller than he thought he was; and a little more humble. And as bright sunshine sparks renewed vitality in the awakening land a new awareness registers on the mind and the low, mournful howl of a timber wolf no longer produces a shudder, and instead interest in the distant hunter awakens in the man and he is impelled to leave his shelter and once more go out into the wilderness. And he is glad, consciously glad, and perhaps for the first time, that he is alive and here, sharing creation with its beings.

Yet man is still the intruder. He is a stranger. It will take time for the wilderness to accept him again as it once did. And some men cannot spare the time and after a short courtship with the wilderness they go back to their own orderly world and perhaps never return. But others have the patience and find the time and they come again and again and slowly the land welcomes them and shares its secrets with them.

Big swollen snows bloated the woods. Overhead the weakened fire of February's sun glanced harmlessly off the ice crystals, filling the wilderness with brightness, but failing to do more than cow a thin layer of the uppermost white ice, and that only in protected places. It was noon and the winter still of middle day lay heavy over the area. Now and then a blue jay flaunted the cold with its screaming, nasal cackle and three grey and white and black chickadees peeped nervously as they searched hungrily for the insects that had not yet come. In the big poplar, beside the scimitar-shaped hemlock, the red-shouldered hawk's nest stood empty save for the topping of snow that filled its stick cavity like a great white egg. Beneath the frozen earth the chipmunks and the groundhogs were sleeping. The turkey vultures, black and bald-headed, were still gliding through summer skies in the southland.

The buck deer, emaciated but preserving well his strength in spite of the winter, stood on the northern flank of a small rocky clearing, an almost circular area of granite upon which only blueberry bushes and sumac and moss could successfully find permanent foothold; other plants grew there, too, but these, like the dwarf pines and the black poplars, were stunted, twisted and sick, for the thin topping of soil was not enough to nourish them. The buck had made a long journey that morning. He had jumped and plodded through six miles of snow country, away from the big pines in which he and the other whitetails in the area had spent most of the winter, to come here and look at his spring and summer range, perhaps hoping to see traces of warmth in this clearing.

Two miles away, towards the north-east, behind the beaver lakes, a big lobo crouched under the lee of a granite upthrust. The rock, tumbled by the forces of ice, was twelve feet high and was eight feet thick; it backed to the north and its sunbathed southerly front was a favourite place of the lobo's. Here the snow was trodden down and there were bones and pieces of animal skin littering the iced surface, remnants of old kills which the timber wolf had carried to this place, tidbits he saved from the ravening jaws of others like him, brought more as playthings than as saters of his hunger. Now and then the wolf stopped gnawing on the thigh bone of a deer and glanced at the sky placidly, but there was an air of expectancy in his eyes.

In the thick, tall pine whose upper branches looked like extended human arms, a porcupine was sitting. It was a female, pregnant from last year and sleepy. Her round, shoe-button eyes were mere slits against the sunlight, her paunch, full now of pine tips and poplar bark, was protuberant.

These and a multitude of other creatures, each doing in its own way what life demanded from it, unknowingly waited on that February day for the slow decline of winter and the germination of another spring. And thus is was with the red squirrels of the forest, the small, active loners who scurry, summer and winter, through the upper pathways of the trees, always busy and inquisitive, alive and anxious, bedding only during the cold months at those time when the weather wears its surliest frown and then only until the fullness of time makes smooth the airwaves and banishes the storm.

If you stand during summer on the highway that passes The Place and you turn your face to the north, you will see before you a rusting page-wire fence that borders a half moon of ageing highway. This is a piece of the old Monk Road, abandoned since the modern thoroughfare was widened and straightened, which was built in the 1800s at a time when peace between the United States and Canada was uneasy. That road was intended to provide a throughway for men and arms in the event of threat from the south. The danger passed, the settlers came and axes bit into the forest and some of the land was cleared and grass was planted and cattle were turned out to graze; and other parts bordering the Monk Road were spared annihilation because great granite boulders and flats filled the earth, swept there when out of the might of evolution the pre-Cambrian Shield of Canada rose to take its place in the history of geology. Through the years man came and harvested the big trees, cutting and slaughtering indiscriminately but never quite able to denude the rocklands. Here they spared an ageing forest giant because the black carpenter ants had already bitten deep into its bowels and hollowed its massive trunk; there a young pine, fresh and healthy and already thirty-feet tall, was still too slender for the sawmill's rip. Over there, in the mouldering tangle of mulched vegetation, the top of a huge pine crashed sixty years ago and the ripened cones with their small, winged seeds remained after the horses and the men had dragged away the dead body of the tree; squirrels and chipmunks found the cones and many of the seeds were eaten. But some fell between the cones and many of the seeds were eaten. But some fell between the browning needles and took root and now there is a cluster of young trees, already as thick around as the body of a man, that grows over the graveyard of their sire. And when a raped tree was unable to reproduce itself in death, the shade area that it maintained in life was banished and the seeds of other species landed there, blown by the winds or dropped by a careless squirrel or carried there in the bowels of a greedy bird to be voided, encased in the waste of avian life which nurtured it through its first growing time. And so this land, which was once peopled only by great pines, is now a range of mixed timber, of spruce and balsam and white pine and red pine, of maple and oak and bass and poplar and birch and of hemlock.

From the page-wire fence and the dying roadway you may at once see the mixed breeds of trees, but if it be summer, you will see little else. Below the trees are the ferns, tall, fanned and dark green, the fiddlehead, or asparagus, variety that conceal many things under their frilled, graceful fronds. Then there are the bushes; the cranberries and the hazels, the vines and pin cherries and the brambles, with their dark red fruits. But, pausing further to study The Place from this view-point, you will notice, despite the concealing wall of trunk and leaf, that the land rises, inclining its plane to the north, slowly, but unmistakably. If you had visited The Place two years ago and penetrated the labyrinth of growth, it is likely that your steps would have been instinctively guided along a narrow game trail that begins across the old highway, on the other side of the ancient drainage ditch, and threads a straight course through a region of deep shadow; on the left a thick stand of hemlocks forms a dense, brown-and-green wall. On the right, created by the axe of man, a straight edge of bush and ferns and poplars stretches to the east, its tangle broken by a few majestic white pines that, somehow, escaped the logger. Following the game trail in a north-easterly direction you would have discovered a thin trickle of water near a patch of poison ivy. This is not a stream, but the overflow of one of several beaver lakes in the area, its waters controlled by the curious creatures that build like no man can. The trail did a sharp right turn here and your face would have been pointing to the birth-place of the sun. On your left a ravine; a low, moist area between ridges of rock and earth in which grow red maples and hemlocks, and pines and poplars and birches and cranberries; it is a fertile ravine, this, kept thus by the water harvested by the beaver and generations of mulching, rotting leaves that fall year after year to nourish the dark earth at this spot. But ahead, due east, the land rises more steeply and the trail turned and twisted several times, once past a round grey rock, again past a low place, near which stands the scimitar-shaped hemlock and the poplar upon the crown of which the hawks nest.

At last the trail breasted the hill and met bare rock studded only by a few gnarled poplars and a scattering of seedling pines; this place is flat, moss-covered in areas. Blueberries and wild strawberries grow well in the sunny soil and there is protection from the winds given by a ring of big pines that border this flat place. The trail is lost for perhaps thirty yards, for the granite will not take impressions, but soon, still continuing east, it is visible again, a five-inch, slight indentation punched by the hoofs of deer and the pads of beasts into the thin coating of earth. Again the land rises, then, abruptly, it flattens upon a table-top plateau of solid granite, bare of all but the tenacious moss. Seen from the air, this plateau is shaped rather like a human kidney and it is some sixty yards long by about half that distance wide. Behind is the first flat, around it are the pines, east of it there is a hollow filled with fine red earth upon which grow a profusion of blueberry plants, their shiny, small, olive leaves clustering around the still-green fruit that face the sky, rotund heads cup-like, as though waiting for the rain to fall into their shallow depressions. Six white pines form a protective half-circle on the north side of this hollow; their sire, a striated colossus whose many rough arms are almost dead, sits just out of the hollow and the carpenter ants which are slowly disembowelling the monarch make busy black lines upon the ground as they endlessly search their neighbourhood for food. Twenty feet from the ground a yellow-white hole in the pine's great trunk is weeping tears of gum and there are yellow, sticky splinters of the tree's body littering the ground, dropped there when the pileated woodpecker, the husky logger of the forest, rammed his powerful beak into the trunk in search of ants and other insects, probing the depth of the hole with his long rapier of a tongue, a serrated weapon used to skewer insects and hold them impaled until they can be withdrawn and swallowed.

Near by stands another pine, almost as large as the wounded patriarch. It too, is suffering from age and the depredations of the carpenter ants and woodpeckers have carved hollows in its body and in one of these, an old wound some two inches in circumference, the brittle points of dry pine needles and the curled, almost pearl-grey fringes of lichen moss peer timidly at the outside.

It is the nest of a red squirrel sow that shows through the hole. She is old, this small dame of the woodland, and she but recently whelped five minute beings that lie snug inside their shelter of moss and leaves and pine needles, and if you had at this time followed the wilderness trail to this place, you would have reached the still-empty site of the small cabin which I was to build here with Joan's help. Before you, and at your back, and to your right and left, the wilderness would stretch, as it does, to infinite horizons. North-east lies the first beaver lake, half a mile distant, and behind it is its twin. East of them is the hamlet of Uphill, four miles away, if you follow the Monk Road; but north, stretching for many changing miles, is the true wilderness, the home of the lobo wolf and the whitetail buck, and of their kindred.

This, then, is The Place, a patch of forest-green welded to the wilderness. It is here that my wife and I came one evening in autumn, and it is here that I came to know the true wilderness, to feel it and sense it, to learn its moods. It is here also that the wilderness and its beings came to know and accept me, watching fully at first; with reservations. Gradually relaxing, testing patience and soul, shaping a newness in the human mind.

χ

When man, with his passion for order and explanation, sets himself to describing the ways of the wild beings, he insists on ascribing certain defined traits of manner, colour, size and similarity which apparently exist in all individuals of the same species. In so far as this is a useful means of generally identifying animals and birds and insect and plants, I will not quarrel with its soundness, but if man is ever to know fully the ways of the wild, he must be prepared to sacrifice this orderly process of reckoning and accept each creature and growing thing on its own value. Too often man applies his convenient yardstick to even his own kind, and he is frequently quite wrong in his assessments. Just as there are cowards and heroes and rogues and gentlemen in the world of man, so these characteristics exist in the world of animals, birds, insects and plants. One creature may be savage, ill-tempered and impatient, exhibiting all the undesirable characteristics of the maladjusted human, while another of his species may be as oppositely gentle as the nicest, most Christian, human grandmother. It is well to remember this, for in the pages that follow these differences in the nature of my beasts will become evident.

Two

On a blustering day in middle of March three years ago the old sow squirrel accepted a mate and was impregnated for the last time with the seeds of life. The snows still blanketed the earth and although there had been two or three warming winds and some of the crystals had melted, still winter lingered that year and in the region of the old squirrel's pine, food was growing scarce. Already the warming sun had signalled to some of the chipmunks, rousing them from their fitful slumbers deep within the earth and these scurrying devourers of seed were busy, on the day of the squirrel's mating, searching out the lost food particles dropped by some of the careless squirrels of the area. Now and then, one of the pastel-stripped 'munks would discover a midden, the food store which all squirrels make near their nesting places, and the agile raiders stole from their distant relatives, sneaking quickly under rock or into rotting tree trunks, there to gobble seed until the capacious cheek pouches were full. And often, in the long days that were to follow, the old squirrel was to go hungry while the microscopic flecks of life that were growing within her feasted unconcerned upon the provisions of creation.

Then came the day, quietly different from all others, when winter turned in flight and the newness of spring descended upon the wilderness. Almost three weeks had elapsed since the mating and the pregnant squirrel had suffered much during that hungry span. Robbed by the chipmunks, her energies sapped by the young in her belly, she emerged from her tree nest on that morning of spring emaciated and ragged, her once glossy fur now dry and brittle, her back with its red-grey colours faded, her white belly hairs yellowed and balding so that her scaly dark skin was visible in several places. Her dugs, four noticeable swellings on each side of her body beginning with the larger breasts low on the belly and ending in small, only-slightly protuberant nipples high on her chest, were already active in the manufacture of the milk that would nourish her brood during the first seven weeks of their life, and this, too, further robbed the mother of her vitality. She was slow and listless on that first day of the new season when she emerged from her nest, but something in the air and in the sun and in the trees around her spoke of the awakening mood of the forest and she responded to it.

She paused on the pine, ten inches from her nest, her tail pointing upwards, close to the bole of the tree, her hind feet, spread with claws of which adhered firmly to the tree trunk. Her black nose quivered as the nostrils tested the air. Her mouth was partly open, revealing the long, slightly orange incisor teeth, worn now, but still chisel sharp, their edges brittle and chipped in places from a lifetime of use on the hard shells of hazel nuts and the rough pulp of wood.

For perhaps half a minute she remained thus, an immobile, indistinct shape twenty feet above the ground, and during this time she scanned her country, using her bulbous eyes—protuberant orbs that projected on either side of her head and allowed her at least partial vision within the radius of a full circle—fixed their keenest focus on the skies above, seeking the shape of predator birds, although this was still too early in the season for the return of the hawks. And while she looked at the heavens, her eyes were still able to distinguish the blurred shapes of the world around her, indistinctly, like a man peering through the fluidity of water, but yet with enough clarity to detect movement below or to the sides. Her rounded ears were also busy. Sounds too faint for human notice reached her small brain, were classified and catalogued, and her nose, so sensitive that it could detect the presence of a tiny maggot hidden within the flesh of a nut, drew in the smells of her country. All this in half a minute. Then she knew it was safe to descend to the ground to seek the nourishment she so badly needed.

The young squirrels were born during the night thirty-eight days after they had been engendered. It was late April and the snows were gone and the grasses were showing their spearheads above last year's leaves and needles. Now there was food; tender fern shoots, and grass and poplar buds. And there were the maples, with their sweet sap and tender skin that needed only a quick nip of the sharp incisor teeth to start a small flood. Everywhere around The Place the young maples wept, for their blood runs fluid in Spring and the squirrels need the vitamin-rich sap to rebuild their depleted energies after the long cold.

The birds were back when the squirrels were born. First had come the crows with their complaining, nasal cra..ahs and their sharp hunger and ruthlessness equalled by few hunters of the wilderness. They came in a large flock, fifty and more, their ebon pinions flashing over the forest as they descended to rest and seek food after their last northward flight. For several weeks yet they would stay together, a screaming band of scavengers for ever on the hunt, but then they would pair off and nest, having performed their mating rituals, fought each other and at last chosen their mates for this year. But while they roamed as a flock they were a constant threat to the small beings of the wilderness. Their beaks, heavy, sharp and black, were always ready to lance into grass snake or frog, or to grasp some careless small bird or squirrel; their round, black eyes, gifted with acute powers of sight, were incessantly searching the woodland.

Ducks, numerous flights of them, had come also with the crows, but unlike the black birds, most of these touched down briefly on the beaver lakes before resuming their flight to the north and the west, to their ancestral pastures. Yet some remained to live on the small lakes for that year and of these many of the older birds were already paired, each partner of last year having survived the threats of hunting and migration. Some there were among the old ones who came alone and these soon found solace with others like them and they prepared their nests, while the young ducks, born on these lakes last summer, began their strange courting rituals.

They were mallards, these ducks, the females mottled brown; inconspicuous birds who watched as the iridescent drakes began their dance. Near one of the beaver lodges, swimming proudly over the dark water, one drake started it. He was large and young, one of last year's brood, a handsome creature, his beak dark green and broad, with a black triangular tip that curved downwards, meeting the lower bill and ending in a slight point. His head was a luminous green-blue that changed shades as he moved it and around his neck was the white collar of his kind, clean and shining as he went through the careful manoeuvres of his dance.

Sitting placidly a little distance from him, bobbing on the gently-heaving waters, his duck watched, but pretended no interest; now she preened one already-pristine flight feather, apparently engrossed in this unnecessary task while her mate shook his curling tail, rocked his body gently up and down and shook his tail once more. Immediately he swam a little way towards the duck and bowed his neck and breast and head, stopped suddenly and was immobile for a flash of time; then he whistled a thin, reedy call and dipped his beak into the water. Withdrawing his bill he tossed his handsome head upwards, releasing the water he had held in his mouth, which showered over him and on to the water around in glistening globules that splattered like drops of rain. Again he remained still for a fraction of time, then he grunted and repeated the movement, again showering himself with droplets of moisture, and, hardly had this settled, he shook his tail again and folded his wings high over his back, showing their light underparts, while his tail, with its twin curled feathers, was also lifted high, its end concealed with the proudly-displayed wings. With that he glanced at the duck and again swam towards her, making his little bow, then as though to doubly impress her, he twisted his head so that his beak was almost pointing skywards and she could see the multi-colour sheen of his head feathers. Then he began again, performing the same movements, in the same order, not adding to omitting one single move, while other drakes around him emulated the dance and the ducks watched, each in her own way.

Two swiftly-gliding shadows passed over the lake while the mallards were dancing for their ducks. It was the hawks, big, rapacious birds gliding easily over the last of the distance that separated them from their nest in the poplar beside the scimitar-shaped hemlock; the nest they had built there three years before, and though they were planing the air waves as they did when hunger sent them in search of prey, they were doing this now more out of habit than need. They had eaten well earlier that morning, dropping swiftly and terribly on two blue jays and a grey squirrel and this flight of their was mainly intended to take them home. But as their shadows flowed over the water stillness descended on the lake and the mallards stopped their dancing and a whiskered beaver who had been swimming slowly towards the rushing dam quietly submerged, not really afraid of these birds, but exercising the care that had sustained life in his forty-pound body for almost seven years.

The old squirrel saw the swift shadows just a little later. She was climbing a narrow maple, seeking its blood, when the birds glided over; the dark of their passing was broken here, its outline knifed by tree branches, yet the old squirrel knew the shadows for what they were and she flashed to the ground and climbed into the sanctuary of a thick spruce. There she stopped, not afraid now, for she knew the hunting birds could not reach her here, but she remained immobile, waiting and scenting and listening, knowing the hawks, for she had been here before them and had seen them each season on their return and had evaded their savage rushes many a time. She knew why they were here and where they were going and she heard them as they alighted on their nest of sticks two hundred yards away, and she moved again and climbed the maple and sucked from its sweet juices.

Inside the squirrel's nest the five young ones were crying. They were hairless and pink, resembling miniature pigs, except for the string of tail that projected from their naked little rumps. They were two days old and already the shadow of their hair showed upon their shiny pinkness as each follicled growth struggled to thrust its finely-tapered end through an invisible aperture in the skin. Three of the babies were males, the other two females and one of these was smaller than her brothers and her sister. Blind and helpless they were then, mewing feebly for their mother, squirming over and under each other, holding together for warmth inside the matted ball of nest made painstakingly by the old sow. But the squirrel was not to heed them for some time yet. She had quenched her thirst for maple sap and was scampering through the higher reaches of an aspen, picking off its buds and eating them, filling herself for her young. Once, while she was up there, she saw her mate pass below, running swiftly along the ground, jumping from rock to downed tree, from log to bare earth, until he disappeared from her view. She cursed him as he went, for now they were strangers and red squirrels are jealous of their range and will fight their own kind if these intrude upon them.

The male heeded not her angry cherrrr, but continued his journey, intending to feed on the buds of a young birch he had discovered the previous day some two acres away from his nest in the dead poplar. He knew he was passing through the sow's territory and he would not have dared this route if she had been near her nesting tree, but he knew also that she would not pursue him if he continued to run; he would be gone from there before she flashed down from the poplar. Passing under her nest, he was about to jump to a budding hazel bush when he heard the wail of his children. He stopped, holding his small head up and his browning nose quivered as he scented them. Their noise reached him again and their smell and he could not resist climbing the scaly pine, curiosity overcoming his instincts. It is not likely that he would have harmed the young, though he did not know they were his, but he did not reach the nest. He was only half-way up the pine when a screaming, chattering fury overtook him and the sharp teeth of his mate sliced through the skin of his left thigh and tore a narrow gash into its muscle. With a wailing cry of rage and pain he raced around the thick bole, the female in pursuit and they sped around and around the tree several times, their bodies twin flashes of speed, their cries shattering the quiet of the forest. Twice more the sow nipped him as he gradually descended the tree and at last he was on the ground and running hard, his mate chasing him. He cried again and again, shrill, whistle-like screams of fear that rose above the spiteful chattering of the angry mother. At last she had chased him far enough and she stopped, her haunches low, her front legs stiff, head up, and from her quivering throat came again the angry cherrrr, both and insult and a warning to the male.

Fearful of her brood the mother climbed the pine and eased her supple body through the hole and at once the young redoubled their crying for the smell of her and her full dugs entered through the twin pinkness of their noses. She nestled amongst them and spread her legs and they crept into her and each seized a dripping black nipple and the small female baby, despite her blindness, was sucking first, her bud-like mouth firmly attached to one of the fuller back dugs.

In the big poplar in the ravine the red-shouldered hawks were examining their nest while the young squirrels were feeding. The male stood on one edge, craning his neck downwards, his head askance, the eye closest to the ageing brittle twigs peering intently at his mate as she shuffled her body in the nest cavity, forcing aside with her wings and legs and heavy, clawed feet the sticks and leaves that had accumulated in the cup since she had last squatted there late last summer. Soon she would leave this task and fly into the trees around her home and begin to gather new sticks with which to repair the damages that time and weather had wrought on the structure where her eggs were to be laid. Each year she had done this and after each migration the nest grew a little.

The male hawk lifted his head and thrust his body into the air. Up he rose, his wide wings taking him beyond the reach of the tallest trees. He flew slowly, completing two circles about his nesting mate, then he landed on the scimitar hemlock. He sat his perch, his body bent forward like that of an ageing man and his big head with its fierce eyes and curving rapine beak moved slowly from one side to the other. His beak opened and he emitted a clear whistle. Kee-yerr. He repeated the call several times, coaxing his mate from the nest. When she answered she was already winging towards him and he joined her in the air and both drifted away south, towards the winding river.

TWO

χ

Summer had come and the young squirrels in the pine were seven weeks old. Now they were one-third the size of their mother and their shiny fur was tinted with the red of their kind and the grey on their flanks and the white on their bellies were smooth washes of colour. The morning was young. The sun was a deep redness as it climbed slowly above the trees. The old sow left the nest first, hung on the trunk for her usual pause and climbed swiftly when she believed the day free of threats. Once, at the foot of the tree, she stopped and looked up and the smallest of her daughters was framed in the opening to the nest. She scolded the baby, but it was a perfunctory chatter that she flung upwards before turning to seek food. The young ones were now old enough to leave the nest and agile enough to find their strength romping in the branches. Still the sow felt concerned for them, but it was less of a burden now and the needs of her empty belly were greater than her worry over her brood. Already she had started to wean the young ones, allowing them only brief suckings at her shrunken dugs and this morning she sped away, a blur of charging fur as she ran through the brush and ferns that had come to life in this place since the squirrels were born.

By man's clocks it was five-forty-five on this day, early by city standards, late for the old squirrel, delayed at her nest by the clamourings of her brood. Since earliest dawn her kin in the woods and the black squirrels and chipmunks had been out, searching for food during the safe time, the dusk-dawn when the owl cannot see as well and when the hawk is scarcely ready to launch its body from it eyrie in search of new prey. Light is treacherous at this time in the forest and predators are more apt to misjudge their death-leaps. And the day is still fresh and there is dew on the plants that quenches the thirst of the small creatures that live far from water.

A raccoon, a female whose young lay concealed inside the rot of a downed poplar, paused to eye the old squirrel as she darted under the ferns. The raccoon was not old, but motherhood had made her fur dry and brittle and her old wool was still moulting and some of its hanks rubbed off on small bushes as she went, and lumps of the fawn-brown hair, matted and balled, hung from her carcass as she waddled along, making for the log and the young ones that waited there.

Somewhere near the raccoon and the squirrel there was a skunk. The cat-like creature could not be seen, but the smell of it offended the morning, strong and sweetly-acrid and yet only a faint emanation from the black-and-white creature's powerful anal glands, for the skunk was not roused and had not sprayed her stench into the morning air; still the smell of it was felt as the oil of its chemistry, slight as it was, permeated the atmosphere. The raccoon swerved away from the smell at once. The squirrel, small and cautious and a meal for the skunk if she was not careful, stopped in her tracks, lifted her slight body on her hind legs and peered towards the smell, her small nose wrinkled and sniffing. Satisfied that the hunter was not close enough to pose a threat, the squirrel dropped back on all fours and scampered away, steering an irregular course through the big ferns towards the hemlock grove near the old road, a place she knew would be full of sustenance.

As a rule she avoided the grove of hemlocks at this time of year because to reach it she must pass through the hunting territory of the hawks and these, she knew, were planing the sky above the crest, seeking meat for their three snowy eyases. But the squirrel was hungry and late and she did not want to leave her young ones too long, for they would be easy prey for the hawks. So she took the trail that leads over the rock and down, through the area of maples and poplars and past the tall aspen in which the great stock nest dwells. She ran swiftly across the open rock, her busy tail undulating, bobbing up and down as she galloped, a decoy intended to deflect the diving aim of the hunting birds should one of them fix its unblinking stare upon her hurrying form.

She reached the safety of the maples. In a trice she climbed a young tree, skittered up the smooth branch and reached the swaying top. She climbed out along a slender branch. Her slight weight was too much for it and it bent, slowly, describing a falling arc, and as it seemed that the squirrel was about to drop to the ground, she sprang, using the tensile branch much as a diver used a spring-board. For a fraction of time her body seemed to hang in the air, legs spread, head up, her tail, upon which she depended for balance when climbing, trailing back, its hair spread, fan-like, its shape curving up and down, resembling a question mark on its side. Then, as she fell, her stretched forefeet with their spread fingers and ready claws, gripped twigs at the end of another branch. Five aspen leaves spiralled quickly to the ground and there was a flurry of agitation around the slender branch as the squirrel's fingers gripped it and her back legs swung in, seeking footholds, and her tail swung upwards, balancing the fast-moving body. In another second the squirrel danced agilely on a heavy limb. Thus she progressed, now that she was racing through the tree tops. She was a constant flash of movement and her passage was almost silent. Only the tell-tale trembling of branches traced her journey and each time she jumped so quickly that a tree branch was yet swaying when she was three trees away from it and this was another stratagem of safety, for a sky hunter would have to pause for a split second to determine the direction in which she was moving and generally this was enough to allow her to scramble out of harm's way if she noticed the gliding shape against the light of the sky. Now and then she descended a tree part way and stopped, allowing all movement above her to still. Standing in a position of attention, her ears and her nose working, and her sharp eyes scanning at once the sky above and the ground below, she remained immobile, proceeding only when she felt sure that no danger lurked near. And at last she reached the hemlocks.

Her journey had not been a long one as human distances go; perhaps only three hundred yards. But it was an event for the squirrel. Death hovered almost every inch of the way; it waited in the air, and on the ground, where the weasel dodged its supple body on a course parallel to that of the squirrel's. But under the dense canopy of hemlock branches the squirrel was safe and a million tiny hemlock buds hung waiting for her teeth and there were many of last year's cones too, small, delicate shapes, the open ones resembling roses, brown blooms made of brittle wood-substance that hung their heads downwards, seemingly eager to see below, because the canopy of the trees forbade vision above.

Here the mother squirrel stopped and satisfied the hunger that had driven her to this place. Below the hemlocks the weasel's slender brown shape slid in silence through the underbrush ferns. The small killer had gorged this morning, eating its way into the chest of a snowshoe hare after it had drunk the creature's warm blood. The lungs and heart and liver of the hare had been consumed, then some of the intestines and lastly part of one back haunch and skin and fur had been swallowed with the meat. But the supple creature had the blood lust. It had heard the squirrel and smelled it and it had followed, interrupting its return journey to its lair, drawn to the live thing in the trees as surely as a magnet draws steel filings. And now it prowled under the trees, its nose following the squirrel's every movement, its eyes, meantime, flicking here and there, unconsciously seeking life for the quick, savage fangs to take. It knew the old sow was in the tree, but it would not dare the heights, even though the presence of warm flesh up there drove its killer instincts to a fever pitch.

Presently another scent reached the quivering nostrils. It was a strong, fetid odour that signalled to the weasel's brain. A grass snake was near and it had senses the presence of the weasel and, as these reptiles do when startled, it had ejected a small amount of colourless, rank fluid from its vent glands, a feeble defence which now drew the brown nemesis unerringly to it. The snake, a killer of frogs and earthworms, measured thirty inches; the weasel was eight inches long from its sharp nose to the black tip on the end of its tail. It paused a moment before plunging in pursuit of the already-fleeing snake which was slithering desperately over the mould and debris that littered the floor of this area of the forest. This was a bad place for the snake. There were few patches of tall grass and fewer downed trees, and no rocks. Only the smooth mulch and a layer of aged maple leaves and brown needles. There were ferns and trillium plants, but these growths were like giant trees to the snake and its killer, they could not conceal the fleeing reptile's green and yellow and black shape. And the fluid it had discharged still lingered around its vent and this linked it to the weasel's sensitive nostrils as surely as one highway connects two cities. The weasel had not need of the slithering sounds made by the escaping snake. It had no need even of its eyes, for it uses its nose more than its sense of vision. The snake had only one advantage—greater speed. With its short legs, the weasel is a comparatively slow runner. In motion, snakes are not of the swiftest, yet they are faster than a running weasel. But this snake was doomed, for what the killer lacked in running speed it made up in cunning and the ability to twist and dodge with surprisingly agility. Soon it abandoned a straight chase and instead twisted to intercept the fleeing creature. Three times the reptile changed course and on each occasion it lost some ground. At last the weasel closed. Its chocolate-brown body flashed and its needle-sharp canines were fastened behind the snake's head. The reptile twisted in agony, lashing its tail and body, the force of its struggles throwing the weasel off its feet. The snake coiled itself around the small killer and tried to squeeze, to crush the ribs of its tormentor. It might have killed the weasel, if it had been given time. But death came too soon. The fangs on its neck met through flesh and bone and the snake died.

The weasel took two bites. It ate one mouthful of the snake's body and then turned its back on it. Now the squirrel was forgotten and the killer started for its lair. Incautious and arrogant it trotted past the hemlocks and followed the game trail to the start of the rise leading to the rock plateau. It passed the giant white pine and stopped by it, sniffing and getting a faint smell; it was the odour of chipmunk that reached the small brain, but it was a cold scent, made two hours earlier. The weasel moved again, its short legs pushing it along casually and giving its hump-backed body an undulating motion. It reached that part of the trail that turns east towards the rock flats, and it followed this, fearless, for there is no creature that can intimidate the weasel. It carried its head high and its fierce black eyes held deep lights in their depths. And then it stopped; a motionless brown dot against the green of wild strawberries and ferns. A whistle had reached the weasel's ears. It was a high-pitched, double note. *Kee...yerrr.* It was repeated twice more. This was the call of the hawk and the weasel recognized it. Still it was not afraid. Foolishly it moved again, a little faster, seeking more concealment, but still visible to the keen eyes of the male hawk as it circled high above the forest.

From the great nest atop of the tall poplar a swift, graceful shape launched itself into space. The female had heard her mate's call and had answered on the second note. Now she was joining him, intent on helping him in the hunt which his signal had foretold. And it was she who was first over the weasel. Planing fifty feet above the pine under which the weasel had stopped for the smell of chipmunk, the hawk used her wings to give almost imperceptible momentum to her flight. She hung motionless for a split second, her head held to one side, her left eye perceiving the brown form of the weasel, its size decreased by half through the distance. The hawk righted her head and now both eyes were fixed on the small killer below. She folded her long, wide wings and dived, rapacious legs carried at first under her body, claws curled, but as her angle of vision narrowed over the target, her legs came forward, spread and her claws opened and the long talons were ready to grip. Down she dropped, a feathered thunderbolt, directly over the weasel. Her eyes worked independently from one another. If she wished, she could look at one object with her left eye and at another with her right. Now she used them both; each was fixed on her prey. Closer and closer she came and at last she was right over the weasel and she could no longer see it and this told her that now was the moment for the powerful legs to snatch downwards and for the claws to sheath themselves in the body of the weasel.

The brown killer, twisting and frantic now that death hovered, heard the sound of the wind as it screamed through strong flight feathers, then it heard no more. A thousand needles pierced his vitals and he was lifted from the ground and the needles became daggers and life fled from his body when the hawk was still only ten feet off the ground.

The huntress flew upwards, towards the swiftly-coming shape of her mate and he whistled his sharp call and the two turned in flight and glided towards the nest where three chicks waited small and white and downy, with black lips and black beaks, but already showing in their round eyes the gleam of lust and the pitiless savagery that would be theirs within another month. The male hawk landed on the scimitar-shaped hemlock; his mate flew to the side of her nest and at once her brood scrambled for the kill, their small beaks open and lunging, their eyes frenzied with the meat need, their movements still feeble as they jostled one another in their eagerness to reach the kill which their mother gripped in her right claw, which rested on the side of the nest. The weasel's warm, limp body dangled over the side and one of the eyases, the largest, which by her size proclaimed that she was a female reached it first. She pecked at it with her hooked beak and some of the brown fur flew and was picked up by the wind and drifted out of the nest downwards to be caught by a small twig. The chick could not penetrate the weasel's tough skin and the female hawk bent her regal head. With one deep, swift thrust she tore the weasel and its blood spilled and the chicks went wild as they dived at the wound.

The male hawk launched himself out of the hemlock. He *kee-yerred* to his mate as he winged over the poplar on his way to hunt again. Now that the eyases had been fed, he would hunt for himself this time and if he was in luck and he made a second kill soon after the first, he would bring it back to the nest. Below a wingspan that was two feet wide the forest passed in fast kaleidoscope. To the hawk the objects that impinged upon the retinas of his eyes were of natural outline and size; to one accustomed to soaring effortlessly one hundred feet and more above the highest tree, height held little meaning. But could a man cast himself into such space and glide at that easy pace above such a forest as this, his eyes would per-

Secure atop their stick nest these young red-shouldered hawks are about two weeks old. White and downy still, the eyases, as young hawks are properly called, have already developed the piercing eye of the predatory bird.

One of the eyases, on his first flight from the nest. An ungainly bundle of feathers, it landed like a stone and clung to a young silver birch.

ceive a world of broad, apparently stunted trees and land that was flat and stretched to horizons more infinite than any he had ever seen. Man and his small vision would become bemused by the light and shadow, the movement in the trees and bushes and the shapes of creatures smaller than a matchbox would be lost upon him.

Not so the hunting hawk. He flew in lazy circles over his territory and he knew intimately every bush and rock, every rise and fall of land, every shadow area, every open place of sunshine. He knew where the chipmunks had their burrows; he knew where the squirrels lived. The game trails, indistinct lines seen through his eyes, were familiar routes, each memorized and catalogued. He knew the trees, intimately. The white pines, with their open, spreading branches at the top that allowed a quick dive, and their thicker, dry-branched bottoms that offered safety to squirrels, birds and chipmunks; and the spruces, the cones of prickly green that were hard to penetrate quickly enough for a kill; and the poplars, the easiest to dive on with their soft, trembling leaves and open tops.

Knowing all this he hunted easily. As he passed over each section of his territory a quick glance below told him what was moving life or growing thing. He looked downwards now, as he flew between a spruce and a pine and his eyes saw a flicker of movement. It was small and fast and green-yellow. It was a leopard frog which had leaped once, from a stone to the shadow of a fern as it struggled with the mighty forest around it on its way to the beaver pond. It was never to reach the water. Down came the hawk. It hovered two feet over the frog, its talons already reading. In another instant the right foot found the coldness of the frog's skin. The great black claws contracted inwards and the softness of the frog was holed and the hawk was lifting again. It flew to the nearest tree, a dead elm whose grey, naked arms spread bone-hard in the sunlight. The grog was quickly eaten and again the killer-shape passed over the forest, its shadow gliding black over the ground.

Presently more living movement caught the hawk's eyes. This time it was a flash in a clump of red maples, young trees that bent easily with the weight of the old sow squirrel. She, too, had seen movement. She knew that swift shape above and she became afraid, for there was scant cover in the maples. Desperate, she ran out along a small swaying branch and leaped into space, trying to reach the safety offered by a nearby spruce. Her reddish body was half-way to its target when another shape fell upon it. Hawk and squirrel plummeted to the ground and the old sow's shrill screams of fear and pain caused a stillness to grip the forest.

The hawk had fallen on its side, but both his claws were clamped firmly about the writhing body of the squirrel; and before she could turn her head to bite at her attacker, the hawk righted himself, turned his head slightly to the side and plunged his tearing beak into her neck. Blood spurted from the severed jugular and the hawk flapped upwards, disturbing some of the dusty top-soil which rose in a thin, almost invisible spiral as he lifted. With the body of the old sow gripped firmly by the talons of his left leg he made his call, telling his mate that he was returning with a fresh kill. *Kee-yerrr*. The call was repeated three times and then there was silence in the forest.

THREE

The wilderness is lavish in all that it does. It creates life in a million forms and it causes death in as many.

It will beam upon its world with the kindness of the seraph and snarl and tear with the savagery of the most blood-thirsty killer. There are no in-betweens in the wilderness and this, perhaps, is the hardest of all for man to understand. Man, with his reason and his pity and his love is unable at times to grasp the message of the wilderness. Rarely does he witness a forest killing, but all too often he hears about such things and he feels hatred for creatures like the hawk and the weasel and the wolf. He forms societies for the protection of squirrels and chipmunks and song birds and alone or in one of his many packs he sets out to kill those that do the killing. In his powerful automobile he roars along smooth highways and never misses an opportunity to run down 'killers' that may be crossing the highway upon which he is driving. To man this is justice. He, the rational creature, the mightiest mammal on earth, becomes at once judge and jury and executioner. Thus the balance of creation has been disturbed throughout this world of ours. Thus have certain species of bird and mammal become extinct and thus, too, are many more creatures threatened. Because man, in his great ignorance of the wilderness, feels pity for the hunted and hatred for the hunter. And yet, if he were to seek the wilderness and get to know it, he would soon realize that there are no heroes and no villains here; these types are reserved only for the limited world of man. Justice there is in the wilderness, and reason and even love, great, self-sacrificing love that makes human affection pale before the radiance of its image. But above all there is co-operation in this wilderness. This is the force that welds life, the strongest, most demanding and more relentless 'law' of the forest. One creature dies that others may live. One hunts and the other is hunted. But in the end, creation takes them all, changes them, keeps them for a time and sends them forth again, renewed and replenished to continue the balance of things in the living green that is a forest. There is no room for human pity here, but there is space for sentiment, for feeling; and the wise man, the patient one that courts the wilderness, finds reward in the discovery of this secret.

The red-shouldered hawk male has killed a squirrel and its young are already feeding upon the still-warm carcass. In their nest of sticks are blood splashes and small pieces of meat and sinew and bone. Below the nest the grass and shrubs are bedecked with the remains of the squirrel and the weasel and particles from other creatures that have been carried lifeless into the great nest this year and last year and for many years. Often squirrels pass fearless under the poplar and they pause and nibble at some morsels dropped from the nest. And chipmunks, too, come by this way and stop to eat and perhaps it is of their own kind that they are eating. And small birds alight swiftly and peck and insects come and feed and the soil sucks at the life that is dropped upon it and the plants around take sustenance from the soil and their cells manufacture the juices of life that keep them green in spring and summer and autumn and form the leaves that are fodder for many creatures.

In the nest of the old sow five young squirrels are huddled in midday sleep. They have romped through the trees and they have eaten green buds and insects and they have fought each other and now they are exhausted and they snore faintly through the heat of this summer day. They are unaware and when they wake to a westward travelling sun, they will seek their mother for a time. But soon they will grow impatient and their hunger will drive them into the tree-tops again and they will begin to feed, for although they would like to taste again the sweetness of their mother's milk, they no longer need it and they will sate their hunger on that which Creation has ordained for their living.

Perhaps some of the young squirrels will die, as their mother did, for death must be, but others will live to breed and re-create their own life and their kind will go on. And perhaps next year, or the year after, their young will become food for the young of the eyases that ate of their mother and this is as it should be. It is the law here.

Night is black silk studded with the sequin-glint of stars. It is ebon atmosphere and phosphor-green planets; it is the stillness of dead space and the immensity of unreached dimension. It is the gentle swaying of grey tree-tops and the soughing of summer wind. All this and more is night in the wilderness, for now, during its time of sleep and wakefulness, the order of things of the forest changes and those who know it during the hours of sun fail to recognize it when Castor and Pollux vie for notice with the tracery of the Milky Way.

Joan and I lay awake upon our air mattresses with the shelter of the green tent. Inside it was blackness, but above, etched against the canvas, the moving shadows of summer maples danced their changing patterns and the canvas walls of our shelter were readily visible against the backdrop of the stars. A wolf howled somewhere in the depth of the bush. It was a melancholy sound to us, yet, I knew, it was made by a growing cub and carried the ebullient playfulness of carefree youth. Closer to us, infinitely more noticeable, a whip-poor-will chanted its monotonous dirge at the night; *whip-poor-WILL, whip-poor-WILL.* A constant cry which characterizes night in this part of the wild and is made by a sleek brown bird, an insect eater whose round orbs shine ruby red in the beam of a flashlight.

This was our first night on The Place and we were excited by it. There was a feeling of peace and quiet, despite the noises of the forest, such as we had not shared before. I had listened to Canada's night wilderness, but it had been in other parts and I had been alone. Joan, less accustomed to the wild—though of recent times we had taken to camping out in other parts of Ontario—had not really heard the fullness of a night such as this. Undoubtedly she thrilled to the experience, but she was nervous also. There was that wolf howl, repeated again, and there were other things. Black bears, she knew, roamed through this forest, and skunks, with their great smell, and porcupines, with their barbed quills of fire. Her city instincts dwelled upon these things and she saw dangers in them. And yet there was excitement and newness, and adventure, and pride in this piece of land we had so recently purchased.

Our tent nestled under the lee of big white pines and slender red maples. On three sides we were ringed by trees and beneath the canvas floor of our shelter lay dormant a multitude of pine needles and mulched maple leaves. In front of our zippered doorway, to the south, was the first rock flat and a ring of granite stones that still contained warm black embers from the fire upon which we had cooked our first supper here. It was mid-May and still cold at this hour, for though winter has retreated by then in this section of Canada, it has not entirely capitulated and often leaves a frosty rear-guard to remind that one day the snows will come again driven by the north wind. In our sleeping bags we were warm that night, but the body had to remain hidden deep within the quilted shelters and an incautious nose peeping over the coverings was quickly reminded that the temperature outside had dropped to twenty-eight degrees. Still we slept well.

In the morning we awoke to the sound of swift feet pattering across the roof of our tent. It was a chipmunk exploring the new landmark that had blossomed on his home territory. Up the wall on one side, across the roof and down the wall on the other side he journeyed, scurrying back and forth several times, curious and impudent, his tiny feet sounding on the tight canvas like a feeble tattoo of rolled drums. Outside the sun had tipped the trees and was attacking the frost in open places, but beneath the trees and in areas of shadow, crystals of ice shimmered and were able to catch the reflected rays of sunshine and cast them forth again, changing their yellow to green and red and blue and filling the day with a million flecks of winking colour. Breakfast was good that morning.

Mid-May is a blessed time in the forest. It is still a time of transition, of small buds, yellow green, forming on the ends of bare branches and twigs; of visible new growth on the evergreens, and of tender grass shoots spearing from the earth, and of hairy ferns rising two inches out of the mould, their curled fiddle-heads tight. The flying pests have not arrived yet and the creatures are strangely fearless of man as they run, or fly, or scurry through the still-thin vegetation. And this is the time of new life for many of the animals and birds have returned and are busy collecting old grass and moss and twigs for this year's nest.

The Place was no exception on that day. At the beaver lake there was a renewal of activity. The ice was well gone and the muskrats and beavers were out collecting fresh fodder after a diet of water-soaked poplar—in the case of the beaver—and almost anything vegetable that contained even the slightest sustenance in the case of the muskrats.

That was the day of the hare for Joan and me. It was Sunday and we were returning to the city that evening. The tent was packed and supper dishes done and we were lingering, taking one last look at our new property. I stood behind the rocks which I had piled to serve as a fireplace and movement in the gloom under a pine caught my eye. It was a snowshoe hare and I have written of it elsewhere, but this history of The Place would not be complete without a recapitulation of the tale of our hare. As I watched the nibbling brown-and-white form it started hopping towards me. I remained immobile, thinking I would panic the creature if I moved, but to our great surprise the hare hopped right up to me, smelled my right shoe, nibbled tentatively at it and then hopped past me to take a look at Joan, who was standing a little distance away. After an inspection which lasted about five minutes and during which time neither Joan nor I remained particularly still, the hare hoped away to disappear in the underbrush. Until that evening, and though I had seen a great many snowshoe hares in Canada hitherto this, I had never been treated to such a show of fearless nonchalance by an adult varying hare, as these creatures are also called.

The varying hare is the staple food of most of Canada's carnivorous animals. It is food for the wolf and the fox and the bobcat and even the great cougar; the lynx loves it and the hawks and eagles and great horned and snowy owls search for it ceaselessly. In fact, I sometimes wonder how these gentle creatures happen to survive at all, since, apart from their natural enemies, man with his snares and guns takes a further toll. But survive they do, breeding and having their young, which are fully furred and alert moments after they rid their grey-brown fur of the birth moisture. Of course, prodigal though the wilderness can be, there are at times serious shortages in snowshoe hare populations. This happens during the mysterious 'fur cycle' when for reasons which naturalists have not yet been able to determine, hare populations begin to decrease until they reach a peak of near-extinction level in some areas. When this zero-cycle is past, the creatures begin to reproduce again and generally build up to a season of great plenty. This 'feast and famine' takes place about every nine years and my guess is that nature, always a careful farmer, has beset the varying hare with sicknesses that ensure an even balance of food, habitat and species in the wilderness, for there must be room for all here. If the varying hare was allowed to multiply unchecked—for somehow, predators do not seem to decimate its numbers during peak years—the animals would overrun the forests of Canada, browsing themselves and many other creatures right out of existence.

Those who have seen the results of plentiful snowshoe populations upon a Canadian forest in winter will know what I mean. The animals nibble off all available ground vegetation during the fall and early winter and the, as the snow piles higher, they start gnawing the bark of young poplars and birches and pines and cedars, and, in fact, almost every species of sapling tree they can reach. They prefer birch and poplar, but when they run out of these they can eat almost anything. Continued reproduction without nature's periodic check would mean destruction of Canada's forests and the life that these harbour.

Our own hare, christened unimaginatively 'Thumper,' for want of a better name and no doubt with still-vivid childhood memories to prompt us, came to see us again the following week. By then I had changed the circle of rocks into a crude but serviceable granite fireplace, complete with tin stovepipe and metal hat—to keep sparks from our precious bush—and as we sat beside the glow of the fire, backlighted by the light from a Coleman gasoline lantern, Thumper appeared the following Saturday night. He hopped around us, keeping only about ten feet away and stopping often to scratch or wash his face with his front paws. I found a slice of bread and threw several pieces towards him and after he had found them, using his nose more than his eyes, he evidently decided this new food was to his liking. He sat and ate for some twenty-minutes, breaking off now and then to go and eat grass, presumably because the dry bread made him thirsty and he was able to secure enough moisture from the vegetable.

From then on, while we were camped there, before we built our cabin, Thumper was a regular weekend visitor and after some three weekends he would come to us and take bread from our fingers. Joan at once began worrying over his safety, imagining his fate between the teeth of a fox or under the talons of some bird of prey, but Thumper had evidently been around long enough to learn how to look after himself. One Saturday night, though, he was late and Joan made all sorts of fearful forecasts. A fox had eaten him; he had been run over by a car crossing the highway; perhaps the red-shouldered hawks had got him. None of these were good guesses. He came later than usual and brought with him two friends. I say brought with him and I mean just that. Hares in late spring are quite gregarious and can be seen two-or-three-strong cavorting around in small clearings during late evening. Evidently Thumper had been frolicking with his kin when hunger overtook him. Instead of breaking off the game to begin eating grass, he obviously decided he would visit the campfire that was rich in the new food he had so recently discovered. At any rate, he turned up, and the other two followed him.

As was his habit he hopped right up to us, passed under my chair and sat between us. I gave him some bread and he munched it right there, then he noticed that his friends had come rather close to the campfire and were feeding from pieces of bread that Joan had thrown to them. This, evidently, was not good enough. The hare did not mind sharing a little of his good fortune with these two interlopers, but he was quite determined that they should not worm they way in to the preferred spot by the campfire. Grinding his molars and making a hoarse, groaning sound deep down in his throat, Thumper attacked. For several minutes the space around us seemed filled with the forms of jumping hares. Round and round the campfire they ran, all three now grinding their teeth and groaning and every now and then, first one, then the others, would leap straight up from the ground, grotesquely-long legs held stiffly downwards, backs arches, heads held out, and always the grinding and groaning. At last, having shown these two that he was the boss around the campfire, Thumper returned for more bread. While he munched he kept a strict eye on his friends. If they were content to keep their distance and eat of the bread Joan continued throwing to them, all was well, but the moment one of them crossed the invisible boundary line that Thumper had evidently set, away he went, repeated his previous performance until he felt they were suitably subdued again. In the end they all ambled off together, apparently the best of friends, but Thumper must have regretted his generosity for he did not bring them around to see us again.

We saw much of the hare during the next five weeks and we learned much from it. It was the first wilderness creature to accept us and though these hares are apt to be incautious during the spring, showing themselves where normally they would remain hidden, I feel, nevertheless, that Thumper knew from the very beginning that we meant him no harm. Why else would be so quickly acclimatize to our presence and come to our fingertips for the bread we held out to him? And this brings me to a theory which I have now held for several years.

During my early encounters with the Canadian wilderness I carried a rifle or a shotgun, depending upon the season, and hunted deer and bear and cougar and moose and caribou. Ruffed grouse, ptarmigan and spruce hens fell to my twelve-gauge, and snowshoe hares, too. I hunted in

Ontario and Saskatchewan and Alberta and British Columbia and in the North West Territories and during those years I took keen pleasure in the sport. At first my 'bags' were either limited or altogether fruitless and I still recall my first duck shoot, in southern Saskatchewan. They came sailing in, mallards and Canada geese, flock after flock of them and yet the net results of my efforts was one duck down in a slough and fourteen shells wasted. It was a humiliating and frustrating experience.

I recall also my first deer hunt. It was November in the Lake of the Woods, a wilderness area of north-western Ontario where game is still plentiful. My companion, a local farmer, went one way, I went the other. At an agreed time I stopped and waited while he walked through the heavy bush towards me hoping to drive a deer or two in my direction. He did. I was sitting under a jack pine cradling my rifle and feeling excitement at the prospect of bagging my first whitetail. I wanted to smoke desperately, but I restrained my urge and presently I heard stealthy movement coming out of a clump of evergreens. The two yearling bucks high-stepped out of the bush and into the small clearing in which I sat. Up went my rifle, crash, and down went the leading buck. The other ran, bounding six feet or more as he cleared brush and shrubs and stumps and my last view of his frantic escape was the waving of his broad white tail.

At the time I felt no pity for the deer. That was to come later, when I recalled the event and when details which had entirely escaped my conscious mind during those moments of lust crystallized and I saw again those two deer; their grace and beauty, their reddish-fawn coats and their white bellies and the slim legs and black hoofs and the big, green-blue eyes, perfect ovals that held softness and beauty in their depths.

Slowly I went hunting less and less and eventually I put my guns away and when Joan and I came to The Place hunting no longer held any attractions for me. And that was when I began to notice the difference. Hitherto, walking stealthily through the wilderness seeking a target for my gun I caught few glimpses of wild life. I found targets enough, of course, but great patience, knowledge of my quarry's way and determination were needed before any of my shots found their mark. But since I no longer hunt and a camera has replaced my rifle, there is no a day when I am out walking in the wild that I do not see something to photograph. And yet my progress through the forest is much noisier than it used to be. I don't, of course, go charging about like the proverbial bull in a china shop, but I gear my outings to an easy walking pace and because I am always thrusting through heavy forest the noise of my progress is sometimes quite considerable. Before I was always conscious that the hunting season was limited and great care and caution had to be exercised if I was to make a kill. Now my 'hunting' season is year round, and I can come back again and again if I miss my first 'shot'. But I rarely miss that first 'shot' and I see many birds, animals and insects during my wanderings.

This has caused me to think. I began to wonder if, somehow, wild animals can sense the 'predator urge' and can likewise detect the harmless from the dangerous. It is a known fact that certain creatures, such as dogs and bees, can actually smell fear on the skin of a human. Then why should it not be possible for wild animals to smell the lust to kill? Fear stimulates the adrenal glands of the body and these cause certain chemical reactions which wild animals can smell. The urge to kill does similar things to the human mind and body. I know for I have experienced both. The stomach muscles seem to contract and the heart races. There is dryness in the mouth and the nerves are bow-string taut...these are my reactions to fear; and they were also my reactions when I was hunting to kill. Only the mind reacted differently. Fear attempts to disrupt the mind and introduce it to panic and severe discipline is needed to conquer an impulse to run. The urge to kill also distorts the mind, but now instead of panic there is savagery, the predator instinct to pursue. If a domestic dog can smell fear on a man it is not unreasonable to theorize that a wild creature, infinitely more keen in its perceptions, can detect the killer instincts upon the body of other creatures, including man.

This, at any rate, is my theory. And it is linked with another. Just as fear leaves its tell-tale mark upon man, so, I believe, does kindness. The kind person invariably carries a certain air of calm benevolence which is apparent and often contagious. I believe wild animals can also detect this in man. If man walks through their world and there is benevolence in his being, I believe the creatures of the forest become aware of it and will not flee his presence. This has been my experience. How else can I explain my recent meeting with a mother bear and her two cubs? They sat and looked me over, the little fellows walking towards me, the mother, dancing slowly on her hind legs, grunting softly to them, concerned perhaps for her little ones, but obviously not alarmed by my presence. Yet, in the past, I have been in danger during a similar situation, when the mother was prepared to charge and the cubs scampered away from me, crying with fear. And, last autumn, during the hunting seasons, when the whitetailed deer were being chased everywhere by men with guns...why did the doe walk right by me, slowly, sniffing at me until she had passed, then stopping and looking at me from only thirty feet of distance? And the other three whitetails, a week later, which saw me and continued eating and allowed me to photograph them before they moved leisurely away? There have been too many such instances at The Place recently for me to dismiss them as coincidences.

By early summer during our first year on The Place we had settled on a site for the cabin I intended to build; and choosing the right place was no small job! Those who are familiar with land measures will know that seventy-three acres of wilderness forest is a fair-sized piece of land and when most of it is unknown and must be explored, finding the proper site for a cabin can become a trying affair. Joan and I started looking in the autumn and after two weekends we felt we had found the perfect place; then we did some exploring and found another 'ideal' location, so we changed our minds. As winter made progress and the land changed its dress, other places were found and by this time we were becoming very confused with the plethora of ideal building spots. But at last, and by accident, we found the right site. It was midwinter by then and we had brought some friends up with us for the day and had stopped to cook hot-dogs over an open fire surrounded by snow that was about two feet deep. After our open-air meal I doused the fire and we went for a walk and soon found ouselves in a section of The Place we had not visited before. This was it.

It was here, that summer, that I began building, up the hill, over the first rock flat and at the foot of the second, just inside the ring of white pines near where the old sow squirrel had raised her last brood. That year, working almost every weekend through June, July and August, I put up a cabin twelve feet wide by eighteen feet long and because we planned to use it all year round I insulated the walls against the big colds of winter. The following year I finished our wilderness home, adding another room ten feet wide by eighteen feet long and so far that is how matters stand.

Now that the building is finished I have time for my cameras again, and I use them liberally. When we arrive here Friday evenings I come prepared for two full days of wilderness living and I have come to know The Place like the proverbial back of my hand. But still it holds newness for me; every weekend it has at least one surprise. Life teems here. Mammals and birds and reptiles and fish and insects are plenty; plants and flowers and trees and shrubs and fruits continue the abundance of creation. And it is now that I realize how pitifully little I knew about the wilderness before I bought The Place! And yet I prided myself on my knowledge of Canada's backwoods; I thought I knew almost all there was to know about them! How wrong I was! In the past I had been walking through the woods blind. I had cursed the flies and mosquitoes and stamped my way through delicate things, so perfect that man's best artistic efforts are insignificant beside them. I had eyes, but I did not use them, and I could hear yet I was deaf and even my nose was dull and senseless. One day, for want of something better to do, I took a magnifying glass and focused it on a piece of granite. I was amazed at what I saw there. Since then I often top to examine the things around me; the earth and the flowers and the moss and the insects and even the water and always the glass reveals to me wonders that I did not know existed.

I have at last been made aware that even three lifetimes would not be enough for one man to learn all the secrets of the wilderness, and this awareness has increased my desire for knowledge, for there is so little time! The insect world, for instance, has opened up vast new fields of study for me; and these were the things I cursed and stamped on so often in the past! Then I was only vaguely aware of them. Now I know that more than eight hundred thousand different insects have been identified and described by scientists since the Swede, Linnaeus, gave us the famous system for the naming of plants and animals—the two-name method which first gives the genus to which the creature belongs and then the species, or type, of that particular genus— during the sixteenth century. And though this number is large, it is not even half of the number estimated to exist on earth, most of which are yet unknown. In fact, it is thought that eventually some two million distinct species of insects will be 'discovered' and described by man, and, such is the astonishing capacity of evolution, it is more than likely that when the two millionth 'bug' has been described, other unknown species will have evolved.

It is a fascinating, mysterious place, this world of the insects, and the creatures themselves, some so small they cannot be seen by the naked eye, others so colourful that they defy description, can be a fascinating as any of our most intriguing mammals and birds, if one is aware of them and has some knowledge of their history, which began, says science, some three hundred million years ago, long before man came to share their world!

Insects can be found almost anywhere. In places where the thermometer plunges to thirty degrees below zero Fahrenheit there are insects; in hot climates and even in hot water there are insects. Since Creation first put the spark of life in their minute, chitinous bodies, insects began learning how to exist, adapt and survive in the face of the longest odds. They have learned unique and wonderful ways of protecting themselves from their enemies, as we shall see later and, what is more important, they make up the dominant group of all living things on the planet earth.

Without insects man could not live. They are the host that descends each spring and, just as soon as the first blossoms appear, the insects begin to pollinate the plants. Insects are food for animals and birds and fish and amphibians and even for other insects. They give us silk and honey; they serve science for research; they help keep the cycle of life turning by scavenging that which others leave and even their tiny bodies often drop to the earth and are soon converted into needed energy.

Some insects, as everyone knows, are harmful. Others are nuisances; yet others seek our blood. But despite the pests, insects in the final analysis, are not only beneficial to humanity, but are an absolute necessity for the survival of our world. And if the harmful species, the ones that get most of the limelight, cause much damage to crops and spread a number of epidemic diseases it is well to remember, when judging these creatures, that out of the present grand total of almost one million identified species, only two hundred of these are actually harmful to man which, for those interested in statistics, is a small average of less than one twenty-fifth of one percent!

July had come softly to The Place. It was evening, the time when the sun has not quite left and the fading of its light seems mixed with the blue of dark night. This is a shadowless time when movement is grey and indistinct. It is the time of the nighthawks, those swiftly-flying insect eaters that harry the sky and report to each other in nasal whistles. They were visible that evening as they raced through the twilight, feeding on insects, catching them on the wing high over the land. Sleek, angled wings of indistinct, mottled olive, each splashed with a white bar, flitted in graceful arcs overhead. Tails with broad white bars and mottled brownish-white places were spread wide as the birds flew; mouths gaped open, swallowing insects, showing clearly even in that light the arrow-shaped splash of white on the throat. Now and then one of the birds would climb high, fold its wings and dive, a deep, booming sound would pervade the evening. Like a miniature aircraft breaking the sound barrier, the nighthawk's explosive sound is made as the bird pulls out of its steep dive, and it can be clearly heard almost half a mile away.

Below the birds the wildlings of day were making their last journeys. The red squirrels were gathering just a few more titbits with which to stock their hidden food caches; the groundhogs, fat, cautious and afraid, were nibbling at new shoots before dark drove them into their burrows. And the night creatures were stirring. The whitetail buck was cropping grass in a natural clearing and two does, each nursing twin fawns, browsed on tender growth in the raving near the hawk's nest. This was the time of softness. Of soft light and soft shadow; of soft wind and soft sounds and each creature moved in unison with this quiet spell. And then, almost unnoticed, it was dark. Heavy dark ate the last tendrils of light and there was complete silence for a time. The stars still slept and the moon was not yet new; clouds there were, but now they drifted concealed by the blackness.

A slow-winking green light flicked between a young poplar and an ageing maple. It came and went regularly, but each time it appeared in a new place. More of the luminous winks were added to the night as the fireflies came out to dance their nuptial ceremonies, special rituals that prompt the insects to flash their cold-light during the summer nights. If one looks closely enough, one can soon notice that the flying lights correspond with other, similar, flashes which are stationary, perhaps on a twig, or high up on a blade of grass. These are the females of the species, wingless, the glow-worms, which are lifting their tails high, bending them right over their backs, to display their luminous underbellies for the attraction of a questing male.

The fireflies, coloured brown with red-and-yellow markings are constantly seeking a mate at this time, yet not all females are attractive to them and some, the older ones mostly, whose light is less brilliant, may flash their mating signals in vain. When a male insect is attracted to a glowing female, he folds his wings and drops upon her with the accuracy of a bombing sight. The half-inch long insects then mate.

What causes the light on the insects' undersides? A substance called luciferin, which is manufactured in the cells of the light-producing organs, oxidizes and is turned into almost one hundred per cent light and *no heat,* a feat which human scientists would dearly love to emulate.

Four

IN THE DEEP WOODS a brown, chicken-like bird with purple-blue ruffs on either side of her neck is walking through the ferns. Behind her strut nine chicks, each the size of a small bantam pullet, all coloured in inconspicuous shades of wood browns. It is early evening in the month of July and the ruffed grouse hen is taking her new family to the hidden nesting spot, picked out two weeks earlier, under the protection of a dead balsam fir. Some distance away, perched on a downed poplar log which is hollow and covered in moss, a cock grouse is getting ready to drum. He struts up and down the log several times, head and body erect, his black-blue ruffs fanning out on either side of his neck and on his head the brown crest is fully erected. His wings hang low on either side of his body and their flight feathers are spread; his tail, normally resembling a human hand, fingers opened out straight and close together, is now fanned into an almost perfect half-circle. Soon he stands still, neck and head up, and his wings begin to move up and down, picking up a fast, vibrating rhythm as he increases the tempo of his beat. *Boom...boom...boom...boom-boom-boom-boom-boom;* the hollow, booming sound, mistaken sometimes by humans for the false start of a two-stroke engine, rings out into the evening. This action by the cock grouse is triggered by the mating urge, only answered by the hen during the spring. Now he is just letting off steam, replete from eating wild strawberries and early blueberries and tree and bush buds and he does not really expect a female to come in answer to his drumming. But another cock half a mile away has heard him and he answers and soon the two birds are engaged in a concerto, each seeming to be trying to outdo the other in rhythm and loudness.

Meanwhile the hen is cluck-clucking to some of her chicks, the more venturesome, who have lagged behind and are busy pecking at a little cluster of wintergreen, attracted to the shiny, olive green plant by the round scarlet berries that hid under the small, pointed leaves. The hen stops and listens, calls to her chicks again and starts back towards them. She hesitates, for now her other children are forging ahead, but the laggards abandon their game with the wintergreen and run to join their mother and the feathered procession continues, the hen again taking the lead. Presently the hen stops and stands still. She has heard footsteps some little distance away; she knows these steps, for she had heard them often, they are made by a man. The chicks are pecking and scratching at the earth, unconcerned and noisy and now the hen utters a series of loud, piercing whistles, not unlike the hunting call of the red-shouldered hawk. At once the young ones freeze. Crouched into the ground, some under the cover of ferns and small bushes, they are impossible to see. The hen leaves her chicks and continues emitting her whistle, alternating it with deep clucking sounds and her progress through the heavy brush is surprisingly noisy for a bird that can pass through the forest, most tangled undergrowth as silent as a ghost. The man nears and the hen redoubled her whistling and clucking and she thrashes about, apparently suffering from a broken wing. She rushes this way and that, calling stumbling, her left wing trailing on the ground, a useless appendage. The man sees the hen and stops, smiling. He remains still and slowly the grouse's frantic movements calm and her wing recovers as though by a miracle. She stands still and silent for a moment, eyeing the man, her crest erect, her bright eyes fixed upon the intruder, then she retreats, going to her chicks and she is again whistling, but this time there is a slight, almost unnoticed change in the quality of the sound and the chicks respond to it. Like miniature rockets they charge out of their concealing places, each flying about two feet above the ground, all going away from the presence of man, while the mother stands her ground, whistling and walking quickly back and forth, seeming to be counting her chicks as they explode out of the ground and race away to safety. When the last one has gone the hen looks once at the silent man and she thrusts herself up into the air, powered by the stubby wings that whirr and rattle, beating the air into drum-like soundwaves that fade quickly as she descends to the ground two hundred feet away. Two or three quiet clucks are heard as she gathers her young about her and then there is silence in the evening bush and the man goes on his way, turning from a course that would again cause him to disturb the family of ruffed grouse.

χ

The hen mated during late May and soon after began searching for a safe place in which to lay her eggs. It was cold on The Place and the trees were still leafless. The ground was soggy yet, replete with spring moisture and there was much light reaching the dead leaves, even in the densest area of bush. For two days the hen grouse searched constantly, finding a number of locations but rejecting each as unsuitable after a short inspection of the site and its surroundings. Then, on the morning of the third day of her search, she discovered the right spot. A slight depression caused when two forest giants toppled to their death years earlier, was sheltered by the dead arm of another tree. The two big trunks had rotted long ago and now showed as moss-and-fern covered mounds. The area around was strewn with layers of dead poplar and birch and maple leaves, and when the trees and bushes regained their foliage, the nest site would be well screened from above and below and from the sides. Into the small depression walked the hen grouse. She turned around in it eight or ten times, pushing her body downwards and with each turn her breast and wings and feet scooped out some of the leaves and pine needles that lined the hollow. Soon she had deepened the place and after getting out and eyeing it carefully, she began collecting dry leaves and a few sticks with which she built up the walls. This done, she left to feed and did not return to her new nest until that evening. At dusk she was back and sitting in it and from four feet away she was an invisible blob of brown flecked life. By morning she had laid her first egg and even in the strong light of day she was almost impossible to see. A man, carefully searching the nest site from a distance of ten feet, might have just been able to see the brownish, slightly shiny beak and the black dots that were here eyes, but he would have needed to look closely indeed.

The hen had been on her nest nine days when Alvin Adams almost stepped on her. Alvin, a neighbour of ours and the most handy handyman in the Uphill district, had come to help me erect a two-strand barbed wire fence around the immediate area of our cabin. This was to keep his brother Len's cows out of my building, for Len has been grazing his cattle on The Place for some time and when I bought the land I honoured the unspoken agreement made by the previous owner. Len and Alvin and I had passed not two feet from the sitting grouse at lease six or seven times while we were stringing the wire in that area and the hen had remained immobile and invisible while we worked and talked and joked, making an infernal noise around her. We had finished stringing the wire and Alvin was returning to where he had left his axe when his right foot landed within six inches of the sitting bird. She exploded out of there, her wings whirring loudly, and Alvin saw the nest. We crowded around it and counted the nine eggs and I raced for my cameras and captured the nest on film. After the Adams brothers had gone and things had settled down around the nest site, I returned, walking carefully and trying to make as much use as possible of the scant cover that lay between my outhouse (near where the nest was situated) and the hollow between the mounds. It was no use. Just as I stepped through a bower of pines, the hen left the nest. But now her movement was not the explosive, sudden flight that had startled us earlier; she was stealthy and it was only because I was walking slowly and had my eyes glued to the nest that I saw her move at all. From that distance I was not at first sure that she was in the nest and was about to raise my telephoto lens and focus it on her when I noticed her slip over the top of the nest and almost literally tiptoe away from it. She seemed to actually slither over the rough ground, making no sound, and try as I might, I could catch only occasional glimpses of her as she progressed through the ferns away from me and her eggs. When she was about fifty feet from the nest she suddenly changed her tactics. Now she crashed her way through the underbrush, making plenty of noise and clucking loudly and she was circling around her eggs and working her way towards me. I got the message, for it was quite obvious. She *wanted* me to notice her now that she felt she was far enough away from her nest. Her idea was simple. Lure this intruder from the eggs, take him for a chase through the forest with the broken-wing and noise act and then take to the air, circle and return to her eggs.

I did not put her to all that trouble. Retreating to the cabin I left her alone all that day and well into the next, then, at noon, I gathered my camera again and set out, going even more carefully this time, determined to get at least one good picture of a ruffed grouse sitting on her eggs. But again the hen detected me and she repeated her stealthy performance and followed it with the noise, the clucking the broken wing ritual, and in the end I never did get the picture that I wanted. I managed to photograph her several times with my telephoto lens, but the distance was so great and her colouring blended so well with the area she had chosen in which to nest that on looking at the thirty-five millimetre negatives over light and through a powerful magnifying glass all I could detect of that bird was the hollow of her nest, a vague outline of her beak and the pinpoint circle of one eye.

Every weekend I persisted in my quest, still anxious to photograph her but by then greatly intrigued by her unvarying performance. There was only one conclusion I could draw from her actions. On that first day, when the three of us had been passing so close to her, she knew we were not aware of her presence. But later, after Alvin had almost stepped on her, she knew also that I had spotted her nest, and while her first hurried flight from the nest was prompted by necessity, by the nearness flight from the nest was prompted by necessity, by the nearness of what was to her an enemy at that time, her subsequent manoeuvres indicated that she had thought things out and 'reasoned' that if I could not see her on the nest and she was able to leave it stealthily enough, I would be led to think that she had abandoned it. Also, in so far as my presence and almost equally stealthy movements suggested that I was stalking her and the eggs, then, if she could draw my attention away from the eggs by offering herself as a sacrifice, I would, by predatory standards, go after the greater prize, the adult grouse which would offer a better meal than a clutch of ten eggs, for she had laid one more egg after we had disturbed her.

The affair lasted exactly four weeks and on the fourth Saturday I went to see the nest, expecting to find it empty and the grouse and her chicks gone. But there she was, sitting as usual, and I was so concerned, believing that due to my interference all the eggs had addled—for I thought the hatching time was three weeks—that I did not notice that for the first time she let me move in close enough to see her quite clearly. When I did realize this I started back rather hastily, intending to return for my camera, which I had not bothered to bring on what I had thought was a useless errand. At my sudden movement the hen became startled and jumped from the nest, clucking loudly, coming straight towards me and flapping her 'broken' wing, and it was then that I saw the little yellow and brown chicks, two or three already clear of the eggs and almost dry, another three clearly newly-emerged and still soaking wet with the birth moisture and still others either just emerging from the shells or cracking them with the little horny projection that all bird young have on the end of their top mandible.

Oblivious now of all but those chicks, I called loudly for Joan to bring my camera equipment as I hurried to the nest. The hen, meanwhile was almost frantic, poor thing, believing that her young were about to be devoured. She raced back and forth, her wing trailing and one leg occasionally going limp, and she would fall, appearing to be seriously injured and when Joan arrived after what seemed to me to be hours and yet could not have been more than two minutes, she was startled when the grouse appeared almost under her feet. Hurriedly I took the equipment from my wife's hands and began shooting pictures. I took black and white close-ups and coloured close-ups and then, after I was sure that at least one of those precious pictures would come out, I turned the camera on the hen. After this I spent a few minutes watching the chicks and noticed that just as soon as each one dried it slipped out of the nest in miniature imitation of its mother's previously-stealthy movements and disappeared, prompted by the hen's piercing danger whistle. Within half an hour the nest was deserted but for one egg, probably either the first or the last laid, which was addled and I was left a little bemused by my luck, for such a sequence as I had witnessed is not one that man is often privileged to see.

The habit of ruffed grouse is to move from the nesting site immediately the young are able to travel and each night thereafter, until the young are fully grown and able to fend for themselves, the hen leads them to different night places, sometimes returning to an old one two or three nights after they last occupied it, but never going to sleep two nights running in the same place.

Alone with the nest, the broken shells with their leathery, blood-streaked linings and the one addled egg, I was about to go back to the cabin when I thought I would like to keep that last egg as a souvenir of this episode. I picked it up and for several days it lay in a glass jar on the sideboard in the cabin, for I was a little loath to blow it, knowing that its contents would be particularly foul of odour. But at last I took it some distance from the cabin and I pierced both ends, making a small round hole in each. With the help of one of last year's dry grass stems, a hollow reed, I blew lustily through one end, now and then closing my eyes as the contents seeped slowly out and splashed green-yellow on to the ground. When the shell was quite empty I turned to go, quite pleased with myself, and then I thought I would leave the shell in the outhouse for a day or so, to give it a chance to rid itself entirely of its bad smell. This was a mistake.

Four weeks after the grouse laid her last egg her chicks were born. They emerged into the world wet, but within minutes they found the use of their legs and melted into the underbrush.

The mother bird, crest erect, struts around the photographer, trying to entice him away from her chicks.

Two days later, when I returned to collect it, all I found was one tiny piece of shell, no bigger than a grain of corn. The thief had been a red squirrel, seeking calcium contained in the shell after a long vitamin-starved winter. And when I revisited the site of the nest, not one scrap of the old shells was to be seen anywhere, removed perhaps by another red squirrel, or by a mouse, or raccoon, or any one of a dozen forest dwellers, for nothing goes to waste in the wilderness.

Of course, I was not too upset by this. I had the pictures and the following Monday, in my city home, I developed them and was delighted with the results.

During the next two months I met my grouse and her chicks on many an evening as I was returning home with my cameras after a tramp through the bush and although she always put on her act and invariably whistled to her chicks a warning, she eventually became accustomed to me and was content to lead her brood just a short distance away from my path. And I respected her feelings and always turned away from her, letting her take her children to whatever place she wished, for she had earned this touch of consideration from me. Perhaps next year some of her chicks will mate and nest in the area of my cabin and I may get a chance to take some more pictures of them. I hope so, but I will not be too disappointed if this does not happen, for now I am well provided with photographs of Canada's ruffed grouse.

One evening during the month of August I walked through the bush through a game trail that provides a short cut to our beaver lake. I was just strolling, carrying only a compass and my big 'hunting' knife for widening some parts of the trail; it was one of those restful and quietly aimless jaunts that I have grown so fond of at The Place. I came to a tributary of the lake, a canal cut by the beavers to enable them to reach fresh supplies of popular fodder some distance from the lake proper and still remain underwater while they swim to and from their feeding grounds. The canal is about nine feet across in mid-summer and the beaver at some distant time felled a big poplar so that it spans this rather muddy, though shallow place. I use this tree as a crossing place, walking over it with the aid of a poplar sapling, of which I cut two so that I will always have one at each side of the canal. When I got to the far side I looked down at the wet bank and saw the clear imprints left by the human-like feet of a black bear. The tracks indicated that a smallish bear had come this way not long before; I thought it might be a two-year old, recently turned out into the world by a mother who was now busy with a new set of twin cubs. For a little distance the tracks followed the canal, then the animal crossed a rocky area and I lost its trail. Soon I forgot about it for the cry of a pileated woodpecker attracted my attention. Once threatened with extinction through the carelessness of man, this spectacular bird, the size of a crow, is now making a nice comeback in the northern woods and is spreading quite well into more southerly areas. It has a vivid red crest and is dressed in black and white plumage; its great wings beat rapidly, sweeping strokes that have the characteristic beat-beat-pause of the woodpecker family, which, during each pause, causes the birds to drop perceptively and rise again when they continue the beat. The pileated woodpecker has a loud, shrill call alternated by a deeper *kuk...kuk...kukuk* and the holes it digs in the trees are soon recognized by their size. I had seen several of the species flying across The Place and I was anxious to find a nest. Now I searched the area around me and presently I spotted the bird. It was busy at a dead pine still standing in the middle of the beaver canal. Somewhere in that pine were insects and the chisel bill of the woodpecker was already busy when I saw it. The *rat-tat-tat* of its powerful strokes against the hollow tree carried loudly to where I stood and soon great white chips started to fly outwards and dropped to the water.

Presently I heard another bird calling from some distance away and the bird I was watching paused in its labours to answer the call of its mate. I waited, hoping to see the female, but she was evidently busy at the nest (which I have not yet found) and soon the male bird, or rather, the bird I presumed was the cock, dropped from the tree and flapped rapidly away. When he had disappeared I continued my walk, pausing now and then to look at some form or other of life that attracted my attention. Once two nighthawks swooped low over me, emitting their squeaky cries; another time I watched a snapping turtle, a great horny-shelled creature, as it quit the bank and plopped into the water at my coming, to disappear in the murk of the canal. In this way I reached the lake proper and the sun was already beginning its nightly escape.

At the lake I stopped and startled a pair of canvas-back ducks which had evidently tired of their migration flight and decided to settle on this small lake to raise their hatch this year. To get a better view of them I climbed down from the rock upon which I was standing and I bent low and entered a tunnel of wild grass that borders almost the entire lake in the summer; this coarse grass grows to a height of four feet and more and the tunnels are made in it by deer and bear going to and from their watering places. The ground beneath my boots was soft but firm; it was gloomy inside that wall of green and the path twisted repeatedly, following the easiest footing. Once I thought I heard some rustling ahead, but I decided I had either been mistaken or I had disturbed a groundhog or some other small creature. I plodded on and came to a sharp, right-angle turn. When I rounded the corner I stopped suddenly. Ahead of me, standing as still as I was, and no doubt carrying the same startled look on his face as I had on mine, was a black bear, evidently the creature whose tracks I had seen earlier and the memory of which had been wiped from my mind by the woodpecker and the canvas-backs. He was obviously a young fellow, but nevertheless I judged he would tip the scales at a comfortable two-hundred pounds. He was sleek from summer living and his reddish-black coat was already shining with the satin glint that becomes magnificent during the first frosts of autumn.

I am not one of those people who maintain that no wild animal is dangerous to man. I am not afraid of wild things under normal conditions, but black bears, though usually harmless, can be provoked into anger by an incautious person or by fright, and looking at the sleek young specimen not five feet from me I could see that he was quite thoroughly frightened. For what seemed like an eternity I tried to decide what I should do. Stand still and hope for the best? Back away slowly? Or shout and slap my hands, thus scaring him enough to make him turn around and run? We probably faced each other for not more than ten seconds and after that time the bear made his decision. He turned in a flash and thrust his way out of the grass tunnel, climbing obliquely away from it and I was glad to see his waddling, fat rump disappear over a rock ridge. For perhaps another minute I heard his lumbering progress through the bush, then he was gone and I was alone again. I, too, left the tunnel, realizing that the chances of coming face-to-face with another bear were extremely remote, but still not wanting to push my luck any further for that evening. As I have said, normally a black bear is not dangerous and by normally I mean when a man is travelling through the woods; we make considerable noise then, by animal standards, and most bears hear human footsteps quite some time before they can see who is making them. On such occasions they simply change location, thought I have met a number of bears in the woods and each time we have passed at a respectful distance from each other, both abiding by the maximum of live and let live.

By the time the bear and I had trampled our ways out of that tunnel the canvas-backs I hoped to see more clearly had heard us and disappeared somewhere in the reeds. Now and then I heard one or the other give a soft quack, but I saw them no more that evening and I was about to turn to go when a slight 'something' drew my attention to one of the beaver dams. I walked along the dam wall, a sold structure of sticks, moss and mud that would support ten men my weight—and more—and saw that the object of interest was a rusting steel trap. It was anchored to the dam by a chain fastened to a hazel sapling which had been sharpened at one end and driven firmly into the mud. I pulled at the chain and the gin was fully exposed. Gripped inexorably by the steel jaws was the tail of a muskrat, old and rotting, showing the vertebrae that had once attached it to the rat's back. Whether the rat had chewed himself free, choosing to slice through his own living flesh and bone rather than perish by drowning at the end of the cruel steel, or whether a mink or an otter had found the newly-dead beast and had stopped to eat it, I shall never know.

To me this was tragedy; the only kind of tragedy that I ever notice in the wilderness, for when Creation claims back its own there is always a purpose behind the death of each living being, whilst this was senseless killing, the act of a forgetful man, and I found myself hoping that the rat had drowned and at least supplied the meat eater with food, for if it had chewed itself free it would have died anyway, but then its body would have rotted deep in the subterranean chamber of its den where it would have crawled to die, and in such a grave the carcass would do little good for the forest and its creatures. I unhooked the trap and pried the vice-jaws free and the relic of a fur rat dropped into the running water of the lake and was washed over the dam to be claimed by some living thing of the forest and turned into a little energy. At least that much I was able to do for the unfortunate creature. The trap I hung in a clump of young maples and it hangs there yet, rusting and useless now and soon the wilderness will claim it, for the winds and the rains will dig into it and the heat will expand it and the cold of winter will contract it and eventually, a number of years hence, it will become totally absorbed by the earth, particle by particle, and the red rust of its decaying body will give some more substance to the forest, and it will never catch another rat.

Taking one last look at the small lake with its myriad water lilies, their dull-green shiny leaves sparkling in the twilight, their yellow and white blooms curled up, closed for the night, I turned to go home. Now I was following an old logging road which runs south from the lake to the highway. On either side of this road grow new trees, some of them already husky fellows that have come to replace those hacked down by the logger's axe and saw. Here and there still stand ancient pines and spruces, big trees, spared I know not why by the logger, and now monuments that thrust haughtily upwards high over the crowns of the lesser species. Looking into these living walls the eye sees black, indistinct shapes that are low on the ground, some only two or three feet in diameter, other massive shapes thicker than the girth of three men. These are the dead ones. The decayed stumps of the pines that forty years ago stood proud and straight, ancient obelisks placed here by nature two centuries before the axe took them. They could claim sympathy from such as me, were it not that out of their top branches other trees have sprung and out of the decay of their stumps and roots and limbs new life came long ago and spread itself and filled the empty spaces left by the logger.

I like this old road. It is the one Joan and I followed when we first saw The Place and it holds special significance because of this, but it also has a charm of its own. It seems that Creation planned the species that were to grow after the old trees were cut down. West of the road grow mixed soft-woods and hardwoods: maples and silver birches, poplars and basswoods and willow and hazel. East stand the tall pines and a few spruces and balsams and a collection of big birches and poplars. This is the side where the beaver lake run-off courses a winding way to disappear as a small stream under the highway and tunnel onwards until it finds freedom in the gurgling waters of the Head River. Birds love the woods on both sides of the old road. In stumps left when sharp winds snapped off young trees chickadees lay their tiny eggs, hatching their broods in the cup-like depressions which are always open to the sky. Flickers and hairy woodpeckers favour the thicker poplars, drilling in their holes as they probe for carpenter ants or wood borers. Somewhere in this area, in a hollow log or atop a rough granite boulder, a pair of turkey vultures comes to nest each year. I have not yet found the secret of their nesting place but often Joan and I watch the great black birds as they soar easily over our land, bare, reddish heads thrust forward on the sinuous necks, sharp eyes scanning the ground, always searching for the carrion upon which these eagle-sized birds feed, thereby keeping the bush clean. But one day, I know, I will find the big nest and then perhaps I will be rewarded with another series of photographs. In the meantime I shall keep looking, and in seeking it I shall find other interesting things, like the Princes of Serendip who set out to find one thing and discovered many wonders by the wayside simply because they were looking. That's how I found the nest of the white-breasted nutlatch, a small, quick, black-and-white bird with a nasal voice. The bird had chosen a small hole made, I believe, by a downy woodpecker in the side of a diseased poplar. When I discovered it the young had already hatched, but the mother bird, or perhaps one of the then adult young ones, was still using the nest as a sleeping place. I noticed the hole as I was seeking the bulky vulture's nest and I went to explore this little place of darkness, wondering if it contained anything. Before my fingers reached it to commence to probe, the little bird flew out. I then felt inside and my index and middle fingers traced the soft outline of a small, round nest, evidently made of dry grass stalks and moss. The bird was there again the next evening, and the next, but I did not disturb it. By looking carefully I was able to see the tip of its longish black beak as I passed the poplar.

That evening I returned home through the woods. I could have found easier walking by travelling my little road until it met the highway and then following the pavement to my own gravel road, but I seldom take this route, for the bush holds too many interesting sights and the things of night are usually on the move by the time I pass through the rolling, rock-studded land that separates the bush road from my cabin.

Five

THREE OF THE YOUNG of the old sow squirrel grew to maturity before man came to share their world. But two of the youngsters were not to mate that winter for hunger drove a weasel into the lower arms of the pine one morning and one of the squirrels died that way. The other incautiously crossed an open rock area during a day of clouds, when the sun cast no shadows and there was no warning black silhouette reflected upon the ground. The hawk glided in and pinioned the small red body, much as it had done to the mother squirrel.

Of the remaining three, two left the pine and sought solitary nests in other parts of the forest and the small female stayed, keeping to the old nest hole, changing its lining of needles and leaves and settling to this part of the woods. Her territory was not large, but the two acres she had inherited were her sole domain and she guarded them carefully from her relatives in the forest. Now and then some wandering youngster, like herself one of last spring's litters, passed by and tried to investigate the tempting nest hole, but each time the small squirrel sow drove them away, fighting much as her mother had done, and screaming her insults in the same shrill voice and though some of the strangers were larger and stronger than she was, they always left in defeat, for such is the law of nature. The intruder, knowing that he is breaking this law, is weakened by his knowledge and at best puts up but a feeble defence and is ever ready to run and leave the forbidden territory.

Born with the speed and guile and intelligence of her mother and father and inheriting that mysterious sense which directs even the most inexperienced wilding during its time of trial, the small sow quickly learned the best food locations in her territory. She learned, too, of her enemies. The weasel hunted her and failed and she learned his ways and the manner of his hunting and she even learned the whereabouts of his lair and avoided it during the hours when the brown killer was out looking for meat. But especially she grew to know the red-shouldered hawks and their ways. Early she discovered their eyrie and their whistled calls became warnings to her ears and she learned to distinguish between a whistle that was near and one that was far and she learned to recognize the difference in their tone, slight as it was, which told her when the call was made before a kill and when it was made after, as the successful hawk flew home with the body of its victim gripped tightly in clenched talons.

Several times one or the other of the adult hawks tried to capture the small sow. Each time she avoided them and discovered some new thing about them that would help her stay out of their clutches, and when the young hawks set out in search of prey she knew instinctively that they were inexpert hunters and she feared them less. Because she was quick to store knowledge and because she was intelligent, the squirrel discovered that the hawks stayed quite close to their nest during the middle hours of day and hunted far afield in the mornings and evenings. She found, also, that the big birds habitually perched in certain trees in and around their nest area from where they scanned the forest floor for sign of movement and so she avoided these placed, and she lived.

Somewhere in her small brain ancestral warnings told her of other dangers. One morning early, just as she emerged from her nest, her quivering nostrils detected a strange, fearful scent which seemed to be travelling down to her from the upper branches of the pine. Instinctively she ducked back into her hole, remaining at its entrance and probing further with her nose the odour that permeated her tree. For a time she remained thus, but hunger drove her forward again and she left the safety of the nest and glanced upwards. A maze of waving green laced with the greyness of early sky met her eyes at first, but soon she saw that which was causing the disturbing scent. A big grey shape sat immobile on one of the high branches. Its rounded head and huge, yellow eyes immediately identified it in the squirrel's mind, although she had never before seen a great grey owl. The bird had hunted well during the night and a number of mice now filled its hunger. It had been flying to its favourite day-time roost in a maple several hundred yards away when the first rays of light and a fullness of its belly had caused it to alight on this convenient perch. Now it wanted to sleep and would have remained hunched over the branch until dusk came to call it but for the spiteful, chattering red thing that screamed incessantly from its place half-way down the pine. The owl tried to ignore the squirrel's angry chatter, but the constant noise made it nervous and soon it could stand it no more. It launched its chunky body out of the tree and flew away, an angry *zit...zit...zit* escaping from its partly-open beak. The small squirrel watched it leave and it watched also as two tiny birds appeared over the top of a poplar and chased the owl, harrying the cumbersome predator, one on each side of the great body, chivvying it like two fighter aircraft in pursuit of a bomber. Twice the nuthatches hit the owl's body as they continued their determined attack, intent on driving the owl away from their nesting place, and the squirrel watched until the small birds broke away and returned to their tree and the owl disappeared among the distant foliage.

Two evenings later the squirrel had a great fright. She was scurrying along the forest floor, a prickly, green-sheathed hazel nut between her sharp teeth, when a great savage creature appeared in her path. The wolf, intent on the strong scent of a hare had neither seen nor heard the squirrel, for the wind was blowing away from the small animal directly into the face of the hunter. The big lobo was intent on the fresh smell he had been following for ten minutes, for he knew that the hare had stopped nearby, relying on its stillness and colouring for protection. The sudden appearance of the silently-scampering squirrel startled the wolf and it curled back its lips and sent a snarl at the little sow. For a split second the squirrel paused. She saw the great shape more clearly. The black lips were drawn back and the glistening fangs showed in the redness of the huge mouth and one broad paw was raised, in the act of coming down. The squirrel exploded away from the place. It was an incredibly-swift redness that the wolf saw as the small sow leaped four feet into the lower arms of a pine and flashed up the trunk to the uppermost boughs. Now the wolf realized it had missed an easy meal and its growl deepened and it glared at the tree and the squirrel's derisive voice reached it. Too late the lobo remembered the hare. Sitting like a small statue just six feet from the scene, the snowshoe had loped away while the squirrel was climbing the pine and the wolf had not seen it go and spent several moments searching the area. It gave up at last and turned away from the pine and the chattering squirrel, aware that the red-back had alerted every creature in the area with its shrill call of danger.

So it was that when winter came that year the small squirrel had already learned the lessons of the forest. She had grown a little since her mother died, but she would remain small. Creation had decreed that she would ever be a runt, but if it had taken size from her, it had given her a wit that was even quicker than that owned by others of her race, creatures all that are actively alert and sharply intelligent and it was this extra perception that enabled the sow to find the most productive trees; the pines and spruces with their tight, nut-full cones, and the hazel bushes and hemlocks, each supplying a different food. The squirrel's midden, a hollow under a flat granite rock located among bushes near her pine, was well stocked with seeds when the first snows fell.

It was during a later afternoon in mid-November, while the squirrel was perched on her home pine, that autumn turned and winter swept in. Hitherto the nights and mornings had been frost-ladden and ice had sheeted the waterholes and creeks of the forest, but yet the sun had held warmth and the wind blew gently. Now there was no sun and scudding clouds migrated across the heavens; fat, grey clouds, sluggish phantom shapes that seemed to roll as they advanced from the northland trundled sullenly by a cold, gusting wind. The greyness of the clouds invaded the forest, creating monster shapes among the tree-tops which now bowed their heads away from the approaching storm, their crowns tousled, some of their leaves and needles snatched by the wind to be sent hurtling in disarray, tumbling playthings of a mighty element.

The squirrel kept to her tree. She sat on a thick branch with her tail curled over her rump, following the ridge of her spine so that its tip rested against the back of her head. The sow's small body was hunched and her chest and belly rested securely against the rough bark of the tree-limb. Now and then she closed her eyes in fitful sleep and the tip of her nose drooped slowly until it touched the living timber of her perch; then she would wake again, her eyes would partly open and her head would raise, rather like a human falling asleep in a chair only to be awakened by the weight of his head as it rested upon his chest.

She was still there when the clouds burst and let fall the whiteness that was snow and she watched the big flakes fly before the northing wind, some of them finding resting places on the trees and ground growth, others driving onwards, while still more fell from nebulous maws. Soon the sow's fur was crusted with snowflakes; yet she sat there, still, alternately dozing and awakening, her only noticeable movement the dropping and raising of her head. By human calculations this was a

Saturday and a man and a woman would be here on the next day and the squirrel was to discover an unexpected source of food.

The snowstorm had fled by the time Joan and I arrived from the city next morning and in place of the wind and the burst clouds there was a blueness in the sky and the blazing of a yellow sun. On the ground a coating of fresh snow, white, soft; twelve inches of intricately-formed crystals that concealed within themselves shapes of delicate, exquisite beauty. The evergreens were dressed in their best that Sunday morning, showing off the freshness of their green under mantles of ermine snow; the bare trees, the poplars and silver birches, and the elms and maples and oaks, had lost some of their harshness now that the snow clothed them and softened the stark outlines of their nakedness.

I stopped the car and we emerged into a bright coldness; sub-zero frost that was enervating, an elixir of Creation that carried just enough bite to it to remind us that this was a powerful, dangerous element we were meeting on this beautiful day of winter. Now the icy touch of Boreas was merely a caress, but it carried warning. Take away the sun, be careless for one moment then, and the fondling would cease; softness would give way to that frigid grip that can dig deeply into flesh and bone and sinew, and turn the blood cells into scarlet snowflakes of death. And yet this terrible prospect could not remove the pleasure from the day.

Out here in the wilderness the sun was brighter. The air was clearer and still retained its ancient smell of life; birds fluted melodious anthems and even the grim north wind seemed in a festive mood as it plucked soft, murmuring music from the crowns of the trees. This was a day for living.

It was also a day that marked the beginning of our real friendship with The Place. We had come here first during late autumn, perhaps the worst time for the land, for the blazing leaves have curled and fallen and their parent trees are sad reminders that one season has died and a new one, the worst one by human standards, is about to arrive. I always experience bitter-sweet nostalgia at the end of each season. The coming of spring sparks within me a burbling excitement at the prospects of renewed life; the beginning of summer, with its torrid, still days and dense canopies of foliage, causes me to regret the loss of spring, but still it kindles other feelings of contentment; the passing of summer and the coming of autumn carry a new beauty, and another feeling, a soft sadness that fills the mind with retrospect, and early memories of other autumns in other places come unbidden but not unwelcome. But my feelings at the coming of winter have changed recently. Once I was oppressed with the forebodings of 'the dreary season': now, while yet I regret losing the soft beauties of autumn, still winter fills me with a new excitement, different to that which I feel on the eve of spring, yet it is strong, vigorous, and I mourn not for the autumn and look forward to this virile new time. This change within me was caused by The Place and it began on that Sunday morning when Joan and I left our car and began to walk through the snow, climbing the slope that leads now to our cabin.

We did not reach the cabin site on that day, nor did we then know that it existed; three more weeks were to pass before we were to find it. All the same, we must have come close to it that Sunday and we certainly entered the territory of the sow squirrel, for she chittered at us and watched us from the safety of a tall spruce as we sat at noon and ate our sandwiches; and the crumbs and crusts that we left behind must have been collected by her, judging by the squirrel tracks we found on our passing our nooning place later that afternoon, when we were returning, tired but happy, to our car.

Joan and I have never actually discussed our feelings on that day and I must confess, I have not hitherto paused to fully analyze those which held me then. Only now, as I write of that Sunday, am I stopping to recall the mood that gripped me during our exploration of The Place. I think that, at first, my entire sentiments were formed by a feeling of ownership; I owned this land, and human pride motivated my thoughts. And this was the wrong approach, and many weeks must pass before I began to feel for The Place in such a manner that my being reflected the change. And it was then that the wilderness reached out and really touched me, put its mark upon me for ever.

I remember now that I was much preoccupied with the dimensions of The Place and I felt it necessary that I quickly traced my name upon a board which I would fix on our road fence so that all might know that Lawrence owned this land. But later during the day, after we had trudged through the snow and paused often to admire trees and shrubs and contours of land, my pride of ownership preoccupations began to fade and physical and mental enjoyment of The Place edged their ways into my

Winter on The Place and the storm has passed and the sun shines again, revealing the tracks of a snowshoe hare.

The hare tracked to its 'form', a shelter under a dead-fall pine.

being; and by the end of that day I was infused by a new feeling, a neophyte sentiment that I did not then understand, but which yet managed to impart a generous measure of contentment. And, when I drove away from The Place that Sunday the power of the land was strong upon me, and I believe that Joan had also fallen under its spell.

What is it about the wilderness that is powerful enough to smash through the barriers of centuries of civilization and reach down deep into the soul of man? In my mind I know. But can I make it captive so that it will live on as words upon paper? I doubt that I have this ability, yet I must try if I am to make clear my sentiments.

You must remember that on Sunday I was a more-or-less average man, a product of my century. I had been marked by two wars in Europe; I had spent most of my life within the encirclement of big cities, and although I had always felt an attraction for 'the country', as I styled it then, I had not really thought greatly about its effects upon me. I had left England and Europe because of many things, but perhaps the most powerful motive force behind my migration to Canada was a feeling of encroachment; there were too many people in my little country; there was not enough room; the freedoms that were given to me by war were suddenly withdrawn at the advent of peace. Life was orderly, drab, dull; there was no more excitement. Was this all? Was this the course upon which my life was to run; an endless, tired meandering that held no rainbow at its end? I had survived my wars, I lived securely in an orderly land, could I hope for more? And then I though of Ovid: Medio tutissimus ibis. You will go most safely in the middle...the middle course. I was, indeed, following the middle course; and I did not like it, and rebelling against it I left England and came to Canada and for a time nothing changed, just my surroundings; until I went out and found the Canada I had unknowingly sought, the big country, the land of lakes and streams and rivers and tall trees and cutting winds; and small things began happening in my mind, albeit they went unrecognized for several years, while I built up knowledge of the animals and birds and trees of this vast land.

Perhaps the secret of the wilderness lies in that man has ever been a part of it. This is our birthright, the vast womb of eternity out of which all things and all men have come. Once, miraculously, there emerged a spark of consciously-motivated vitality from our of the darkness of a primeval swamp. It grew, this writhing, sluggish thing, and changed, and sought, never pursuing the middle course of safety, but reaching farther and farther, guided by Creation, rising from plane to plane until at last it walked upright and it was called man.

Then this ape-like creature with the often-changing body reached fullness of physical development and only one avenue of growth was left to it: the mind-road. And man turned to it and perfected his brain and his great powers of thought and he became the master of all things. And somewhere along this last, tortuous journey, he began to lose his early ties with Creation. They receded into lost places in his mind, these mysterious senses, and while the brain continued to develop conscious thought, they sank deeper and deeper into the abyss that opened when culture advanced and became almost a fine science. And so man paid his price for civilization. But still the forces of the wilderness would not die and they exerted themselves at certain times, when Creation spoke with silent voice and for short spells penetrated the darkness of unconscious mind and stimulated dormant sensations. Was it thus through the centuries? Is it thus today? Is there a message, a warning, in the bosom of nature telling man to have a care, else his great achievement, his fine powers of thought, will turn upon him and destroy him? Does the wilderness still cry, 'Remember me? I am you, and you are still a part of me. Do not abandon me fully or you will destroy yourself!' I believe this is so.

It was twenty-one days later and again it was Sunday. This time four of us stepped out of my car from where I had parked it snug against a snowbank. Marq De Villiers, a young South African colleague of mine had spent but a short time in Canada and winter in this land was to him, creature of the tropics, a torture to be but barely endured. It had taken much coaxing on my part to bring him here this day. Sheila, his fiancée, was a Canadian, a product of the East Coast and a city girl. I will not soon forget her first words as she stepped from out of the storm, cigarette-smoke tainted air of my car into the crispness of a sunny winter's day.

"My! One can *breathe* here!" she exclaimed, standing spread-legged upon the snow and reaching her face towards the sky, breathing deeply.

You can, indeed, breathe on The Place. You can *breathe* and expand your being; you can relax in the quiet peace of it, bathing in this unaccustomed luxury as you would in a hot bath after a trying day in the city, yet gaining far more from the experience than it is possible to obtain from the mere contact of hot water and soap.

At first Marq was unconvinced. He hunched deeper into his voluminous parka and shuddered at the bit of the cold. But slowly even his tropical sensitivities began to change and by noon, when we stopped to toast our wiener sausages on the flames of an open fire, he had quite forgotten to be cold and had abandoned himself to the pleasures of The Place.

The noon stop over and the fire doused with snow, we set out again, exploring, seeking new paths through our wilderness and it was during this journey that we discovered our cabin site. We came upon it suddenly, from the south, as we were wading through the snow. Breaking out of a ring of heavy timber, large pines, balsams and hardwoods, we saw the first flat, then the slight hill and the rock plateau and beyond this the protecting ring of white pines seemingly sheltering the small plot of flat ground. Of course the earth was deep with snow and I was not absolutely certain then that this piece of land would be suitable, but I hoped, and waited for the warming winds and the sun of spring. And my hopes were rewarded.

Since that time De Villiers has married his Sheila and they are now either somewhere in Europe or back in South Africa while Joan and I are still gripped by the life that is ours on The Place. It is a full life this, for there are many plans ahead of us and there is much to see and do and discover on our 75 acres of wilderness. And, of course, there are our birds and beasts, and our trees and shrubs and the land itself, with its untold secrets; all these wait for us each weekend and by Friday evenings, spring, summer, autumn and winter, we are ready to leave the city and pick up our second life 'up north'. Some of our friends ask if we do not find that our constant trips to The Place are monotonous and I am sure they don't believe us when we answer in the negative. And yet this is the truth. No two weekends are alike. Perhaps only the weather changes and The Place wears a different mood; more likely each week's newness will be provided by our creatures, or by some new 'find' in the forest. But enough of this! Let me now begin the real task which I have set myself here; come with me to The Place and meet my creatures. Come see my land and its trees and shrubs and rocks. Come, you will learn many secrets on this journey!

Six

THIN, WRITHING MISTS WERE CONDENSING from the forest floor, escaping the damp earth to rise skywards, dousing shrubs and early plants with their moisture. Soon now this curtain of floating wet would be sucked up into the atmosphere by the sun's action, for already the crimson of dawn was fingering the east. It was again spring in the forest; late spring, a new morning during early May and our first 'new season' on The Place.

Life was stirring. Low and melancholy the voice of a timber wolf climbed above the trees and floated away into space, seeming to pursue a thin rind of moon that was paling into oblivion against the new light of day. Only once did the wolf call and then his voice was silenced; but even before its echo was lost, fresh sound came to replace it. A barrage of powerful blows intruded itself suddenly on the air in the area of the beaver lake. *Boom-boom-boom-boom*, the hollow drumming was loud, almost vicious after the sad-soft call of the wolf.

Four more drum-like rolls filled the air with vibrant noise, then a nasal bugle call assailed the day. *Whucker, whucker, whucker.* The voice spoke from the top of a tall, thick poplar tree that had been killed years before when its roots were drowned by the encroaching waters of the beaver swamp. The call came from a large, black-and-white bird whose head was topped with a blood-red cockade. Crow-sized, owning a heavy black bill, the pileated woodpecker surveyed his territory after the last notes of his love song died among the trees that were one mile from the area.

Fifteen feet below the bird was a squarish hole some six inches long and four inches wide. Showing against the darkness interior was the black beak, white cheeks and partly-red head of a second woodpecker. The male called again from his perch atop the poplar. He was impatient now, strident, ending his loud melody with a sharp note twice repeated: *kuk, kuk.* In her nest the female leaned her neck forward and thrust her head into the morning. She answered her mate, her call not as loud as his, then she pushed her sturdy body through the nesting doorway and burst into the air. As she left the tree she fell slightly through space, but the downward plunge was arrested as the black wings with their half-white primary feathers spread wide and flapped quickly. Progressing in a sweeping motion the female winged away from the poplar in straight flight.

From the top of his tree the male watched his mate for a moment then launched himself in chase, neck held forward, the broad white stripe that decorated its sides flashing against the backgrounds of his black body and the blue-grey light of early day. He caught up with the female on the bole of a tall pine and spent a moment wooing her and when she did not respond, led her away, deep into the forest, but remaining in their own territory, there to seek the grubs that tunnel through the wood of live trees.

Inside the nest in the poplar lay two white eggs, pigeon-sized and perfect in their oval smoothness. By the next day one more egg would rest amongst them and one or the other of the two birds would take turns sitting on them. This third egg was even at that moment acquiring its last coating of shell lime deep within the oviduct of the female woodpecker, the microscopic seed that lodged within its membranes awaiting the fulfillment of life that would come to it eighteen days after it was deposited in the nest.

The two birds darted through the pines and spruces of their territory, alighting now and then on one of the trees, their black feet with the heavy gripping claws finding secure holds on the bark, their bristle-stiff, short tails pressed against the tree trunk, giving them added security on their vertical perches. Sometimes they shared the same tree, hopping agilely up or around the trunk, at other times they would each select a tree and one or the other of them lanced at the wood with its powerful beak, probing for weaknesses in the organic structure of the tree that would tell of grubs or ants tunnelling inside.

Now the male bird, distinguished from his mate by a red crest that extended from beak to the base of his skull and by a flashing red band of 'whiskers' on his lower mandible, alighted on a dying pine. Gripping the tree trunk some twenty feet from the ground, the woodpecker arched his neck and held his head to one side, as though he was studying the bark. He moved his head, holding it at various angles, but he was not studying the tree. He was listening; listening for the slight noise made by tree borers as they worked with pincer jaws on the sapwood. The female, watching her mate from a nearby spruce, showed sudden interest. Early sunlight bathed her yellow eyes and picked out the blackness of the small pupil; her head with its black front and flame-red creast was held erect as she watched the male begin his attack on the tree, and as the first battering strokes burst out she flew to the same pine.

The male woodpecker paused in his mighty assault on the bark to look at his mate. She sidled up towards him, but moved around the trunk to a position opposite his, but several feet higher. While he arched his flaming head and continued to hammer the tree, sending great yellow-white chips of wood flying to the ground, she imitated his stance, listening, until she had located a likely area.

Now both birds chopped at the pine and the noise of their pile-driver blows filled that part of the bushland. Deeper and deeper the beaks chiselled into the tree and the ground below became littered with wood chips. After a quick barrage of blows each bird paused to examine its work, neck arching backwards, head held to one side; then the attack would begin anew.

Suddenly the male bird's beak burst through into the main tunnel of a colony of black ants. Inside the hole pulsing vibrations came from the frantic ants, aware in their tiny insect brains that a great enemy was at their door. The woodpecker could not yet reach its prey with its beak, but its specialized tongue went to work. Like a dart it shot out more than twice its normal length and its pointed tip, equipped with backward-sloping barbs, flashed into the colony of ants. Four of the ants were speared by the woodpecker's tongue; they squirmed and wriggled, but the barbs held them until the tongue had been withdrawn from the hole and the ants were in the bird's mouth. Then in again darted the tongue and more ants were stabbed and the woodpecker, the great cock of the north, dined royally.

On the other side of the tree the female had also broken through into another chamber and she too was stabbing and swallowing the great black ants that destroy so many of Canada's trees.

When the feast was over they moved to another tree and the tattoo of blows began again; and it is a wonder that any living thing can use its own body to carve into the vitals of growing trees. And yet it is not so strange for the woodpecker; he and his kind have been equipped by

Creation for this task and the jarring blows that would undoubtedly injure some other species of bird have no power to molest the woodpecker, the bones of whose skull are almost as hard as concrete and who has a tongue fitted with twin bony roots that wrap around the cranium and finally become anchored at the upper base of the beak, giving the bird, as it were, a tongue on the top of its head.

It is this arrangement that allows the bird's tongue to stretch to more than twice its normal length and thus probe deeply into the tunnels of wood borers to find the insects upon which it lives. Once impaled upon the spear-thrust of that tongue beetle larvae or black ants find escape impossible, for in addition to the spear tip and the barbs, woodpeckers discharge a thick, sticky mucus from large salivary glands. This 'glue' coats the tongue rather like the compound placed upon fly-paper and insects that are not speared, or are not properly impaled during the bird's blind thrusts into the insect tunnels, become morassed on the tongue's stickiness if they are so much as brushed by this big bird's very specialized hunting tool.

There are several pairs of these fascinating birds living on The Place and one of these, inhabiting the ravine that runs past the northern area of our cabin, has become quite accustomed to our presence, though the pileated woodpecker is a shy creature most of the time. Always we know when they are about, even if we cannot see them, for the noise of their progress is unlike that made by any of the other woodpeckers that inhabit our land.

In contrast to these husky loggers, the little downy woodpeckers are midgets, yet they are as interesting as their giant relatives and far tamer. Through the winter we watch these fluffy fellows as they come to our fat stations and attack the beef suet we always keep on the pines near our cabin. Always they put on a good show for us. Their routine hardly ever varies. First, if we are outside, we hear the tattoo of stubby wings as a bird flies towards us to alight on a tree perhaps fifteen feet from the cabin. From this vantage it takes a quick look around, its feet holding to the perpendicular trunk, its tail, with its strong 'gripping' feathers, propping up the bird as it is pressed hard against the tree. Perched thus, the downy looks to left and right and will perhaps hop around the tree trunk, the better to survey the area. In another moment the bird launches itself away from the tree and flaps to one of the pines that contain the hanging fat stations. Now the downy has a good look around, hopping round and round the trunk, peeking from behind it several times until it decides that all is well. Then it takes the last short flight to the fat and begins its snack, quite unconcerned about the humans who are watching it.

X

The first spring at The Place was a memorable one. At the time we were still intruding upon the wilderness, yet so much newness lay before us that we were too busy just looking to note that there is a sort of spirit in the wilderness, a feeling, if you will, rather like the feeling of personality that goes with an old house that has been steeped in the character of its owners.

We were 'under canvas' at that time, living between our green tent and the rock fireplace I had built, and the tasks which we had set ourselves were making slow progress, for instead of clearing our building site and preparing for the construction of our cabin, we would roam through our forest entranced by the many sights it offered.

At last, when May was spent and June already lusty, we bought our building supplies and had them delivered. I had drawn up my own plans for the cabin; simple plans, providing four walls, a roof and some windows and one door, and although I am what might be termed a 'handyman', it must be admitted that I had not before attempted to draw house plans and estimate, on paper, the quantities of material needed to finish the job. And it is perhaps for this reason that I am slightly proud of my calculations, for I finished two months later with very little surplus lumber. But I must be honest! My cabin posed not a few problems...

To begin with, every piece of wood had to be hand-cut, for there was no electricity (and there still is none) on The Place. Then, despite the yeoman efforts made by Joan and the very real help she provided, there are certain aspects of house building not suited to female physique, and yet requiring two persons for their performance. I had my problems. And there were days when my temper was admittedly vile and my patient wife came in for the brunt of my frustrations. Yet, slowly at first, the cabin began to take shape.

The simple foundations were sunk and levelled; the floor joists and first floor were laid; the two-by-four-inch framing was built on the floor and hoisted into place. And suddenly there was the skeletal shape of our cabin before us. From this point our progress was good and if the peak of

Cabin construction: author setting the rafters in place on the cabin on The Place.

Tending the first fireplace on The Place. Later the fireplace was moved to a new location; later still it was moved again and a more permanent structure built behind the cabin. (Photo: Richard Cole).

The cabin during its first winter, framed by a snowfall that dropped more than two feet of snow on The Place in one night.

our roof has a slight bump in it, we don't mind in the least. We are proud of our small cabin and though it may not have the streamlining of a professional job, still it is sturdy and comfortable, coolish in summer and almost too warm in winter, even during nights when the thermometer plunges to twenty degrees below zero.

There is something very satisfying about building one's own house and though I am not one to attach great emphasis to pride of ownership, yet I get a warm feeling now and then when I return from a long tramp in the bush and see the small cabin snuggled inside its ring of evergreens. And I suppose that this is as it should be and I don't think that my wilderness thinks the less of me for it. We poured much sweat over that cabin, Joan and I, and more than once my blood spilled over it; albeit in small quantities each time, yet I literally bled for the building!

There were weekends when my back would give me no rest after the abuse it had taken during sweltering heat; days when my hands ached constantly from holding saw or hammer; days when the blackflies and mosquitoes marked my body with their sucking tubes so that I carried ten or a dozen itching welts that made sleep difficult. And I still remember the days that Joan and I spent carrying building materials to our cabin site, a distance of some three hundred yards and mostly uphill.

This was the very beginning of our labours on the cabin. I had ordered all my two-by-four timbers (two-hundred-and-ten of them) and the concrete foundation blocks, floor joists and rafters, and they came before Alvin Adams arrived with his caterpillar tractor to build our bush road from the highway to the rock flat beside the cabin site.

The lumber dealer sent me the two-by-fours in sixteen-foot lengths and these had to be taken up the hill on the shoulder. Joan, who is the patient one of the team, was satisfied to stagger away burdened with one sixteen-foot length (and this is a big enough load for any woman), but—and I may as well admit this now—I am impatient; I looked at the pile of long timbers and calculated the number of trips we would have to make if they were ferried up the hill one at a time and I decided to cut this short by carrying several at once. Well, I did. I tried six the first time and got them all up in one trip, but by the time I dumped them off my shoulder I knew I'd have to cut down the number. Two more trips of trial and error (the latter mostly) and I discovered that three of the two-by-fours were as much as I could hope for at one time if I was not going to rupture myself, or something.

To vary this punishment, I alternated my loads. First I carried three two-by-fours, then two concrete blocks; and while I have never stopped to weigh one of those blocks, I would guess they tip the scales at some thirty-five pounds each. Their surface is rough, so gloves were needed; they don't have projections for easy gripping, and although some other object would not be burdensome if carried in one hand, those concrete blocks seemed set to escape my grip at intervals of about ten yards and I was always thankful to rid myself of them at the top of the hill.

I really don't know how long it would have taken us to complete the transfer of building materials from the highway to the building site if Alvin Adams had not come rumbling along on his 'cat'. Fortunately he arrived early one morning after we had spent a week on the job and all else stopped while we got on with the road-building. During that weekend I cleared land ahead of the cat while Alvin maneuvered the machine, levelling here, digging out a rock there, pushing over this tree or that one, always handling the cumbersome tractor with such skill and accuracy that I maintain he could, if necessary, manicure his fingernails with the blade.

When he finished work that Sunday night he made a forecast.

"Don't promise, mind, but maybe you'll be able to drive up next week," he said matter-of-factly.

Looking at the morass of earth and rock and chewed vegetation I did not believe him. I wanted to, of course, but I just did not believe he could do it. He did. Joan and I arrived early the following Friday evening. There was our brand-new road, smooth and level and already holding one layer of gravel, waiting for us. Gingerly I nosed the car on to it and we rode for the first time to the site of our cabin. It was delightful.

Next morning I drove the car down and started loading building materials on to it; but there were problems here too. Cars are not made to ferry sixteen-foot lengths of timber, and they will not accommodate too many concrete blocks at one time. But Alvin came to the rescue again. He arrived with his truck, drove to the pile of supplies and one trip later all was stacked in readiness.

Come to think of it, in those early days Alvin Adams was an almost indispensable extra around the place, and in so far as he pops in and out of this narrative, perhaps I had better tell you something about him and his family, for these are nice people, good neighbours to have, and it is their kind that tamed Canada so many years ago.

Alvin is crowding forty, a quiet, calm man with sandy-fair hair and blue eyes. A smile is never far from his lips and he dearly loves a joke, or a small prank. He is slim, for such men are, and there is the bush country etched into his eyes and in the crow's feet that crinkle their corners when he smiles. He is tallish, stooped slightly and carries himself loosely; his arms dangle a little when he stands, as though they do not quite know what to do when they are idle. He has large hands. Capable hands, those, calloused, of course, and strong. He speaks softly with a good voice and his accent is filled with the dialect of the northwoods.

At his home in the village of Uphill, four miles from The Place, his wife Audrey pursues her philosophical life surrounded by what at first seems to be a veritable host of children. In fact the Adams have six, in this order: Peggy, tall, boisterous and in her late teens; Jim, a shy, slightly gangling replica of his father who is close to Peggy in years; Shirley; thin, thin Shirley, bright, perky, pleasant and the dancer of the family, such monstrosities as the frug and the watusi being among the most cherished antics of this fifteen-year-old; edging up to Shirley is pretty Marylin. An owlish girl this, serious, perhaps even studious, certainly quiet, but with a smile that lights up her face when it makes its not-too-frequent appearance. Marylin is twelve. The next small Adams is John; he is eightish, a handsome boy, spirited, with apple-red cheeks and a bloom of health that comes built-in with country lads. And then, of course, there is Sandra, the baby; last, but by no means least of the Adams clan. Sandra and I are to be married in some fifteen or twenty years time, or so, at least, says Sandra. And, according to this elfin six-year-old, my wife Joan may live with us and do the cooking. Mind you, neither of us has consulted Joan about these arrangements yet, but time will tell, I suppose.

Audrey Adams as much as her husband requires a place of her own in this book. Audrey is hard to describe. How does one illustrate the elements? How does one capture the features of the south wind? Audrey is full of contradictions, to begin with; she is frail, because there is a heart condition, yet she has stamina, and courage, and there is humour latent under a fire that can rise quickly. She is quiet and boisterous, one mood racing in on the heels of the other; she is, above all things, friendly. She would be the first to agree with me when I say that she is not beautiful, yet she has a good face and there is that in her smile and in her eyes that means more than the superficial glamour of the pin-up girl. They are a fitting pair, this Audrey and her man Alvin. We like them. And we like their children.

χ

One weekend in late August of our first year on The Place I hung the cabin door, built a make-shift front step and put away my tools. I was glad to be done; yet I had no regrets as I walked with Joan around the small building on a final tour of inspection. It was evening on Saturday, hot, but not unpleasant, and in the wake of the setting sun there was a promise of a fine star-filled night.

In the cabin the furniture crowded our quarters for we had brought enough to furnish the building when we got around to enlarging it into two rooms. Connected to my chimney was the tall, round Quebec heater which was to stand us in such good stead that winter. There was an enormous, ancient sideboard covered in awful machine-made 'carving' which we had bought in the town of Orillia for ten dollars; and the equally ageing dining-room table, too large for the cabin, but sturdy and serviceable. Our twin cots, separated by a plywood tea chest which did duty as a feed-storage container and bedside table, were placed under the north window. We were a bit short of seating in those days, quite short, in fact, but two apple boxes filled our needs at the dining table and if we really wanted to relax indoors we dropped on our beds and usually fell asleep. Outside we had a couple of garden chairs and an outdoors table I made, all three near the second rock fireplace that I built, to the south of the cabin.

At that time our animals and birds still held aloof. Thumper, our first friend, did not visit us as often, possibly because we had moved the tent and abandoned the old fireplace, but now and then he would amble up out of the woods and munch bread or seed which we put out for him. But although the forest was full of creatures, they fled at our approach and we would get only occasional glimpses of them, quick shapes through the trees.

So the first summer on The Place faded and the nights began to carry a tinge of frost. The last wildflowers of that year opened to the sky, withered and dropped; the mushrooms and toadstools bloomed, shrivelled and melted back into the earth, their brief passage through the land marked by dark brown, jelly-like stains upon their growing places. And the leaves began to turn. Yellow-green became the heart-shaped, shivering poplar leaves; pale yellow crept into the silver birches; the oaks browned and wrinkled, hanging in seeming shame upon their branchlets. And the maples...hues of pink mixed at first with the emerald texture of those great five-lobed leaves. The pink then deepened and the green fled and at last blazing scarlet blushed through the wilderness wherever a maple stood.

The birds were leaving. Indeed, many species had already fled and daily flights glided over our cabin as the migration continued. One Saturday morning when I walked near the home of the hawks I noticed that the birds had gone, the only trace of their tenancy the big nest and two slightly-barred breast feathers that were fluttering feebly upon a cranberry bush. That same evening a great flight of geese arrowed above us, dark silhouettes against a paling sky; these were Canada geese, big black-and-white birds, strong fliers who sped south in an almost perfect V, honking their husky farewell high in the heavens.

At last they were all gone; the thrushes and the robins; the phoebes and the king birds; and the grackles; and the cardinals and orioles and the flickers and the towhees and creepers...an endless procession of delicate, colourful songsters, all hurrying now that their big journey was begun anew, leaving us with some of their more hardy relatives to face the advancing cold of a Canadian winter. I felt nostalgia as I looked at the ground and saw the curled, dead leaves that carpeted it. Now the broad-leaved trees were naked and even the scarlet sumac had shed its last flashing spears, leaving the seed head, brown and sere, standing lonely vigil above the dying plants.

This was the end of autumn, a requiem for 'the fall season', and the wilderness waited for Borealis to catch his breath and inflict his frost-laden exhalation upon all things. The forest was a quiet place then, its silence relieved only by the screaming chatter of the jays and the mutterings of the red squirrels. Yet there was newness, for the land changes when the broad leaves fall from the trees, when the bushes go naked. At this time the eye travels farther through the cloisters of the forest and what was last month an almost impenetrable wall of green becomes an open space seen through a trellis of branches. Only the evergreens stand clothed, and even these sturdy species have changed their hue slightly and lost some of their needles.

SIX

The time of autumn's death which ushers the birth pangs of winter is a strange interlude in the cycle of life and, so I believe, just as this in-between period has power to imbue a man with a feeling of inadequacy, so it can invade into the being of all wild things. For a short time the birds and animals of the wilderness are subdued and more than usually timid; the deer walk much and are restless, the squirrels spend more time just sitting, dozing on their favourite perches; the winter birds fly more busily but their voices are softer. The wolf howls more frequently and his voice carries a new note, perhaps a warning of what is to come.

On such a day a man may stand contemplating nature and hear a wolfish voice begin its mournful dirge. The ululation is sad to human ears and its has the strength to enter into the innermost reaches of the mind and set the brain to wandering through memories mildewed by passing time. I had often wondered about this and wondered, too, if it was just the mysterious cadences of the wolfish song that alone had this effect upon me. How would I feel, I asked myself on occasion, if I could but find the calling wolf and see him launch his song? Would my sensations deepen, or would sight of the creature break the spell?

One autumn I was able to resolve these questions. I was in muskeg country in the northland and it was late afternoon. I sat upon a downed tree smoking my pipe, reflecting, at peace with myself when the wolf called. The sound was loud; the wolf near. The green muskeg carpeted my steps and I circled so as to get downwind of the creature and I moved slowly towards him, guided by his intermittent call.

I saw him. He sat upon his haunches on a bare, grey obelisk of granite, bushy tail lying in a loose curl beside him, hips spread, his front legs close together and set squarely between his extended back legs. When I first saw him the angle of his back travelled straight towards his head, which was held so that its muzzle pointed downwards. He was big, but no giant, an almost coal black creature whose flanks were salted with a blur of white hairs. He sat alone, silhouetted against the evergreens and as I watched he raised his head, slowly...slowly, and he raised his muzzle, until it pointed directly at the sky. His mouth opened wide, so wide that I could see the gleaming fangs and the red of the tongue and gums through the glasses. He howled. Long, tremulous, loud; this was a haunting melody and the sight of its utterance more haunting yet. I felt a chill enter into my body and the hair on the nape of my neck prickled and I was unable to move; but this was not fear. I have felt fear too often to fail to recognize its ugly form. This was some new sensation come to visit me in the presence and sound of that wolf and for ten minutes I stood immobile, watching and listening as the lobo on the rock called and paused and called again, until at last he received an answer and his flattened ears lifted and he howled once more, a short call. Then he raised himself and leaped from the rock on to the muskeg and loped away into a tangled evergreen copse, travelling towards the answering call that still seemed to linger around me.

I left, released from my trance and ever since that day there has been new meaning for me in the howl of the timber wolf. Now, when I hear him call, a slight sadness still comes to me, but the ancient, evil folklore with which man has managed to surround the wolf is no longer there. That is no evil, rending beast that calls. It is the spirit of the wilderness, preserved since time began in the vocal chords of a wolf.

SEVEN

OUR SECOND WINTER upon The Place arrived with the boisterous vigour of a yearling moose. It was rowdy, and powerful, and capricious, and the big white mantle that it spread upon all things announced, by its density and quantity, that the time of cold had come to stay awhile. Overnight the forest was transformed from a sad place of garish shapes into a veritable fairyland and it was easy to see how Andersen contrived to depict so much fantasy in the telling of his tales.

Intricate designs in virgin white were wrought by the wind and the snow and the trees and there was much to marvel at in the manner of their sculpting. Those who are accustomed to the wet snows of more temperate zones know that many shapes can be moulded with it. But this is not so in the northland. Here the snow is dry, brittle, a powdery substance that will not hold form when pressed by human hand. Pick up a handful of the white crystals, squeeze it together and you do not obtain a snowball; instead you will discover, upon opening your hand, that some of the crystals have melted and stuck to you, attracting a thin layer of white to themselves. But the bulk of the snow remains powdery and cascades back to its place on the ground. Few snowmen are built in the northland in the midst of winter. Yet, what man cannot do, nature does. Comes the storm and the snow is blown here and there, aimlessly. And watching it driven by the gusting wind one could well wonder how this slippery, evanescent substance could yet band itself into so many intricacies by storm's end.

During our first weekend of our second winter the heavy snow arrived. It came during Friday night and by Saturday morning it had become a dense curtain and the land was washed with white, and the trees were ghost shapes through a swirl of snow. A brisk northern wind swept over all things and the cabin was good that day, its fire a sacred element that had power over the cold. Through one of the windows I watched the storm build, reach its climax and slowly go into retreat when the wind became tired of its game. The pelting flakes slowed their mad dance, hesitated, blowing irresolute in confused directions, then lifted their density and began floating towards earth in lazy tempo.

Soon the descending curtain lifted, leaving only scattered confetti-drops that were dregs emptied from ravished clouds. Then even these rear-guard remnants ceased and as the last wasted cumulus was blown across heaven by a wind unfelt upon earth, the sun of noon took its rightful place in the sky and smiled. Uncountable crystals of ice came to life and flirted with the sunlight and the forest was transformed and it beckoned to me and drew me away from my snug fire into its frigid midst.

I went outside, my face blooded from the heat of the stove, my body dressed warm, snowshoes attached to the suppled softness of the mucklucks that encased my feet. Before me was the wilderness. I went to it, lifting each foot high, swinging each leg, bending the ankles to ease my steps from the burden of the long, wide shoes of rawhide webbing. And as I walked the wilderness of this country took hold of me and the untamed that lives chained in all men eased its fetters and burst through the tenuous threads of civilization. It must have been thus with those first white men who came to this enormous land and willed themselves to exile within its unchartered vastness.

Before me, beyond the boundaries of the land that I owned, stretched a white forest that knew not the taint of human weaknesses. No evil lurked ahead; there was none to lie, or steal, or cheat; here there were no fine speeches cloaking the lust for power, or greed; no blood would be spilled here needlessly, uselessly...Why did I think thus then? Why do I think thus now, as I write of this day that has passed? Perhaps the peace of mind that came to me out there reached into hidden recesses of the mind...perhaps. I know not. But I felt alive on that day; alive and glad that I had found this wilderness and I think now that if there ever was a time of demarcation, a time when the wilderness accepted me as part of itself, that time occurred on that day.

For three hours I tramped in my webbed feet across the snows of the forest, now through stands of pine; through balsam thickets, over ice-bound creeks and down into small valleys choked with a welter of hazel and cranberry and spindly aspens. I tramped across the beaver lake and beyond it, to the second lake that is home to the ducks of spring and summer and autumn. Sometimes I paused to listen to the call of a chickadee,

More tracks in the snow; this time those of a red fox, at left, those of a person's snowshoes at right. Crossing both sets are the prints of a snowshoe hare.

or the drilling of a woodpecker. A porcupine eyes me myopically from the crown of a sparse pine; tracks in the snow told of a white-tail's travels not long before. Occasionally, glancing back over my shoulder, a strange feeling of loneliness took me as I saw only my own tracks etched deeply into the snow.

Beyond the second lake a spectacle of death waited. The telling crimson of the act became evident while I was still almost one hundred paces from the scene, a small place between two young spruce trees. Five timber wolves had ambushed a yearling deer at this place, said the writing on the snow. Two of the wolves had run the young stag while the others had skirted around and ahead, intercepting the fleeing animal. The drama was clear. Leading in direct line to the death place were three sets of tracks. The deer's, small punch marks in the snow, widely spaced; those of the pursuers heavier, each paw-hole followed by a drag mark as the shorter legs of the wolves did not quite clear the top layer of snow; the tracks extended, showing the long, tireless, loping stride of the hunters. Then a welter of tracks. Three clear sets coming in from the opposite direction, converging on the deer. And a wide, roughly-circular amphitheatre of snow broken and scattered, where the kill and the death struggles had taken place.

Then the final script. The scarlet blood, gouts of it sprinkled around the edges of the kill, flowing quantities of it bedaubed upon the snow, mixed with it, diluted to light crimson in places as the heat of life melted the crystals of winter. The grey-fawn, hollow hairs, scattered in profusion, the base of each clustered bunch ivory yellow, where, in life, each filament had been anchored to the hide by its microscopic, bulbous root. And the last remnants, the leavings of this kill; bits of sinew and flesh, shreds of bone; two vertebrae intact but gnawed clean of flesh which I picked up and still have; a section of the skull showing the button-marks of the antlers. The cups of the antlers told me that this had been a stag; the vertebrae, by their smallness, told me that this had been a young animal.

Human emotions returned for a moment at the scene of death. I felt sorrow for the deer and was on the verge of anger towards the wolves. But the wilderness was too close for these feelings to last. I still regretted the passing of the graceful young buck, but there was need in the living bodies of the wolves and this was the law here. One had died so that five should live; one creature was fashioned by nature so that others should nourish themselves upon it. Who was I to wish to alter this law?

Pocketing the small bones I turned and followed my tracks back to the cabin on The Place.

χ

We met Nutsy and Beau Brummell that first winter and others of their kind, and this was the start of our real friendship with the beasts and the birds of our forest and Joan and I were made captives by them, for this was the beginning of our understanding.

Nutsy was the little sow squirrel whose mother had been struck down by the hawk. During the early days of that winter we saw her often from the windows of our cabin as she came to eat of the breadcrumbs and other table leavings we were then putting out for the forest creatures. As one weekend followed another she became more accustomed to us and one day she did not run chittering to her pine when we stepped out of the cabin. By the next weekend she was waiting outside, sitting in the snow with a look of expectancy on her bewhiskered, elfin face. I had bought peanuts that Sunday and I threw one to her.

Her nose told her that this was good. She sidled up to the nut, sniffed it once and picked it up with her mouth. Then she twirled it neatly and rapidly between her fingers, getting the 'feel' of it until she was evidently satisfied with its balance, for she put it into her mouth again and gripped it with her long teeth and made off with it. Minutes later she was back, having hidden the nut somewhere in her territory, and I threw her a second one. Again she repeated her previous performance, twirling the food between her fingers and finally grasping it between her teeth and taking it away.

Three weekends later she was taking peanuts from our fingers and before spring's arrival that year she could be counted on to enter the cabin whenever she had a chance, search out the peanut bowl and help herself. Besides this, if there were no peanuts in the bowl, she was not afraid to climb upon Joan or me and search about our persons for the nuts. I always carry a supply of them in the back pocket of my trousers and Nutsy, as we christened her because of her fondness for the nuts, would often clamber on me and seek out, by smell alone, the supply in my pocket.

Then, one fine winter's morning, Beau Brummell turned up. At that time Beau was the only male in our immediate area and he was so beautiful that no name less than Brummell's would fit him. He was big, and his coat shone with vigour and its colours seemed always to be prime; he was the handsomest of squirrels—and the local coward. No matter how small the other squirrels might be, if they chittered angrily at Beau he ran, emitting shrill squeals of rage and frustration and invariably hard pressed by one or the other of his kinfolk. But if he was short on courage, Beau has ever been long on determination. No matter how often he was chased away from the handy food supplies that surrounded the cabin, back he would come again from another direction, sneaking in to run up to me or to Joan and snatch a peanut from our grasp.

His system for taking peanuts from us is practised by no other squirrel in our area. First he comes up and makes sure that we know he is there, and this is generally accomplished by the simple process of dashing right up to us, stopping dead at our feet, looking up into our faces with a very reproachful look on his own, and squeaking. Then, undoubtedly working on a theory that a stationary target is easiest to hit, he streaks away to come to another brief stop six or eight feet from us. One more survey from this point, and if the coast is clear and we are bending forward holding out a peanut, he zeros in with the speed of a striking cobra, back legs held out stiffly to each side, his run a strange, hopping motion. Thus he sights on the target, dashes in, leaps from two feet away, grabs the extended peanut and beats a hasty retreat to the place where he intends to bury the offering. He is neither gentle nor scientific about his home run and once, when he was evidently in more of a hurry than usual, he missed the peanut and his razor-sharp teeth connected with the skin just above my thumb. Retrieving the nut which he had dashed from my grasp I extended it again and he repeated the run and this time made off with the prize and only then did I notice the neat incisions on my hand, so sharp are his teeth that neither pain nor blood came for several seconds after the wounds were inflicted.

Of course this was an accident. Beau is gentle and friendly towards us and if he had not been turned into a sort of nervous wreck by the machinations of his vigorous young wife—Nutsy—he would never make his lightning dashes. Whenever she was not around, which used to be rather rarely, for that damsel missed very little around the cabin, he would bide his time about taking his peanut; but, as I have said, these occasions were rare.

Nutsy and Beau Brummell have taught us much about 'wild' animals and their world and perhaps the first and possibly most important lesson was that of recognition. Strangers visiting us have never been able to notice any difference between one red squirrel and another, but just as there are variations in the human race, so there are in the realm of the animals and birds. And so it is with our ever-increasingly family of squirrels. Beau, apart from being a coward, had, when we first knew him, a number of distinctive and readily-recognizable characteristics. The way he ran; the way he called; the colour of his body; the shape of his head; the rather flat nose with a brownish blemish at the end. Joan and I can pick him out from amongst a dozen red squirrels at a glance.

It was so with Nutsy. She was small, her colour was peculiar to herself; her face was 'pretty' and had its own cast of character and, above all things, she was a holy terror. No other squirrel could intimidate our Nutsy, and she was utterly disdainful of danger from the predators.

During our second summer on The Place my father-in-law arrived for a visit with a hulking, black, Labrador retriever—Joan's father raises these enormous brutes—and, while I must admit that the dog was a model of canine behaviour, I must also place on record that our Nutsy was distinctly jealous of this great black stranger that was allowed space inside *her* cabin. The poor dog sat obediently in the center of our small living-room (we had built the addition by then) and eyed the open door. Near him, but at what we considered was a safe distance, was the bowl of pink plastic that we use as a container for the current supply of peanuts. Soon Nutsy came a-calling. As usual she announced her coming with a series of shrill screams that were intended to alert us to her needs: 'Come on, you people! Break out the peanuts and open that confounded door,' her calls managed to convey quite clearly.

Well, on this day the door was already open and Nutsy hopped up the steps and paused momentarily on the threshold. Instantly she spotted the interloper and Joan and I though that she would retreat. But this was the obvious, the only thing that a half-pound squirrel could do when faced by eighty-pounds of massive, tough, hunting dog. We knew this, my father-in-law knew this and Blaze the dog knew this. But Nutsy did not know this.

Shaking her head with the disdain of a beautiful woman being eyed by a repulsive male, Nutsy impudently marched right up to Blaze, paused inches away from his shaking, eager body and, adding insult to injury, swept regally past him, walking right under his nose and brushing his muzzle with her erect tail, continuing her nonchalant journey to the peanut bowl. And this mind you, when she did not need to go near the great dog to get her peanut!

The poor dog was completely demoralized! He sat shivering with hunting eagerness, knowing he must not chase this brazen little tramp, and, I suspect, completely flabbergasted that such a thing could happen to a self-respecting hunting dog. And he had hardly got over his first shock when Nutsy returned again for another peanut and another go at the dog. Deliberately, pitilessly, she baited Blaze, this time hopping right around him, aware that he was watching her with eyes that seemed to have turned bloodshot with lust, but yet pretending that he was not in the same room. When a little while later she repeated the performance I closed the door, fearing for the dog's sanity more than for Nutsy's life. Whereupon the hussy treated me to a round of her most royal insults, shrilling and screaming like some medieval fishwife until I opened the door and threw a good handful of peanuts on the front steps.

I knew, of course, that by putting out that handful of peanuts I was not buying peace. But at least, then, the object of Nutsy's wrath was not I, for now she transferred her not inconsiderable vocal powers upon the dozen or so other red squirrels that attempted to cash-in on the offering I had just made.

There she sat, the little harridan, eating a shelled nut, holding it daintily between her two ridiculously small thumbs, turning and twirling it around and around while her sharp, nimble teeth nibbled at it; and all the while shrilling and howling at the pack that circled around her but never quite dared to steal any of her precious peanuts. With one accord, the jealous horde that faced her knew that this regal little being that sat swearing upon our doorstep was the boss of at least that section of forest. They wanted their share of peanuts—not that they were hungry, for there was plenty of seed in the feeders—but they were not prepared to incur Nutsy's rather fearsome anger.

During the years that we have lived on The Place we have acquired enough knowledge of squirrels to fill a good-sized book and though I do not plan to write in such depth of our squirrels in this narrative, still I feel that I must tell something of these perky, interesting little wildlings.

From natural history books and other writings you may obtain much general knowledge of these creatures, but there will be a great deal that the books will not tell you. For instance, it is said that squirrels have from one to several middens in which they store their supply of winter seeds and, while this is true, never have I seen mention of the squirrel's more predominant habit of just plan hiding foods that he does not plan to eat in the first convenient location that he can find.

In fact, squirrels, like many other animals and birds, are compulsive hoarders and while they do have one or two main larders, perhaps in a hollow tree, but more likely in a downed log or under the ground or under a rock, in times of plenty they will ferry nuts and seeds, one or two at a time, and scurry off to hide them anywhere within a radius of two hundred yards or more, and rarely in the same place twice. What makes them do this? Obviously this is a habit born into these creatures, Creation's way of ensuring survival of certain species of trees and bushes that might otherwise die out in a particular region. It is also Creation's way of sharing her supplies of food with others in the forest.

One pine seed hastily buried under leaf-mould by a busy squirrel can be forgotten and is as surely planted as any cultivated seed sown by a human farmer. If it be summer, chances are the seed will sprout before autumn and though the frost may damage the upper part of its growth the rootlets are already formed and will lie dormant until spring comes to stimulate their growth anew. If the seed is 'planted' in autumn, it will lie dormant and by spring will burst its shell and send down root tendrils while it pushes its green parts through the earth and out of it, into the free air.

This is one reason for the red squirrel's habit of burying the food. The other is easier to see. Watch a red squirrel scurrying away into the forest with a nut and you will see one or two blue jays, or a perky chickadee, following closely above him, flitting from tree to tree, hovering each time the squirrel inspects a likely hiding place, following again if the redback rejects the planting spot and seeks another. Often the squirrel is aware of the robbers above him and takes evasive action. He will pretend; digging a hole with flashing paws and covering it over again, patting the earth down firmly with his small hands much like a miniature grave-digger tramping a newly-dug grave. But there is nothing buried in this place and the squirrel makes off with the nut or seed still gripped in his mouth while the jay plops down from the trees and inspects the area, scratching at the newly-dug earth in vain for the titbit it believes is there. Meanwhile the redback has buried his seed somewhere else, perhaps securely, perhaps under the keen gaze of another jay.

In this way I have seen Beau and Nutsy and others make several dummy holes in order to fool as many as three birds, one after the other. So why does the squirrel continue to bury the food in the open, where the birds can dig it up again? Why does the creature not find a hole, or a dead tree or a rock crevice for these individual supplies? I do not rightly know the answer to this question, unless it be that the squirrel out of habit buries much more food than he can eat and some of this would be a wasted supply if some other creature did not get it.

On the other hand, a squirrel's proper midden is often raided by other squirrels and by chipmunks and above all things, by black bears, who delight in uncovering a bushel or two of hazel nuts, salted away for the winter by a cautious squirrel. So perhaps the squirrel is practising that old, human adage and not putting all his eggs in one basket. By having two or three main middens and by burying or hiding individual seeds or nuts helter-skelter, the small wildling is making sure of his dinner when times are scarce and his hoarding habits are so acute that even when food is plentiful, as is the case around our cabin, he must bury all that he cannot eat.

Another interesting aspect of the squirrel is its way of eating. Agile and seemingly dexterous though he is, the squirrel has not yet learned to use his fingers as do other animals, such as raccoons, monkeys and humans. He picks up objects with his mouth quite easily, but when it comes to holding these same objects with his hands he is relatively clumsy about it. His thumbs have evolved through many, many years of use, his tiny stubs, rather like extreme miniatures of a human thumb, which, unlike the rest of the squirrel's fingers and toes, do not have long, sharp claws but have instead a tiny thumb-nail more like a human nail than that of an animal. If you were to take a cob of corn, fold both your thumbs towards your palm and hold the corn between the first joints of each thumb, you would be emulating a squirrel holding a nut or a seed. In this

One of our young red squirrels. This is a favourite pose of those little creatures, who hang on to the tree bark with their back feet while they eat nuts or seeds.

This baby red squirrel has met a peanut for the first time.
It did not take him long to discover what to do with it.

way he brings the food to his mouth, while his fingers with their long claws are employed to hold shells, husks or other food. But if, let us say, the squirrel has found just one hazel nut and has gnawed through the shell, discarded this and is left with the meat, he leaves his fingers idle while his thumbs guide the food to the chisel-teeth.

This manoeuvre is complex enough for this little primitive—I have tried to copy it with only limited success—but what is so fascinating to me is the dexterity with which a squirrel uses his tiny, stubby thumbs. With a rapidity that baffles the eye he twirls and twists his morsel of food this way and that with such seeming ease that an observer would at first swear the entire hand was in use. I thought this, until I observed the red-back more closely and noted that it was only the thumbs that manipulate the actual food portion, but though I have watched carefully and often, the amazing speed that this little fellow uses in twirling his food has so far defied my best efforts. You see what is happening, but you cannot see how it is being made to happen and the nearest I can come to describing the thumb action is to ask you to imagine a tiny lathe the spindles of which are clamped on a nut; when the motor is turned on, the spindles rotate and, of course, so does the nut.

As is so often the case with the workings of Creation, this small woods creature who is so plentiful in some areas that he is condemned and hunted and relegated to the category of pest, is yet full of marvels. He is so common in the sight of man that few humans take the time to have a really close look at him, but he is worth the study.

His intellect is highly developed and he has his very own personality. In the forest he is policeman and scavenger, farmer and news broadcaster ,,asking little in return for his services and providing besides many hours of fascinating study for those naturalists interested enough to study him. *Tamiasciurus hudsonicus* is his Latin name; red-back, boomer, pine squirrel or many another epithet are the colloquialisms applied to him by unscientific man. He is shot at for fun, because he is a pest, for the pot, or just simply because there are some humans who must, it seems, kill something every so often and *Tamiasciurus hudsonicus* is available and obviously will not shoot back and killing him can be done with impunity, barring the odd time when one nimrod, practising a remarkable degree of zeal, shoots another of his fellows because, says he later to the police, 'I thought he was a squirrel.' And those of you who think I am joking, don't laugh! There have already been any number of deaths and injuries in Canada and the United States because of just such mistakes.

Be this as it may, Canada's red squirrels were the first to really make me think about that mildewed, senile, yet still lively cliché: Animals don't think, they act on instinct! I wonder who first said that? I wonder what sage decided in the fullness of his human mind that animals do not have the power to reason? And I wonder why? It must be readily granted, of course, that man's powers of reason are far superior to those of other animals (that's why we call ourselves *rational* animals—though at times of recent years I have wondered whether that adjective is really the correct one, what with the H-bomb and all). But for somebody, eons gone, to have stated once quite categorically that the so-called lower orders of terrestrial life act only upon instinct is to me the height of human egotism. Or is it ignorance? Or ignorance and egotism?

If we are to say that animals are motivated by instinct, it would be just as true to make the same claim on behalf of the human race, for man, in many, many ways, is so motivated. He points, blinks, swallows, groans, drools, laughs, grins, cries, inhales air into his lungs, etc., etc., etc., through instinctive action rather than conscious thought. And so do animals. But man also *thinks,* he reasons, in other words, working things out for himself by an orderly process of conscious mental effort. And so, say I, do animals and birds. Man, likewise has laid claim to another rather wonderful trait, the ability to think backwards—the highest refinement, surely—and remember. And so, say I, do animals. And I can prove this quite simply through the actions of a humble woods creature—a red squirrel.

Autumn had come and gone and rigid winter gripped The Place and Beau Brummell, undoubtedly well supplied with peanuts and other seeds he had been carting away from our cabin feeders to his secret places in the forest, stopped coming to see us. Now and then in the months that followed Joan and I thought we saw him; quick, dashing glimpses through the snow-crusted trees, but he did not approach the cabin or seek the peanuts we used to hold out to him. And so we gave him up and I rather thought he had fallen victim to one of the many predators that roam through The Place.

Then, as the ides of March fell away and the first calendar day of spring came and went and the weather began to moderate, Beau appeared out of nowhere, scrambled up our door, as he had been accustomed to doing during summer and autumn every time he wanted to attract our attention, and waited patiently on our doorstep for the peanut he knew we would give him.

Naturally we were only too glad to oblige for, alas, our sprightly Nutsy, the little harridan of our woods, had fallen victim to the forces of Creation. I opened the door and there he was, almost as beautiful as ever, certainly as saucy as ever and absolutely certainly having full remembrance of us and the cabin and the food that came from it. I handed over a peanut and it was just as though winter had never been. He reached up, standing on tiptoes, took the peanut, gently now, for there were none there to chase him, and away he went, as spread-legged as ever, as jumpy and fast as he had been last autumn. Beau had returned and he kept on returning, as familiar and friendly as ever. Instinct? Or reason and remembrance? I prefer to think it was the latter; I leave it to others to invent a dozen explanations for Beau's process of thought.

χ

That second winter on The Place was an ever-changing kaleidoscope of fascination and for the first time in my life I was almost sorry to see the cold retreat before the pushing of a warm wind coursing north from the torrid zones of this continent. But even this retreat of frost and the invasion of warmth held great interest. The transition was slow and it was this slowness that provided new thrills for me and led my mind to hitherto unexplored avenues.

I remember that March was ageing and we were in the middle of a warming spell. The first robin had appeared one morning, the tree sparrows were congregating, massing for their northward flight to their breeding grounds; the squirrels were active and numerous, coming out of their hiding places to scurry around the cabin, nibbling at seed and chasing each other through the tree-tops in an exuberance of mating lust. Finally it had come, I said to myself one Saturday morning; Spring, the harbinger of life, was here. Even the poplars and maples and willows and hazels were responding, I thought, noting their tinge of yellow and orange as sap long-stored in the root systems began travelling upwards preparatory to its new adventure with life.

Almost convinced that I could change the snow tyres on my car and return to the conventional treads of good weather, I was walking casually through the bush, my boots leaving big prints in the melting snow, when I saw a snowshoe hare. Sight of him brought me up short, for the creature was still snow white. Could it be, I asked myself, that this varying hare was wrong? All the signs said that spring was here, yet this hopping, uncaring fellow still sported his fine winter suit and there were no signs of the brown hairs of spring lacing the pristine purity of his white.

Sunday morning came and it was even milder and brighter than yesterday and by noon of that day I was convinced that something had gone wrong with the hare's metabolism. The idiot thing, said I sagely, was going to die a quick death, for his white coat would show up just fine against the browns and greens of the spring forest and the hare's safety depends almost as much on camouflage as it does on the speed born in his great long legs.

Sunday evening did nothing to alter my view of that dolt of a hare whose system had played him false and placed his life in jeopardy, but two days later the hare was vindicated by the frost that crept back into the air, even in the city, one hundred miles south of his home range. And by the following Thursday a fresh topping of snow, eight inches thick, again cloaked the bush and against this blazing white background the snowshoe hare was nearly invisible.

How do these creatures know? One day, perhaps, we shall have the full answer to this question and to many others like it. All I can do just now to shed some light on the mystery is to say that somewhere deep inside the beings of wild creatures there is hidden a 'time clock'. By this intricate yet unknown mechanism the hare's body knows when it is time to begin the moult and no amount of 'false' spring days is going to alter its timing. Thus the beaver knows when to begin his logging operations in the autumn, starting early one year, late another, in both instances his actions forecasting a hard, long winter or an easy one. It is so with the marmots and the chipmunks and with the squirrels and the skunks and raccoons and the deer and the bear and it is even reflected in the howl of the wolf. In fact, so it seems to me, man is the only creature that must depend on the often incorrect weather forecast before he knows what kind of coat to wear when he leaves his house. But it is not always so with the birds. Birds can be fooled, like the fat robin that appeared too early during that second winter. He came during that weekend when the hare was still white and he sang his fool head off all during Saturday and partly through Sunday, for all the world as though he, personally, was ushering in the new season. Quite obviously he left in a hurry, for there was no trace of him a week later when we returned to The Place and found the new fall of snow.

Three more weeks of cold were to drift by after the robin stole a march on the south wind and if the cold was not as intense as it had been in December and January and February, still it was a respectable sort of frost that nipped at the body and only partially retreated during the sun hours, grudgingly allowing the yellow warmth to thaw some of the snow, then cutting in quickly when Sol drifted away behind the western tree-tops.

The days of winter's stubborn retreat and spring's hesitant arrival are known to many as the doldrum days and doctors tell me that at those times there is a rash of colds and influenza and rheumatism and you-name-them sort of complaints amongst city dwellers. Having written about such times as a journalist, doing the usual 'late winter' stories on epidemics of disease, I have learned from medical men that the human system finds itself short of vitality and therefore subject to the attack of 'bugs'. I accept this, I must, for I am no doctor and the men I have spoken to were all competent physicians, but still I wonder if it is the body that is made low or the mind? Can it be that the mind, becoming fed up by home-to-office-to-supper-to-television-to bed-to office routine of winter is putting up a bit of protest and is telling the body to 'act up' so it will be noticed? I do not really know and I do not propose to pontificate on this one, I am content to let the mind men figure it out.

All I can tell you with any certainty is that since I have fallen in love with the wilderness I do not get the usual attacks of 'flu and colds and creepy horrors of pre-spring and no great waves of noxious miasmas come trooping into my bedroom at night to invade my poor, weakened body. Instead I am reasonably fit (apart from a slight tendency to sleep in off-hours lately, occasioned, I believe, by the demands of my publisher and the equally persistent requirements of my job as a newspaper man) and I look forward just as eagerly to my weekends now as I do in the middle of winter, the start of spring or the middle of summer. And if there is a moral somewhere in this, you are welcome to it!

I progress through those days of city doldrums until one morning I wake up and there is a 'thing' inside of me and I get restless and a bit more irritable than usual and I feel like arguing more and there is a far-away look in my gaze. Sternly I tell myself that it is still too early, but the 'thing' inside me will not be denied and I start thinking of long train journeys at night, when through a daze of jolting sleep I hear the engine shriek its ghastly, lonely whistle at the country through which it is puffing; I think of the song of birds and the soft blowing of temperate winds; I see again the waves, green and translucent, splashing themselves to rest on the hard, wet sands of a moonlit beach. I think things when the 'thing' enters my mind and I become impatient with the weekdays and feel like packing my four-wheel drive and heading for the backwoods on Tuesday night, instead of waiting for Friday.

Still, to a degree, I can control the 'thing' and manage to keep my mind at least partially devoted to the livelihood which enables me to eat regularly, and for ten days or so life flows on and my activities are more or less normal. And then, perhaps one evening as I am driving home from the office, I look up at the sky. There are clouds up there, bluish, greyish clouds, torn and tattered by swift winds and in between them there are patches of limpid blue flecked by occasional milk-white cumulus. And coming in across those clouds I see two ducks, dark silhouettes against the skyline, but recognizable as mallards. They come in strong, their wings flashing, their long necks stretched straight out, their duck's bills pointing the way to some unseen patch of water that will be their landing place and refuge for this day. Sight of those ducks does it. The 'thing' takes over and what was moments before a reasonable human being becomes transformed into a scheming, idle lout whose only concern is to escape to a place called The Place, where, he knows, the pussy willows will be decorating the forest and the buds will be popping their gussets as they try and beat their own system and where the birds will be risking laryngitis as they flute their calls all over The Place. Where the raccoons will be out chittering at night, the males fighting, the females watching and waiting and last year's young males dancing about wildly, feeling frustrations of aroused but unrequited passions. And where the skunks employ themselves in similar fashion and now and then perfume each other in their excitement, usually under the floor of the small cabin on The Place, so that man must get out of his cot and smoke his pipe to minimize the aroma of skunk romance.

The 'thing' is king then and I know that spring has arrived. It is a small spring yet, needing a bit more growing time, but it is here, and it is exciting and if nights become frost-nipped still, the mornings are something to behold, up there at The Place. And it must be the 'thing' that puts strange thoughts into my mind about this time and I begin to wonder why it is that dogs, or wolves, or bears, or cats do not go about smelling the flowers.

Smell is a wonderful thing. It is pleasure, and hate, and love, and horror, and sickness, and death, and life. All these things are smell; but why? And why is one smell obnoxiously horrible to one creature and pure, unadulterated nectar to others? Why do not dogs smell flowers? And why do they love to sniff at so many other strange smells? Why will a dog spend several minutes sniffing at the defecations of one of his kind? Why will it go into ecstasies over some putrefying aroma that would turn a human stomach? Why will it not take pleasure from smelling a flower?

I find such things interesting when the 'thing' takes me in the spring. And I try to answer these questions and now and then I come up with reasonable replies, such as the reason why dogs do not smell flowers. I say to myself then, smells are very, very personal things. They are things that associate themselves with the life and habits and traditions and heritage of the creatures that sniff them. For the dog a flower has little significance; he may or may not like its smell, he does not bother about it. But the manure of another dog, or the putrefied carcass of a bird...*there,* now, is pure paradise in the canine nostrils. The manure's aroma tells him whether it was a male or a female that defecated at that particular spot; it further tells him when the act was committed; it also tells him whether, if it was a female that passed the spot, she was receptive to romantic advances or whether she would be likely to administer a good hiding to a presumptive male. The smell of rot tells the dog that there may be something deliciously palatable kicking around unclaimed and it stimulates his taste buds and if there be nothing left but the smell, he lingers over it, sniffing like a connoisseur of rare herbs. But flowers? Why should *he* bother to waste his nose on such dull, inedible objects? He is prepared to let humans and bees and birds enjoy the smell of flowers, and of course, to these creatures, flowers are heavenly, clean, pretty, wonderful objects that supply each with a different value. The bee finds nectar for his honey, the bird finds insects nesting in the flowers and it finds seeds mayhap and it even finds nectar, too, if it be a humming bird. Humans, as everyone knows, find all sorts of enchanting things in the smell of flowers; like love, and art, and beauty, and remembrance, and sadness, and happiness, and even death.

X

Have you ever heard a mouse sing? No? Well, I have. Of course, it was no ordinary house mouse, so perhaps that's why it sang, but there it was, the voice of a mouse raised in tiny, plaintive melody. It was a night a new spring; one of those velvet-soft spells of dark that can only be truly appreciated in the heart of a Canadian forest. Above, green stars sparkled in a sky clear of cloud; below, the quiet of a bush night, that silence that is not stillness, but rather a subtle harmony of natural sounds.

Rising over the murmur of aspen leaves the occasional snapping of a dry twig told of the passing of some small creature. Somewhere hidden in a thick stand of balsam firs a grey owl spoke, deep yet soft its sound. As I stood enjoying the wilderness a quiet singing thrust itself upon my notice. I thought at first it was a cricket, but the season was not yet come for these and the notes of the song were not quite like those made by the cicada. It was a small voice, yet rich and melodious, and it reached into the night from under a granite boulder.

What manner of creature was this, I asked myself? Certainly it was a new 'song' to me, and I crept closer to the granite and the voice chanted on, a wonderful, trilling little song that was as intriguing as it was mysterious. Squatting about three feet from the rock I listened closely to the unknown balladeer and I thought that had this been Ireland two centuries earlier, I would undoubtedly have decided that I was listening to a solo by one of the 'little people'. And then I saw the songster. The glow from the stars and the meagre glint from a thin crescent moon showed me a tiny shape which had just emerged from under the rock.

Little people indeed! They do not come much 'littler' than the white-footed mouse, that cheeky, pretty little chap that breeds like a plague and provides food for all manner of meat eaters in the forest. I had read that these mice can sing, but I had not heard one before and I must confess that I had not really believed the claims made on behalf of the singing mouse by its naturalist fans. But there he was, squatting rather like I was, resting his weight on his meagre little buttocks, his white 'socks' clearly visible, his tiny hands held against his chest, his long, tapery-thin tail stretched out behind, visible as a faint, string-like outline against the mossy ground. He was facing me and his sharp face seemed to be aware of my presence but the reedy little voice with its curious melody continued.

How can I describe this pretty melody of the wild? To say that it was akin to a shrill buzzing does not do it justice, for there was more to it than that. Yet I can find no syllables capable of giving even an approximate idea of the sound. It was rather like an incredibly high, yet soft, crooning that lasted between five and ten seconds, stopped and was repeated again; but despite its softness, this mite of a bush voice carried, for I had first heard it without recognizing it while I was still some fifty feet away from the rock.

I do not like the term 'mouse' applied to *Peromyscus,* the Latin name of these little chaps. Mouse has for too long associated itself in the minds of humans with the unpleasant, dirty, disease-ridden species that have followed man ever since he fell out of the tree. But *Peromyscus* is not like that. *Peromyscus* is clean and never slovenly; he or she preens its fur, is indefatigable to the point of prudery in its insistence upon hygiene. It sweeps and combs and brushes and scrubs itself and its young and its nest and anything it comes into contact with.

It is said by naturalists that *Peromyscus* is a shy, retiring little creature, but I cannot readily agree, for there are many of his kind living at The Place and I have made frequent and friendly contact with them on many, many, occasions. In fact, the first of the species that I met stole half of Joan's pretty, blue nylon blanket in order to build herself a posh, fluffy nest in my tool box and she was so insistent on her choice of home site that she resisted three times any and all my efforts to house her and her stolen blanket in more appropriate lodgings. It was only after I went to a great deal of trouble to build her a palatial mansion out of a cardboard box that was properly roofed with pieces of the same asphalt shingle that protected my own dwelling that she became content to quit my tool box and occupy the new house.

Since that time, several years ago, any number of these songsters occupy various spots around our cabin and at one time took over our modest outbuilding, stealing yards of toilet paper with which to line their nests and setting up a miniature, indignant stamping with their tiny front feet every time we had the audacity to enter our little building in response

White-footed mouse babies huddle in their nest, made from kapok stolen from my lifejacket.

to the ancient call of nature. But when Squirt arrived and appropriated the outbuilding for himself and cleaned out the erstwhile tenants, driving them to other hidey-holes and only grudgingly allowing them to help themselves to the occasional supply of toilet tissue or to little lumps of kapok stolen by both Squirt and *Peromyscus* from my perfectly good, buttercup-yellow lifejacket, which I foolishly hung in the outhouse and is now no longer either perfectly good or serviceable for its original intention.

Now, upon entering our outhouse bent upon urgent missions, Joan and I are no longer treated to the tiny stamping of *Peromyscus;* instead we are greeted by rather loud stampings and the spiteful chitter of Squirt, who is a red squirrel, a son or daughter (we don't know yet) of Nutsy, who while not actually biting the hand that feeds him, still objects somewhat to its presence in his home.

Because of this Joan is now engaged in a new project while passing the time away in the city. She has this small, mandarin-orange box and she is devotedly applying herself to converting this wooden structure that found its way into our home after a long journey from its origin in Japan, into a home for Squirt.

"Well," she said defensively not too long ago when I asked why. "I'm trying to stop him (woman-like she has already decided that Squirt is a him) from scaring me every time I go to the back."

Perhaps there is logic in this, somewhere. At present Squirt has some eight or ten homes. One is inside the remains of my good, buttercup-yellow lifejacket; another is inside an orange box that was *once* filled with tools that I do not use daily and *now* is filled with tools that I do not use daily *and* a supply of kapok and finely masticated toilet paper, in four colours; another place that Squirt calls home is behind a tall, white-enamelled water-cooler that we no longer use as a water-cooler but which now does duty as a container for our toilet paper, supplies of which were difficult to maintain when they were conveniently kept upon one of those rotating things which, despite the great strides made by man in the field of science, have altered not one whit from the days of great-great-granny. Now that rolling contraption hangs empty and while we keep the tissue in the water-cooler, I am convinced that Squirt uses the rotating thing as a gymnast uses a trapeze.

However, to get back to Joan and her present project, I do not doubt that Squirt will accept it as a home, for he seems to have a real fad for collecting houses, but I do not think it will solve her problems. Squirt, I am sure, will continue to pop up just at the wrong moment and Joan will continue to become startled at his expectedly-unexpected, and most inopportune, appearances. But then, such is life...and after all, squirrels, too, are entitled to a place they can call home, and anyway, the poor little beggar had to have *somewhere* to live and at least neither he nor his relatives, nor the tenants he so recently *ousted—Peromyscus et al.*—have invaded our cabin...yet!

All this sounds as though Joan *hates* squirrels and mice, which of course, is not true. She goes all silly over the squirrels, goo-gooing at them all over the show, commiserating with them when they do not need it and leaving tidbits of food for them wherever she discovers a likely place, including, naturally, our outhouse, the shelf of which—the one over the rolling thing that *used* to hold the toilet paper—is constantly littered with either entire peanuts in their shells, or entire shells without their nuts, which are never, but never, cleaned up by Squirt after he has finished gorging himself following one of Joan's trips.

Watching the arrival of what I call our first proper spring on The Place (proper because we were now established, cabin and all), unforgettable experiences came to enrich our lives. Again I was conscious of the forces of Creation and for the hundredth time I was struck with the feeling that the forest that housed me more closely resembled my ideals of a place of God than any church or cathedral I had visited.

Once, years ago, during the blood and sweat of a war far away, I assisted a woman in childbirth. She was an Arab, a waif of war caught in the ruins of a tiny mud village that was baking in the afternoon heat. I was on patrol, expecting death from enemy guns and instead finding this poor soul already held rigid in the cramps of birth. There was nothing for it but to help and after it was all over, when I had handed the dusky, haggard and wizened, monkey-like baby to an army medical officer, I felt a warmth come over me. I had helped life emerge. It had been bloody, at times nauseous work to a youngster such as I was then, but in the end something about it had touched me lightly and I felt good for a time and the desert did not look so barren.

It was so during my second spring on The Place. But now the feeling was stronger; it reached more firmly and marked me and though I was now a spectator and not a participant, yet the birth of a forest had more power over me. And there was so much, very much to watch and ponder over and touch and smell. I did not know where to begin to look first and I was afraid to linger over each wonder in case I missed some new miracle. I watched the growth of a fern, not all at once, of course, but slowly, savouring each visit to the shade spot in the ravine, watching first a slight disturbance of the soil that parted the brown pine needles and revealed just a touch of light green that was sheathed in furry silver; returning again hours later to note that now a tightly curled 'fiddle-head' was protruding ever so slightly above the needles; going to the same place next morning, early, when the dew still shone over the growing things, and seeing now the curled head, still bowed towards the earth that bore it, still dressed with its sheen of fine, silvery bristles, but now a little taller, perhaps a little prouder as it stood atop the thin hairy stem that carried it aloft.

Each time that I visited that shady spot there was a difference and at last the full plant stood proud, broad leaves, fretworked designs of wonder, fanning into a graceful curve that tipped downwards to the earth at each point while the soft, pulpy stem I had seen come to life out of the earth womb now stood rigid and tough and seemingly smooth to the naked eye, until I looked at it again with a magnifying glass and saw the hair still there.

I watched the coming of grouse eggs and the birth of the chicks and I watched a wonderful wild mother hen as she fussed and brooded over the product of her inner self until the fluffy yellow chicks arrived four weeks later.

I watched a litter of white-footed mice, grey, squirling, helpless mites that looked like tiny, tiny pigs, so through their growing stages and emerge whole and splendid.

There was an infinity of things to watch that spring and, of course, I could not watch all. Nor shall I ever manage to watch every single miraculous happening during the birth of a forest and I must content myself to look a little more each year and learn a little more each year and perhaps record some of it so that those who come later will not have to start at the beginning. Of course, there are other ways of learning these secrets of Creation, if one is willing to sacrifice the pleasures of the forest in exchange for fat tomes, many of them, couched in the unromantic language of the scientist. In these one will find such words as 'tropism' and 'geotropism', but their mouthing is dull and uninspired and they do not really convey the excitement of the wilderness.

What do these words mean? Well, a tropism is, to quote an authority, "a response to a stimulus that comes from a given direction"; and geotropism means, in the same language, "a growth response to gravity", all of which is very well and good, but means what? I first became interested in these words before I knew their meaning, and it happened this way: I was walking through the bush and I stopped to look at a flat, thin slab of rock.

I wondered what might be lingering under this granite and I lifted it gently. Sheltering under it was an assortment of small beetles and spiders and ants, all seemingly at peace with each other. I was about to replace the rock when I noticed a sprouting seed, a tiny thing, not much bigger than a pin head, which had swollen and was even then sending out root tendrils and shoots. This seed, of a variety unknown to me, had fallen down through the crack made by the rock and the earth, had come to rest on its side and in that position changed its dry, husky, dormant body into an embryo of life. Not much to wonder at really, except that I noticed that the root tendrils had emerged from the upper part of the seed, had grown outwards and then turned down to seek their proper place in the soil, while the yellow shoots had grown out of the bottom part of the seed, pushed their way outwards and had also turned, but upwards, in the direction of the surface.

Closer inspection of the seed showed that each growing part, the rootlets and the shoots, had emerged from their proper places, but because the seed had fallen on its side, their natural growing positions had been reversed. What had guided these embryo threads towards their proper places in life? Why had they not grown, the roots towards the surface and the shoots towards the ground, thus perishing because neither could survive out of its own elements? Faint stirrings of long-forgotten lessons of biology whispered tropism, a word I had not encountered for some twenty years and which, though it persisted in my mind, failed to awaken any response, so that for the rest of that weekend it tormented me and drove me to my biology books as soon as I returned to the city that Sunday night.

The books gave me the interpretation of tropism and this led me to geotropism and I knew why a seed, no matter in what position it may be planted, always grows so that the roots drive downwards into the earth and the shoots upwards towards the sky. I learned again that the tropism (stimulus) responsible for this in the root is the force of gravity, while the tropism responsible for guiding the shoot upwards is negative to the force of gravity and therefore allows this growing part to 'float' up in a seeming attempt to break away from its parent body and reach the sky and only being prevented from doing this by the root and its opposite pull. This is what is known scientifically as geotropism while each individual geotropic force is called positive geotropism (the root), and negative geotropism (the shoot).

Now, all this was of much interest to me, but still there was a big question left unanswered: what invests each of these tiny, insignificant beings, this baby root and this baby shoot, with the marvellous force that, no matter what, always guides them in the right direction? I know not. I know now how Creation has managed to implant such forces into objects so small that in some species two or three may not occupy more space than are covered by the head of a pin. I know not and I marvel greatly and at times I wish that man, with his immense brain and his great powers of reason, had been granted a similar boon, for how many of us can claim that no matter what the circumstances we will always follow the right direction?

Often, when I discover some new wonder of Creation, the words of Bliss Carman's *Far Horizons* come to me:

> Lord of the far horizons,
> Give us the eyes to see,
> Over the verge of sundown,
> The beauty that is to be.

Carman was Canada's poet, a visionary, a dreamer, a man who penned great wisdom in those four short lines. The eyes to see are indeed necessary for those who travel the forest in search of values and there is an extra bonus in the last line, for the beauty that is to be is often hidden from the eyes of the casual looker and only comes alive when one does, indeed, look over the verge of sundown. And while the poem is perhaps metaphoric and intends to introduce the reader to the spirit of the wilderness, yet it is so wisely penned that it may be interpreted as an invitation to seek wilderness beauty anywhere, under any circumstances. That, at least, is how I see it.

During the first days of that spring I had been so busy watching plants and trees and shrubs that I almost forgot to watch other things, until the honking of northbound geese and the quacking of ducks reminded me that the birds had returned.

Of a sudden the forest seemed alive with bird sound. Flights of courting crows cawed noisily overhead; thrushes, woodsy-coloured birds camouflaged in the deep part of the bushland, flung their clear, sweet melodies into the air; robins vied with each other, singing and chanting, the cocks disputing with each other, quarrelling over the affections of their coy hens; the ruffed grouse thundered their love through the forest, drumming their wing beats again and again, challenging their rivals, wooing their hens; the night birds were come, the noisy whip-poor-wills with their monotonous chant after dark; and the swift night hawks with their sleek wings and strange boomings; over by the beaver lake the pileated woodpeckers redoubled their short calls and the bitterns launched their strange, bass cries: *oonk-ka-woonk, oonk-ka-woonk, oonk-ka-woonk*, like noisy pumps trying vainly to suck water out of some cistern; and the great blue herons, the birds of stilts with the long, sharp bills, with their hoarse cries. *Crawnk, crawnk, crawnk, crawnk,* their calls echoed across the lake while the quacking of mallards and black ducks and pin tails was thick and gossipy from the reeds. They are legion, these birds of mine, and would fill an entire volume if I let them,

My hawks are back, also, and already busy with the big nest of sticks in the crotch of the poplar tree and their shrill, nasal calls filled the forest and put fright back into the smaller creatures, the mice and the chipmunks and the squirrels and the birds and into Joan, who worried over our small friends.

Of course, the flying things came too. The tiny blackflies that sneak into your clothing and plunge a stealthy needle into a skin pore and suck your life's blood, leaving a neat, blood-back center to the wound that is soon surrounded with a purplish circle that plagues with its persistent, swelling itch. And the mosquitoes, the big, harmless males blundering in search of a female and these smaller viragoes forever searching for blood so that the results of their union with the males should not be wasted, for blood they must have if their eggs are to bring new life to the swamps and the grasses. The moths came, those blundering, soft-dusty creatures that must dash suicidally against a light, drawn there by some unknown force. And following the moths, the bats...

Great secrets fly with these two creatures; the humble moth and the supposedly-evil bat. Everyone, or almost everyone, knows of the marvellous radar system of bats, that intricate device that enables the creature to fly blind through a maze of twigs, wires, or poles without hitting one of them; that allows him to fly into the blackest night and locate his insect food through the aid of his sonar. But what about the moths, his natural prey? How do these creatures avoid their enemy?

Many, of course, do not and become food for the hunting bat, but each moth is equipped with 'ears' that have been especially designed by Creation to capture the ultrasonic sound waves launched by a bat as he searches the black reaches of the forest for his insect food. These 'radar scoops', long in operation before man discovered the techniques of radar and sonar, are located on the body of the moth and are found in pairs near the creature's waist. Each consists of a minute air space that is covered by an extremely fine membrane, which corresponds to the tympanum, or human ear drum, and inside of which are three impossibly-small nerve cells, the sensory organs of the ear.

Sound waves cause the membranes to vibrate and the sensory nerves to warn the insect of danger. As soon as a bat gets within 100 feet of a moth, the ears pick up the vibrations of its sonar, but such is the marvel of this finely-designed mechanism, that the moth can tell from what direction the bat is approaching. The impulses of its ears are not synchronized in the insect's brain and if the hunter is coming in from the left, the vibrations are stronger there than on the right, allowing the moth to steer away from the enemy.

Now, equipped with such fine hearing aids, it would seem that the moth could always evade the bat—which it does at times by either dropping like a stone to the ground upon receiving warning, or by altering course to try and escape the pursuer—but these uncanny companions of witches have, through the centuries, worked out a way of fooling the moth. Knowing that if they approach their prey in straight flight it will hear them and avoid them, the swooping bat flies rapidly from side to side, reeling drunkenly and in a seemingly clumsy manner through space. This action bewilders the moth. It knows the enemy is near, but it cannot decide which way to duck and that, probably, is why it has developed its own answer to the bat's reprisal technique. Being in doubt as to direction, it does the only thing it has left to do, drops to the ground and lies still until, it hopes, the danger is passed.

Yet the story does not end here. Undoubtedly the bat was fooled for a time by this manoeuvre, but in the end, no one knows just how far in the ages, the bat developed another attack technique. Now it seemed to have worked a sort of ballistics calculation so that it learned to intercept the moth even as it is dodging, when, if it cannot take its prey in its mouth, it tries to scoop it up with its membranous wings as it flashes by, though the 'battle' may be considered a sort of stalemate just now, for often the bat misses. And undoubtedly, if man does not become altogether mad and destroys this planet of ours, bats will evolve some more sure way of catching moths, and moths will then begin to work on a new system for avoiding them, for there seems no end to the genius of Creation.

EIGHT

COME, LET US GO ON A JOURNEY. Let us watch a small drama in the ever-changing life of my wilderness. Relax your mind, clear from it the cobwebs of civilization for it is summer, our second at The Place, and we have set out to explore the beaver lake. We have balanced the red canoe atop the car and we have driven down my road to the highway and turned left and driven for another half a mile. Now we have turned left again, through the rickety gate and along the bush road that winds through the mixed woods, a road muddy in places, shrouded by shade and alive with the buzzing of insects and the bloom of wild flowers; full of the aroma of summer in the forest.

We have reached the lake and lifted the canoe from the car and I am walking to the water's edge, the canoe balanced on my back, its thwart resting upon the vertebrae of my neck, for I do not have a yoke to ease its portage, meaning always to buy or make one, but never doing so. Here, at your feet is the water; to your right is the dam of mud and sticks, and before us is a low place, fitted by Creation with a flat, smooth rock, which is the launching place and the spot where we will make our landing on our return from this trip.

The journey has started and the lake is before us. Clusters of shiny, broad lily leaves float upon the surface. Here and there a frog plops into the dark waters as we travel, slowly and silently, towards the upper reaches of the lake, where the reeds grow tall and the shrubs cluster the shores; where the beaver have made their home bigger and have isolated pines and poplars and cedars, so that these now form a tangled barrier upon the water barring passage for all but the light Indian canoe in which we are paddling.

Lily blooms are all around us. Yellow blooms, waxen and beautiful holding their cups to the sky; white blooms, gracious petals, the lotus of mythology and of Japan, and of Canada. We pass by a muskrat raft, tangled floating platform of shredded vegetation and mud and growing organisms, one of many rat places, and soon we are faced by another of its kind, but bigger, much, much bigger, and we must go over it, pushing with our paddles, forcing the shallow-draft canoe over its spongy surface and now and then I must put one leg over the gunwale and push with my foot against the raft and thus we travel, slowly, and quietly, and peacefully, going where few other humans have been before us, seeking anything we may find, expectant; alert to the sounds of the lake, to the trilling of the redwing blackbirds, to the buzzing of the flies. Watchful, noting the small circles made by the minnows as they rise to play with some bit of floating debris that has caught their fancy.

A beaver rises just ahead, beyond the raft, and he looks at us; a bewhiskered, glistening-black water creature, uncontrollably curious about this invasion of his domain. He swims slowly, lazily, making a half-circle and always facing us, his small head held high, so that part of his wet chest is visible. Then, satisfied, he sounds, but because he had not been disturbed, because he has nothing to fear, he does not slap his great paddle tail upon the water to alert all creatures of danger.

We are over the raft of vegetable and mud and the canoe floats again and I withdraw my foot and we paddle some more, slowly, leisurely, for it would be wrong to make noise this middle morning. And before us, drama is about to unfold. ...

The big snapping turtle is almost buried in the slime of the lake bed, some six feet from shore, where the water is not deep. His moss-crusted shell looks like a large, green rock; he is motionless, and hungry. Inches above, on the surface of the water, a mallard duck paddles gently towards the turtle, now and then dipping her head under the water, her pointed tail lifting upwards as she reaches with her clacking bill, probing for the foods that are hidden in the murk.

The turtle watches her. His horny, triangular head is a still projection leading out of the shell. Only the unwinking black eyes move, holding the nearing bird in their stare. Elsewhere in the vicinity life sleeps, lulled into quiet by the heat of a summer noon. The lake, small, and round, like a giant's spit droplet carelessly expectorated into one tiny hollow of the vast bushland, flashes water-light into the empty stillness, now and then casting a fleeting, golden shaft on the untidy beaver lodge that nestles under the shade of a gnarled, waterlogged cedar. A red-winged blackbird flies low over the water to land on a branch in the cedar. It eyes the duck. The bird sings and its fluting melody is strangely haunting. Now it is quiet; it peers about, then preens, spreading one wing to reveal the scarlet that bands its shoulder, like a splash of fresh blood that has been carefully edged with the yellow of a buttercup. The bird watches as the duck moves closer to the turtle.

The mallard's orange feet, their webs outstretched into small paddles, almost brush the green on the reptile's shell and the turtle's ugly snout inches down, shifting into the striking crouch that will allow the cruel, snapping beak to fasten upon one of the mallard's legs and hold it with the tenacity of a steel trap.

The mallard is a widow. This year she has no young to brood over; there is no gaudy drake to share with. Last autumn a pattern of lead pellets cut him down from the sky and she watched him drop, a suddenly-ungainly bundle of feathers that a moment before had been her free, high-flying, colourful partner. The duck misses her drake. He was her first and only mate and she mourns his loss each evening as she circles the lake, calling to him, still hoping to hear his answering cry. And because he is not there, because she has not taken another mate this year and has no young, she is apart from her kind. That is why she is now foraging near the lakeshore.

If the drake were here, she would be with the others, floating at rest in the safety of the reed-bed on the lake's south shore and her loneliness would not have made her careless, would not have robbed her of the alertness that let her survive to fly south during eight autumns, to feed on strange grasses and insects and to return in the spring with her drake to the welcome that the lake offers each year.

The lake is her home. Here she was born; it is here that she will die, and this is as it should be, for in this place she has fulfilled most of her productive years, giving to it of herself with her young; taking from it too, finding happiness in the company of others of her brood soon after her tiny, horn-tipped bill first broke through the eggshell in the nest that her mother built carefully in the concealment of reeds close by the beaver dam.

Now the mallard is almost over the turtle's head. She floats another inch; the predatory beak of the turtle streaks upwards with an agility surprising in such a slow-moving reptile. The horny, snapping vice clamps on to the mallard's right foot. She utters one startled cry even before she feels the pain, then she is silent. She fights, for she does not want to die yet. Her struggles awaken the lake's sleeping form; they disturb the reach and send light shock waves rippling into the main body of water. But yet the lake is not fully conscious; only a small part of it moves as the mallard's beating wings froth the murky water. The lake is like a heavy sleeper being pestered by a persistent fly. That part invaded by the duck's struggles answers with lazy movement, but the rest of it remains placid. It is too hot, too still for action.

The mallard is losing her flight feathers. They float near her for a moment, hating to leave her, but they are pushed away from the struggle propelled by waves that are raised by the frantic wings. The turtle hangs on to the foot. He is old, and an experienced hunter. He uses his great weight to anchor the duck and allows her the luxury of her frenzies. Nothing now can rob him of his meal. Nothing...but the foot is fragile; it can snap off and the wounded mallard may yet scuttle away from him. The mossy-back waits for the right moment and when the duck flops down under the water, momentarily exhausted by her wild threshing, the turtle shifts his hold, sliding his beak higher up the leg. Now the jaws are clamped over the duck's knee.

A beaver, yawning and curious, floats to the surface near his house of mud. He must cruise out to see what is causing this sudden disturbance. His black head cuts through the water in a smooth arc. He circles the mallard, see, is satisfied. He swims back to his lodge, smacks his tail against the water and the ensuring crack, loud as a rifle shot, signals his displeasure with those who have disturbed his noon sleep. He sounds, slipping back into the chambered coolness of his lodge.

On his perch in the cedar above, the blackbird has stopped preening and is watching the battle below. His small head is cocked to one side; he watches with one eye. He sees the floating feathers, some of which are drifting under the tree, and he wonders if he will find some particle of flesh or fat attached to their ends. No—the feathers can wait. The bird knows that, soon now, larger pieces of skin and meat will float upon the water and can then be gathered without effort. He stays on his perch, waiting.

It is an hour later. The mallard's lunges for freedom are weaker. The turtle drags the duck's head under the surface and can now hold it there for seconds at a time until her last waning strength the captive bird lunges up again for a quick gasp of breath. Working slowly and with infinite patience the turtle moves his hold higher and now grips the duck's drumstick thigh. Already a large section of the mallard's belly skin has ripped and blood is tinting the water. Death hovers near and there are those who wait for it. A school of sunfish has moved in close to the killer and its victim; the orange and green bluegills are the lake's gastric juices. Gliding within its bowels they are always ready to dispose of the waste left by the killers in the water, and sometimes they are themselves prey. Now they are excited and impatient. They can smell the kill and one of them slips in quickly to nip at a bit of meat that is trailing from the mallard's torn belly. The little fish must get close to the savage jaws of the turtle, but he knows he is safe. He grips the morsel greedily with his pin-sharp teeth; he pulls, shaking his oval body from side to side, but the flesh resists his tug. Still holding it, he moves in closer, then backs away suddenly, shaking his body more violently. The meat rips free. It is a piece two inches long and perhaps as thick as the body of an earthworm and the fish races away with his prize, chased by the others, who seek to share that which they are afraid to steal from the jaws of the predator. The daring fish gulps as he swims and the duck's living meat enters deeper into his mouth, and he is able to finish before the others reach him, and they all turn back, swimming near the turtle, made more excited by the taste of the blood that is now mixed with the water.

The helpless mallard is exhausted. She floats on the water, her graceful brown neck arched, a look of resignation in her gentle eyes. She knows she is doomed. There is no point in fighting any more now; but the turtle is patient. He is hungry, but he will not risk losing his meal through haste; he continues his mangling hold, enjoying the taste of live flesh, a fierce, pitiless gourmet savouring a rare dish. Now he begins to back slowly towards deeper water, dragging the mallard, submerging her head more frequently…

It is done. The duck's body jerks suddenly, is still, and begins the dance. Swift convulsions seize her as life ebbs away. She is quiet now; her neck hangs, her green beak that has a black triangle at its tip rests limply on the bottom. Still the turtle waits.

Above, in the cedar tree, the blackbird trills again, voicing his impatience with the turtle's caution. From his perch the bird can just see the outline of the big shell that is clouded by drifting ooze. He can see the red life that has escaped the duck's body; its stain is deeper now, it hangs around the turtle in amorphous, slow-moving tendrils that drift upwards, spreading their colour as they near the surface. He sees the turtle's head, a shadowy, snake-like object, as it moves, as the jaws tentatively release their crushing hold. The duck is dead, the meal is ready. Taking hold of the leg again the turtle drags the carcass into water that is deeper yet and he stops by a flat, sandy shelf where he will eat his victim.

The sunfish rush to the kill and begin feeding in crazy parody of their provider. Pieces of meat float to the surface and the blackbird launches off his perch. Skimming the water, the bird picks up a piece of meat and flies back with it to the tree. He picks at his find, then drops it disdainfully and returns for another piece. The meat he has dropped lodges in the tree's bark. Soon the ants come and it becomes black with their feeding shapes.

The lake is asleep again. The lake must rest. Soon evening will come with a breeze, bringing out the ducks that are now quacking sleepily in the reeds. They will come in noisy flotillas and with their coming the beaver will slip out of his lodge and swim a wide circle around the lake, inspecting its shoreline, seeking changes that may tell him of danger. If all is well he will swim ashore, his body sleek with the lake's moisture and he will waddle clumsily up the slipway that leads to the grove of poplars. There he will feed, perhaps gnawing at the small tree that he felled this morning, but more likely he will cut with his strong, sharp teeth some of the grasses or shrubs that live near.

Now the sun is gone. A pale moon peeps over the trees, shy of the old lake. The mallard, too, is gone; only some of her feathers remain pressed against the bank, as if seeking sanctuary from the fury they have seen. The turtle lies replete, quiet. He will stay submerged until his need for air drives him slow and cumbersome to the surface; then he will hang there, head just breaking water, his small nostrils two obscene holes snuffling unclean at the night. In the spruce the blackbird is asleep. He sits balanced upon a high branch, concealed by the tree's scrub, his head buried under one wing. Now and then he utters a small, chirping sound. He is dreaming of his feast.

This is the lake's time. It talks to itself in many voices, each of them carrying a message for those who will stay and listen. The lake has been here a long time and has seen many things...

Dusk makes gargoyles of the shadows as we paddle the red canoe.

Ahead, twenty good strokes away, is the flat rock where we shall land soon, for we have completed our journey; we have visited our lake and witnessed the drama enacted in its bowels. The early moon hangs just above the horizon, in front of us. It is a blood moon, its shining surface bathed by an unseen sun and it helps guide us over the last stretch of water.

As we heave the red canoe from the lake a loon laughs. It is a mad cackle that the loon launches at the evening and, near by, in some reeds, a bittern, determined not to be outdone by the crazy bird, hurls his own bedlam over the water. *Oonk-ka-woonk, oonk-ka-woonk, oonk-ka-woonk.*

We pause, unwilling to break the spell of our journey and the orchestra of night becomes full and rounded. The high drone of mosquito bitches increases its tempo; the bull-frogs croak their hoarseness; tree-frogs chant and treble peep. A whip-poor-will starts its tireless whistle. Invisible, a bat flies overhead, the rustle of his wings a slight melody in the air, while the deep, resonant hooting of a great horned owl carried far into the forest.

We go now. The car's engine ends the serenade, its headlights cut twin swaths through the fast-dark as we return to the cabin, to the quiet of it, to Joan and peace and perhaps a cold bottle of beer and a pipeful of tobacco, sitting in moonlight on the doorstep while the things of night scurry through the forest, and some of them pause to visit, eyeing the two who sit, smelling their strange human scent, but unafraid, for here no man will harm them and they know this.

χ

One evening during summer number two I was returning to the cabin, taking my usual route through the bush, when I spotted a raccoon as it climbed the smooth bole of a poplar. This was a picture I wanted and I stopped under the tree to set up tripod and telephoto lens while the 'coon, curious as only these bandits can be, made himself comfortable in a crotch and watched what I was doing from the safety of twenty feet up. The light was poor, but I shot a few pictures, spoke softly to the old boy in the tree and put away my gear again, finished with pictures for this day.

Evening in the bush is perhaps the time that I like best; this is the in-between period, when the creatures of daylight begin to seek their places for the darkness and when the things of night start moving, beginning their peregrinations in search of food. There is a new smell to the forest,

A wild raccoon, uncontrollably curious, stares down as I take his picture. Ten minutes after this photograph was taken in late evening I met a mother bear and her twin cubs.

an aroma special to the time of twilight and a man can think clearly and see things better aided by that subtle mental process by which a thinker can visualize that which he is thinking.

It is perhaps because my mind becomes more active under these conditions that I am apt to be taken by surprise by some of my creatures and on the evening of the raccoon photographs, while I was busy with a number of small, inconsequential but pleasant thoughts, the mother bear and her two cubs must have been watching me for a minute or two before I noticed them. Even then, it was my nose that drew my attention to them, not my eyes, thought they were standing in an open spot watching my slow progress through a cluster of hazel scrub.

The smell of them broke through my thoughts as surely as the aroma of cooking fills with the drool the mouth of a hungry man. Bear smell is special; it is a strong, somewhat musky fetor that distinctly spells bruin to anyone familiar with it. It is pungent, slightly acrid, but not unpleasant. Five or six years ago I would not likely have noticed it, for my olfactory senses were weaker then and had not yet re-learned the art of distinguishing one smell from half a dozen others. So my nose led the way, and I looked up.

Mama was medium big, shaggy, a deep red-black all over. She stood on her hind legs, her small brown eyes glued to me, her long mouth partly open, showing just a peep of the big canines that could, if she wanted to put them to such a use, make shreds of me. But she was quiet and standing on her hind legs, and no bear attacks from that stance. Her children stood exactly as their mother. The twins were spring cubs, coy, pretty little things, one coloured like the she, standing a little ahead of her and to the right; the other, a lighter, almost cinnamon hue, standing near the old lady. All three were sniffing for all they were worth and I suspect we made quite a tableau, for I too, was sniffing, unconsciously, but my nose must have been wrinkling in cheap imitation of their lusty inhalations.

For perhaps fifteen seconds we stood thus and then I thought of my camera and became aware almost at the same time that there was not enough light to take pictures by. I was too much interested in the bears to feel mortification just then, that was to come later, but at that point the youngsters dropped to all fours and advanced slowly towards me, curious and unafraid, as they had a right to be, for Mama was more than capable of looking after them.

I let them come, wondering how close they intended to approach and their mother did not stop them and I was surprised, for she bears are notoriously jealous of their children. I wish I could write about what would have happened had I been able to stand my ground. Would the cubs have come right up to me? Would their mother have allowed them to do this? I shall never know. The babies came too close for my comfort and when only some ten feet separated us I felt that it was time for me to move, to place myself out of their line of march. Only then did the young bears stop. They stared at me, and I could swear that I was being reproached for my cowardice, and I suspect that they might have altered course to zero in on me again if Mama had not spoken.

Her mouth hardly opened, but she sent out a dark brown growl that had one effect on the cubs and another upon me. The children turned and scampered back to mother immediately. I stood stock-still and allowed the hairs at the back of my neck time enough to settle down after the mad dance they had just performed; and they had hardly settled in their proper places when Mama let out another one of those hoarse orders to her children and my scalp hairs again went wild.

All of this performance by my mind and person was quite unnecessary and reason told me immediately that this was so, but have you ever tried to listen to reason when you are in a deep funk? It's hard to do! But the she was just dishing out orders to her babies. The first growl told them to return to her side and stop fooling with the stranger; the second took the place of marching orders.

The sow dropped back to all fours and led her cubs away, not bothering about me further and, feeling very brave again now that her waddling rump met my gaze, I stayed to watch until they had disappeared in the deep bush and I stayed on after that to listen to their crackling progress, growing fainter, until at last it was gone. And then I became frustrated almost to the point of tears. Here I had been privileged with this rare sight and I had been unable to use my camera. If you are not a photographer you will not know what I mean. If you are, you will understand.

"Bears," a man once said to me, "is funny things. When you think they're a-goin', they're a-comin', and when you think they're a comin', they're a goin'. They's funny things, is bears."

He was an old man, brown and leathery and wrinkled after years of living in the wilderness and he was wise in many of the ways of the wild creatures and, to a degree, he was right in his quaint summation of bears. But only to a degree. It could be said with more reason that 'people is funny things', etc. Bears do have a reputation for being unpredictable and it is true that some of them are, but, then, so are humans, but more so. And why pick on a bear of this doubtful distinction? I like bears. Of course, I like all wild things too, but bears are special. They're intelligent, courageous and when they have to be, immensely strong, and above all, honest. The sows make wonderful mothers, the cubs make wonderful companions, if a little rough, and the hulking, crusty males show an independence of spirit that I frankly envy.

Man has always sought to kill these great creatures; for their fur, for their meat (prized even today by some), because they are reputed predators, or simply because they make such good targets when a hunter manages to get his sights lined up on their shaggy bodies. But bears manage to do quite well on man's doorstep and often they follow their lonely, placid life without disturbing their human neighbours, who quite likely are unaware of their presence. Despite their bulk—a good, fat black will scale as much as six hundred pounds—bears manage to move as lithely as prima ballerinas when they are so inclined and because they are ever cautious when not enraged and like to mind their own business, they keep out of man's way more often than not.

Once, several years ago, I had occasion to watch a black bear mother and her two cubs under unusual circumstances. It was late summer and a farmer friend told me of an old moose that had evidently died a natural death and was then serving as rations for a variety of meat eaters of the forest. My friend had passed near the carcass that morning and had seen bear sign; three sets of tracks, two small, one big.

"If I wanted to watch a bear having a feed," said my friend, "I'd get out there around sundown and climb a jackpine that's right close to the old moose."

The pine tree, he further explained, was easily climbable and would offer a good perch from whence to bear-watch. I was intrigued and he gave me explicit directions and about four o'clock that afternoon I set out, equipped with field-glasses, some sandwiches and a thermos of hot coffee, all packed in an old army haversack and slung over my shoulders. It was a pleasant walk through the forest to the place, some two miles away, where the moose carcass lay, and I let my mind idle as I walked, watching this and that and thinking of the experience that I hoped would soon be mine. The moon would be full early and so far there were no clouds in the sky and I was keenly looking forward to an interesting evening.

An hour later I located the place and immediately became aware that my friend had omitted one important element from his news. The moose, besides being very dead, was very, very high. It was a sweetly-sick aroma, the smell of decaying meat, and the wafting fragrance of this particular potion was as ripe as any that I have ever smelled. I could have found the carcass blindfold, and, I was sure, the odour of its presence must unfailingly draw the bears that I had set out to observe, for there is nothing that tickles a bear's palate more than rotten meat, unless it be rotten fish!

Fortunately the pine that my friend had told me about was located upwind of the moose and the perfume of it would be much less once I was ensconced in its branches twenty feet up. After checking the tree and noting that climbing it would not be bothersome, I steeled myself against the smell of the moose and walked up to the carcass to have a look around. The old fellow had chosen an open place in which to pop off, a place of wild grass and small plants and some moss, with not a few small areas of bare, moist earth that now held perfect impressions of the beasts and birds that had been feeding on the moose. The bear tracks were clear and told me that my friend's surmise was correct at least up to the point that concerned the sow and her twin cubs. But there was a third set of bear tracks, big ones, far larger than those of the sow, that spoke of an enormous boar and I hoped that mama and her kids would arrive first, in which case the old lady would keep the male away, no matter how big he might be, for there is nothing more savage and protecting than a she bear with cubs, unless it be another she bear in like circumstances; and I could count on this lady to give the male a thorough drubbing if he showed his face around that moose carcass while she was there with her young. All bears love rotten meat, but I suspect that male bears love even more the tender bodies of young bears, even if they are their own children, and that is why the females will not tolerate their erstwhile husbands anywhere near their cubs.

It was not until I began climbing the jack pine that it occurred to me that a bear could easily follow me up its trunk! I did not like that thought, especially since I had not brought a rifle with me. But there was no turning back now and I consoled myself with a promise that if mama or papa bear spotted me and decided to come after me, I would seek safety in the slimmest branch I could find; and since I weigh only one hundred and fifty pounds and I could reliably count on either one of the adult bears scaling at least three hundred, I thought everything would turn out all right. Which, by the way, it did.

By the time I had looked around once more and had climbed the pine and settled myself as comfortably as possible on one of its thick limbs, the sun had drifted behind the trees and dusk was slipping in quickly upon its heels. Already a very pale moon was creeping up the sky and the night hawks were calling and ducks and geese were passing overhead on their way to their night places.

I sat with my back against the tree trunk, happy, smoking a last pipeful of tobacco, the moose clearly visible some thirty feet in front of me. And soon the stinking carcass had a visitor. A red fox slipped out of the bush, stopped, sniffed longingly at the moose and hardly bothered to check for danger before he trotted to the feast. I watched him at work and was pleased because these little sharp-nosed creatures are quick to sense man and the one feeding below was obviously convinced that he was alone with the dead moose. For fifteen minutes the fox ate and when he had finished and completed his toilet, licking his chops and his white front and his paws, it was almost too dark to distinguish more than outlines, for the moon was not yet high enough to help and the dark was not yet deep enough to accept the moonlight.

Half an hour passed. The fox was gone and except for the occasional rustle of a mouse as it sped through the grass to pick crumbs off the moose, nothing moved in the clearing below me. Now I could see quite well for the dark was real and the moon was busy shining and that old familiar feeling crept over me. I wanted to whistle or sing, or talk to myself, to keep myself company and banish the eerie things that persisted in their attempts to invade my mind and take it over, driving it back into time, into the age of superstition and black magic, when witches and warlocks danced in the dark of night and drew mysterious cabalistic signs upon the ground. Once a bat flew between me and the moon and the quick, fleeting glimpse of his leathery black body fed boyhood dreads to my mind and visions of vampires and such horrors danced in frenzy inside my head. I became stern with myself and banished these nonsensical whimsies and I thought of why I was there and imagined that the she bear was just emerging into the clearing followed by her two cubs; which was not imagination at all for she was, indeed, coming and her babies galloped at her heels, twin round balls of black fur as mischievous as any puppy dogs.

The sow led the way to the carcass and stopped by it. She looked all round the clearing, standing squarely on all fours, head held high, nostrils testing the breeze as she carefully scanned each section of forest. And once her gaze seemed to rest squarely on my person and I flinched inside, but she had not seen me and she began to feed. She squatted by the carcass and went at it and I could hear the grunts and sighs of relish as she gorged on the rotten meat.

The cubs, too, ate of the moose, but they quickly had enough and broke off to play while the she made a pig of herself. And it must be admitted that sight of that bear enjoying so hugely her repast of rotting meat almost made me retch, especially when she used both paws to dig deeply into the mulched entrails to scoop out double handfuls of putrefaction which she supped greedily. But my interest in the primitive drove civilization from me and I became composed and was able to watch without further qualms as the she finished her meal.

After she stopped eating she sat up and cleaned herself all over, first her muzzle and paws, then her chest and belly and her flanks and she even reached over her back to scratch and dig at her shaggy self; and I believe she would have prolonged her toilet indefinitely if her cubs had not suddenly rushed to her, intent upon their night's ration of milk.

At first the mother played hard-to-get. She stood on her hind legs and danced away from her screeching youngsters as they jumped upwards on clumsy young legs trying to reach her dugs. Quite obviously she was teasing them and just as clearly they were becoming increasingly angry at their mother. Their small voices became shriller and they jumped higher and swatted at her with their front paws until she at last gave way and dropped to all fours again. At once they rushed upon her, one on each side and tried to seize a milk dug as she walked away from the moose, aiming for a young tree that grew near the one that housed me.

Now the sow sat down and propped her back against the tree and let her legs slide forward, for all the world like a human stopping to rest after a long walk. The cubs rushed at her and she fondled them to her breasts, holding each against her chest with her long arms while they seized a nipple apiece and began sucking boisterously. She was rough-haired and smelly and wild and her children were shaggy and dirty and fierce, but sight of her and her young made me think of a human mother nursing twin babies at her breasts.

The nursery scene lasted almost twenty minutes and was not interrupted until the greedy lips of her babies made great smacking noises around the she's empty dugs. Then the mother tumbled the cubs off her lap and got back on to all fours. While she stretched the cubs mopped up each other, licking off little driblets of milk from one another's bodies. At last the family moved away, the mother walking more slowly, the cubs trotting as quickly as ever, now and then racing away from the sow only to be recalled by her stern growl.

When quiet returned to the bushland I climbed down from my tree, not wanting to wait for any more bears that night and secretly glad that the big male had not made his appearance. And it was then that I realized that I had forgotten to bring a flashlight with me. But the moon was full...I enjoyed the walk back and was a little afraid now and then, for in those days I was not yet accepted by the wilderness.

NINE

I FIRST NOTICED GEORGE one bright night during our first winter on The Place. The snow was heavy and the cold intense and I had gone outside to fetch more firewood for our satanic stove. About to open the cabin door on my return, I heard a small noise, a quiet cheep, like that of a sleepy bird, that was accompanied by a minute rustling. I stopped by the door, seeking the sound-maker and a brief flash of white drew my eyes to one of the wire fat stations, placed in a pine that grew near the cabin. Quietly munching fat was George, small and furry and sleek, and fat, and entirely unconcerned by my presence.

I went inside the cabin and dumped my load of wood and told Joan to come out and take a look at our latest visitor, and George obliged us both by remaining where he was and consenting to continue his feeding on the fat. I do not know how long he had been in the habit of visiting the fat stations, probably since the beginning, but this was the first time we noticed him and we were amazed at his lack of fear, at his great unconcern, for he remained feeding while we stood and looked at him from only a yard's distance.

George is a flying squirrel and he is still with us now, four years later and he and his quite numerous clan can be counted upon to flit swiftly and silently through the pines and descend upon the feeders and fat stations any time between first dark and four o'clock in the morning, usually appearing two hours after sunset, feeding for an hour or so and then flitting away to their tree nests to sleep and digest for a couple of hours before returning to feed again until the pre-dawn.

How can we tell that George is still with us? I suppose the answer to this question could be painstakingly detailed, requiring the individual physical characteristics of George which distinguish him from the other flyers. But I would answer instead with another question: how does a man know that one of his relatives is still visiting him every night? There is no need to detail a description; George is George, we know him and he knows us and it is enough to say that he had been visiting with us every weekend, winter, spring, summer and autumn since that first night.

As it was with Nutsy and still is with Beau Brummell, George quickly adopted us, becoming more tame than any of the other flying squirrels, accepting little blobs of peanut butter from my extended index finger, or gently taking a peanut from me. He does not always deign to accept these titbits however! There are nights when George will slither up and down a pine tree while I stand below, arm extended against the trunk, fingers holding a nut. Then he glides to within a couple of inches of the peanut, sniffs deliciously but will not accept it and I am sure that he does this deliberately, just to put me in my place, for he knows that eventually I will tire of holding my arm aloft and I will throw the peanut into the feeder, from where he will retrieve it immediately.

These tiny squirrels are fascinating beings. They are always gentle and unlike their red cousins never quarrel amongst themselves and do not seem really happy unless they are surrounded by their kind, a situation which red squirrels would not tolerate. But it is their speed that is truly amazing. They seem to be powered by a series of coiled springs which, when they are let loose, propel the squirrels with such suddenness and such incredible speed that they literally seem to melt into space. I have watched many of them and often have I had my gaze fixed on one when he has decided to move his presence. One instant he was there before me, the next he had simply vanished. One night recently, when our stove was attempting to dehydrate us and I had been forced to get up and open door and windows, I was leaning on a windowsill, idly looking at the seeds on the ledge feeder attached to the wall of the cabin when George materialized out of thin air. Admittedly I was half asleep and half cooked, but there is no other way to describe George's sudden arrival.

This time he landed as light as a feather. At other times George and his kin sound like small elephants as they thump on our cabin roof, using it as a springboard to gain momentum and altitude for their next leap into space. This, of course, is a game, for I know of no other creature that can control his leaps to such a fine degree as the flying squirrel and if he want to land softly, believe me, he lands *very* softly. But this noisy playfulness is another intriguing side of the character of Canada's flying squirrel.

Like so many other creatures of the wilderness flying squirrels have been misnamed, for they do not actually fly. They glide, using a loose flap of skin that is attached along their sides and to their wrists and ankles which, when their legs are fully extended, becomes stretched out and traps air, billowing like a tiny sail. Using their tail as a rudder they can control their direction, but they can also control the angle of their glide by taking up slack with their flying skin.

I suppose that if the world lasts long enough *Glaucomys volans*, to give him his Latin title, will, in all probability, perfect his wing system, for he does not seem to be prepared to forgo his unusual method of transportation, and he is not really at home unless he is in a tree or flying between two of them. In fact, on the ground the flying squirrel is relatively clumsy and only shows true form when he is skittering about in the trees.

The little chaps weigh only between three and four ounces, but the small brain houses a keen wit and the big round eyes that shine ruby red in a light are as soft as those of a deer. They are charming imps, our flyers, and their soft voices are a welcome sound after dark. Often Joan and I will stand outside and listen to their melodious chatter, a peeping and cheeping that sounds more like sleepy birds than like squirrels, especially after the raucous yelling of their red cousins during the day.

Very soon after our arrival at The Place George connected the noise of our car engine and the swath cut by our lights with the food that we place in the feeders as soon as we get the cabin door open. At first he and his family used to wait until we had unpacked the car and settled ourselves in the cabin, but nowadays they take up dining stations as soon as they hear our car engine turn into the driveway at the bottom of the hill and by the time we stop on the rock above the cabin we can hear them and see them, cheeping and flitting from tree to tree, telling us, as clearly as any human could, to hurry up and replenish the feeders. Often I have hardly enough time to pour the seed into their favourite feeder, the one near the cabin door, before George slides down the tree trunk and plunks himself inside the hollow pine section that holds the seed.

Recently, leaving The Place at midnight one Sunday, I parked the car against the cabin door while I loaded it. I went into the house to fetch the first case, leaving the motor running and lights on and wondering whether I would disturb George. When I came out with the bag George was in the

The chipmunks, first cousins of the squirrels, take away surprising quantities of seeds in their capacious cheek pouches. Here one of them stuffs his cheeks with seeds from one of our feeders.

feeder, inches away from the car, busy stuffing himself. He looked up at my arrival and slid to the entrance of the feeder, sticking his nose out at me and demanding a peanut. He got it and he scurried five feet up the pine and sat eating it while we drove away.

George and the rest of his clan are, I fear, giving Joan and me a reputation locally. Already we are considered a little strange where animals and birds are concerned, but on the whole these idiosyncrasies of ours are accepted gracefully by the Adams family, who are about the only ones privileged to browse through our acres; but when one night last winter Alvin and his boys dropped in for a chat and I cautioned them to 'mind our squirrels' as they were leaving, Alvin treated me to a rather searching look. Most people can spend a lifetime in the wilderness and not see a flying squirrel because of the creature's entirely nocturnal habits; and, of course, everybody knows that red and grey squirrels bed down after sundown—mind you, they are wrong here, too, for the reds and blacks occasionally stay at our feeders well into the night—so I must admit that it may sound unusual when I caution our visitors against disturbing our squirrels during a pitch-black night!

As a matter of fact, though, Joan and I get just as much pleasure out of our night creatures as we do out of our daytime friends. Often we stay awake at night to listen to the traffic outside the cabin and one or the other of us is always popping out of bed to investigate a noise. This way we have met the skunks and raccoons and hares and owls and whip-poor-wills, and white-footed mice and shrews and bear and wolf, though Joan is not too eager to make the close acquaintance of the latter and she is not madly keen to fraternize with the skunks.

I like skunks. Old Josephine in particular. She is a very lady-like skunk who always minds her own business and can be relied upon never to raise her bushy tail and salute an inquisitive human with a spray of evil-smelling oil that is capable of knocking out the strongest. Of course, I am always careful with Josephine. One must never startle her, or speak roughly, or move suddenly, but these whimsies of hers are little enough price to pay for the pleasure of her company and if now and then she gets carried away by the attentions of an amorous swain and spatters a bit of her scent under our cabin, well, nobody really minds. As a rule I keep the windows shut in early spring, anyway, for it is still a bit too chilly to have them open, and we only get a slight whiff or two of Josey's perfume.

She is a fat old lady is our Josey. I cannot recall seeing a plumper skunk and I must presume that she has got that way from the easy living she finds near our cabin. One night last winter Joan announced that she had to go to the little room at the back—which means our outhouse—and, as usual, the announcement became a royal command, for when Joan must make one of her night trips, she likes my company as far as the little house.

The now familiar procession was under way, Joan ahead, I trailing behind, lighting the way with my large flashlight, when Joan stopped rather suddenly and made stabbing motions with her smaller light.

"What's the matter," says I, knowing full well what the matter was.

"Skunks," says Joan, succinctly.

This meant that I had to move ahead, find Josephine with the beam of my light and entertain her while Joan went about her business. So, I passed the time of night with the old lady and spoke softly to her while she proceeded to devour an enormous hunk of cold roast beef that Joan had put out for the 'critturs' that evening. And if our conversation was a bit one-sided, Josey was most genteel, never once raising her plume and allowing me to move up to within six feet of her. In fact, Josey could not have cared less, being far more concerned at that moment with her dinner.

Skunks are very much misunderstood creatures. People fear them, running from them in panic if they greet them in the bush; they kill them if they have a gun and enough distance between the skunk and the rifleman; they mash them on the highway and pay the penalty by having the undersides of their cars liberally squirted with essence; they panic if, as often happens, a quiet skunk pops into an apartment house hallway in a city. People generally just do not get along with skunks. Yet there is no more gentle creature in the woods, none more placid, none less likely to interfere with you and none more tolerant of man. In fact, I am sure that skunks enjoy the company of man.

We have our fair share of these pleasant, black-and-white fellows on The Place and never once in all the time that we have been there have they bothered us in the slightest. I suppose they would become understandably annoyed if we went around screeching at them and carrying on, but since we do not indulge in these hysterics, the skunks and the humans get along just fine at The Place.

I like raccoons, too. So does Joan. In fact, Joan adores raccoons and she still sheds a tear or two when she remembers the twin bandits we adopted and raised until they were old enough to go out into the world and look after themselves. Alvin found them and donated them to us one day in July and a more bedraggled, skinnier, unprepossessing pair of orphans you could not wish to meet. One seemed about ready to die, the other was a savage little devil who had decided that if she was to be murdered by the hulking brutes that towered over her, she would at least die fighting.

When I first saw them they were huddled in one corner of Alvin's truck, the sickly one underneath, the fighter on top, holding her small head high, her mouth open wide, needle-like milk teeth ready to bite. At first I hesitated to put my hand down to those little teeth, but a second look at the pitiful, half-starved little bodies decided me. Something had to be done about these two, I said to myself, and if I lost a little skin and a little blood in the process, well, I had done both before! I grabbed the fighter and drew her to me, cuddling her against my shirt. Immediately she burrowed right in, seeking the warmth of me, no longer emitting the blood-thirsty little growls she had been uttering seconds before.

I reached in and picked up the inert body of the second little 'coon and this one seemed beyond hope, a limp bundle of fur and bones. We were in Adams' yard and Audrey hovered near, so I asked her if she had some milk and a bit of bread. When she brought this I returned the limp one to the truck box and soaked a piece of milk bread and offered it to the fighter. One sniff was enough! Her mouth opened and she gurgled the milk down, sucking on the bread and half-choking over it, so that I had to take it from her.

Then Audrey returned with a pencil at the end of which she had tied a bit of cloth and I dipped the cloth in the milk and gave it to the scrapper to suck, whereupon she immediately pulled the cloth of the pencil. Audrey remembered the last of Sandra's baby-bottles and she brought that out, nipple and all, and I gave it to the raccoon and she gorged.

When I judged she had had enough I turned my attention to the other one, but it would not suck and I almost decided to put it out of its misery, but I did not have the heart to do this. In the end Joan and I bundled them up in the car and started back for The Place and on the way we stopped at the local store and bought a can of unsweetened condensed milk with which to feed the orphans.

In the cabin the fighter had another feed and was doing very nicely by the end of it, so I put her in a cardboard box and tried to feed the limp one. This time the little creature took some milk, so I hoped it would live. Joan by then had fussed around and found bedding for the two and she had lined the box and now they curled up, one tight against the other, and we covered the box, for raccoons like darkness, and we left them for about an hour.

When next I lifted the covering and offered the bottle both orphans fed royally and the limp one had perked up to the extent of outdoing the fighter; in fact, the little brute swallowed so much that his small belly swelled like a golf ball and I was afraid he would burst. But now they both seemed much more content and we felt reasonably sure that they would live.

By that evening the orphans were screaming for food about every two hours and they were blissful when either of us put our hand into their bedroom and stroked them. At these times they purred, loudly and continuously, a strange, hoarse purr not unlike that of a cat. It seemed that we had been accepted as foster parents and the twins were obviously determined to make up for lost time by gorging themselves when they were able to capture our attention, which was so frequently that they got diarrhea and I had to discontinue their feeding until morning and dilute the milk formula to fifty-fifty.

That night in the cabin, while the twins slept, Joan and I sat up discussing names for them. Why must humans always seek names for their pets? I know not, unless it be to associate themselves more closely with them. However, Joan made her suggestions and I made mine and each vetoed the other's and we gave up for the night and settled ourselves for sleep, the baby raccoons already snoring in their box that had been placed between our cots, just like the first-baby's cradle in the human world.

Came morning and the twins were ravenous and their loose bowels were looser and we became worried and diluted the milk still further and this time we added a raw egg to it, for 'coons are notoriously fond of eggs. But if the little ones had the trots, this did not seem to inhibit them at all, except that they were rather liberal in spraying each other with a bright yellow, quite smelly mess which we had to swab off with toilet tissue. However, progress was being made, and that day being Sunday we were due to return to our city apartment, a dwelling which had strict rules about dogs and cats and birds, but in which, fortunately, nobody had thought of forbidding the presence of raccoons; undoubtedly because it never occurred to the owners that anybody would undertake to raise twin raccoons in a city flat.

The twins were models of behaviour on the way back to the city that first Sunday night. Admittedly they were being constantly coddled by Joan, but they gave no trouble at all and were really quiet while I was sneaking them up the backstairs of the apartment building, for all the world as though they were aware of the conspiracy and had both agreed to do their share.

Up in our third-floor apartment we found a wooden box more suited as a bedroom for the twins than the now definitely soggy card-board affair and we fed them and went to bed. This time the twins were placed at the foot of my bed and because they were so small and so quiet we did not think of securing them in their bedroom. A towel over the top would be enough, we thought, until I woke up about two o'clock that morning with a feeling that I was not alone and upon sitting up and feeling my bed I encountered a cold, sticky wetness that spelled raccoon diarrhea in any language and Joan was hastily awakened by my cry of horror. The light showed the limp one happily crawling about my bed after it had evacuated its bowels upon the bedspread.

Soap and water repaired the damage to the coverlet and a wooden cover with my typewriter as weight fixed the babies so that they could not wander any more that night, but still the problem remained of how to look after these two, who were content to sleep in between feeds during the day, but who had been made by nature for the purpose of wandering about at night. We went to sleep on this riddle and next morning, after the twins had been fed and mopped up, it was decided that they needed a larger box. One was procured hastily and fixed so that the orphans could not escape it while Joan and I were at work.

Joan, who was within walking distance of her job, agreed to return home at noon to feed the orphans and at first I thought she was being most heroic about the whole thing, until I realized that she would have walked from the back of beyond in order to spend half an hour playing with the bandits. Thus the pattern of our ways was set for the next two months, while the babies grew and became more mischievous each day and developed their own natures and grew hungrier and generally ruled our small household.

During the first week of their tenancy in the city I found suitable names for them. Alvin had found them huddled together on the roadside near a town called Coboconk and because the locals referred to this place as Coby, I suggested to Joan that we call the twins Coby and Konk, to which she readily agreed.

Coby was the fighter and she was ever quick to use her teeth or her sharp, bear-like claws in fun or in real earnest. Konk was always the more placid, though he was not opposed to nipping now and then and he had a terrible method of reacting to discipline. Raccoon babies are, undoubtedly, the naughtiest youngsters on the face of this earth and they only obey if a sharp slap on the rump is administered at those time when they have got out of hand. Mother 'coons never stand too much nonsense from their young; they are wonderful and patient mothers, but if they are to raise their brood successfully they must use the old-fashioned form of child discipline and give their offspring a good spank or two now and then. This I learned through trial and error and eventually proceeded to put into effect, much to Joan's horror; but it worked to a point, at least with Coby, who, when spanked; generally calmed down, though not without first trying, and sometimes achieving, bloody vengeance upon the hand that did the spanking. Konk had a system all his own. When lifted by the scruff of the neck and spanked, he simply evacuated his bowels, and his accuracy was uncanny! No matter which way I tried to aim his posterior, he always seemed able to twist so that he pointed at some part of my person and at last I simply had to set aside a pair of pants into which I quickly changed whenever there was a need to punish the twins. Not that they were severely dealt with mind you, but there were times...

Looking over the diary which I kept on Coby and Konk in those early days of their first summer, I find these entries:

'Monday, July 18: Gave twins a feed in a.m. and decided that both needed a bath and delousing. Joan came home at noon and fed them. I returned home from work in p.m. loaded with purchases: shampoo, flea powder (two kinds), litter for the bed and feed bottles. (Later) Both clean and set up in fresh quarters. Thriving. Fed them a bit of chopped meat and pablum with fingers. Joan bitten!

Tuesday, July 19: Both toilet-trained. Last night without prompting both used corner of their box where litter was placed. Did their business and have been clean all day. Both now feeding well and know their bottles on sight. Both love plenty of fuss. Marshalls and Adilmans coming to visit them tonight. McTaggarts come Thursday.

'Wednesday, July 20: Marshalls and Adilmans visited. Both kids doing well, but a bit loose still. Changed their diet to dilute Olac on advice of Dr. N.D. Scollard of Toronto Zoo (one to three). Joan bought a teething ring and some dog biscuits, but both still prefer to suck their bottles which they use just before feeding time. Konk climbed out of the box and got into the bedside table and panic lasted while we looked for him. Coby sucks like a vacuum cleaner. Konk takes it easy when feeding, but puts away plenty. Each weighed one pound this evening, according to our bathroom scales.

'Thursday, July 21: Have to clean them every evening, not because they are messy in their personal toilets, but because now they play and roll into their toilet corner. McTaggarts arrived and fussed all over them and the twins took all this fuss as their own royal right. Coby bit Serena McT, not hard. Ken McT on hands and knees making noises at them. Quite an evening and the twins thriving on it all.'

Reading these entries I feel I must recapitulate on some of them, for they were written as reminders for the day when I was to sit down and narrate our experiences with the boys, as Joan still refers to them. That time, of course, is now, and the entries have served their purpose, recalling all manner of strange and wonderful episodes in the lives of Coby and Konk, orphans.

That first bath on the Monday was quite an operation. For those of you who are not familiar with raccoons, let me explain. A raccoon is a first cousin to a bear, although, thank the Lord, much, much smaller. Still they are armed with ten eminently practical claws; tough, black, curved, needle-sharp weapons which they know how to use most effectively. Their teeth are also like those of a bear, proportionately smaller, yet wonderfully suited for chewing and ripping. They differ from the bear in agility, though; but this difference is all in favour of the raccoons. They can twist and squirm with the speed of light and can thrust their furry bodies through apertures that would challenge the suppleness of a mongoose.

Coby became my first victim that bath night. I had previously prepared a bowl of warm water and the shampoo and flea powder were handy to my reach. Towels were draped over my lap. All was set. I picked up Coby and began. First, allowing her to sit on my open hand, I lowered her gently into the water. Now, raccoons love water; they swim like an otter, wash all their food in it most painstakingly and use it as an avenue of escape if chased by a larger predator. But, if our experiences with the orphans are the rule, they obviously reserve the right to enter water when and if the spirit moves them and as soon as Coby felt the wetness creep up past her bushy tail she changed from a soft, cuddly, purring ball of fur into a furious, screeching squirming wildcat that seemed to sprout feet and claws from every angle of her body. She used those claws; she used her teeth, she used her agile body the better to get at my naked arms.

This was my first real lesson, learned the hard way. After several minutes of unequal struggle I had to retreat to consolidate my forces. Coby stared at me, a fishy-eyed, hostile stare, from her box, her little inquisitive brown eyes following my every move. At that moment I was more concerned with the lacerations on my arms and with one rather wicked nip which Coby had inflicted on my breast, almost dead-center on the left nipple.

When the damage to my person had been examined and treated I studied my next move. Obviously there had to be a way to handle that miniature bundle of barbed wire, but how? How, I asked myself idly, would mother ’coon do it? And there was the answer. Mother would grab the little devil by the scruff of the neck and just dunk her. And that is what I did. Holding her with my left hand, I dunked her belly-deep in the bowl and used my right hand to lather her, always trying to keep clear of her reaching claws. This worked very well. The moment you grasp a young animal by the back of the neck, by the loose skin that is there just for that purpose, it reacts to the ‘mother grip’ and lets its limbs hang loose, more or less.

In this way, I bathed Coby, rinsed her and became fearful of the next step, the drying of her. But there was no need to worry. She loved the drying and was in a delirium of joy as I held her on my lap wrapped in a towel while I rubbed away the moisture. She purred and purred and purred and was a perfect lady. Which was more than I can say for her brother. Him I bathed without great difficulty, after learning from Coby, but although he obviously enjoyed the rubbing of the towel afterwards, he was yet determined to take vengeance for the abuses at my hands and just as he was almost dry, he paid me back with a prodigious bowel movement, which necessitated a change of towels, pants and a new bath for Konk. Fortunately he seemed to have run out of waste matter after this and I was allowed to dry him properly on the second time around.

After the rubbing came the delousing, which caused no great problems since I simply allowed the twins to romp around on a large towel while I sprinkled powder over them and rubbed it in with my hand. They seemed to enjoy this game, though they were a little nervous when the powder was sprinkled. But at last they were respectable. Now they looked well fed and were clean and smelled a whole lot better and they were ready for their first visitors.

After the bath and a game it was time for food, as they well knew, and we tried ground meat again and Joan, ever a trusting soul, put some on her little finger and extended same to Coby, who opened her mouth wide to receive it. So far so good; then Joan forgot to do one vital thing. Having inserted little finger and ground meat into the 'coon mouth, she allowed the finger and the meat to continue keeping company, instead of scraping the meat off into Coby's mouth as soon as she had introduced it to the teeth. The result was to be expected, by everyone except Joan, that is. Coby liked the ground meat and she was not a bit particular whether it came with or without finger. With a deft flick of her rough tongue she coaxed the finger with its load of tasty meat between her chewing molars. She pressed, hard, and Joan cut loose with a most unlady-like yell and when I looked up at these doings I saw Joan engaged in what appeared to be a tug-of-war with Coby, Joan's little finger being used instead of a rope.

"Clout her," said I.

"No!" said Joan between clenched teeth.

Coby put an end to the struggle by starting to chew and Joan's finger came free and Coby was left with the meat, which she rolled around her mouth, the while drooling copiously while she sat on the towel looking angelic and not a bit sorry for almost crushing Joan's finger. Naturally, all good stories have a moral, and the one in this was designed exclusively for my wife: Never, never, never introduce one of your fingers, liberally coated in fresh meat, into the mouth of a carnivore, if you want to keep the finger, that is.

I think that it was this incident with the finger that decided Coby to bully Joan. Both the 'coons enjoyed a rough and tumble with us and soon after the finger business it became apparent that whilst Coby was not averse to nipping me or removing a bit of skin now and then with her claws, she seemed determined to amputate any and all of Joan's extremities that came within grabbing distance of her when she was in a playful mood. In vain did Joan scream and run and hop up and down and plead. Coby took after her like a tiny bloodhound on a hot scent.

Konk, on the other hand, while not quite as rough with me, still took occasional and unfair advantage if I was not looking. He had a sneaky habit of waiting until my back was turned and then making a rolling dive at one of my legs, flinging his small arms and legs around me and not being a damned bit fussy as to where he dug his claws. With Joan, however, he was always a perfect little gentleman, and, of course, if I occasionally slapped his backside, driven to desperation by the stabbing pain of his claws, Joan would immediately sally to his defence, picking up the little monster and cuddling him while she made the most revolting baby noises I have ever heard.

On the whole, though, Coby and Konk and the Lawrences got along quite well and even in those early days it was obvious that the orphans had invested in us the affection and trust that they had previously lavished on their lost mother. And we often wondered about their mother. My guess is that she was killed crossing the highway and her twins were left to starve in the nursery. When Alvin brought them to us they had obviously gone hungry for a long time and had been chewing anything that might offer nourishment. Their teeth were broken in places and their gums lacerated. But by Monday night, while they were still thin, they had recovered their energies and seemed perfectly content with the treatment they were receiving.

Next morning, when we awoke to find the twins housebroken, I wondered at their instinctive cleanliness; probably their mother had already initiated the training and once we provided them with a litter box they used it. At any rate, from that time on, unless Konk was taking revenge for punishment, they always used their box, and I remember being particularly pleased with them that day for I did not wish to go through another prickly hour bathing them that evening, before their visitors arrived.

Already, only three days since we found them, Coby and Konk ran to us when they fancied that danger was present. This became obvious with their first visitors, the Marshalls, who naturally bent over to see them. I was holding them and they immediately burrowed into my body, squeezing close to me for protection. They did the same thing with the Adilmans and if they were less cautious with the McTaggarts, still they viewed them with suspicion. This fear of humans persisted and they were never quite themselves when strangers were around.

By the end of that first week each baby had developed definite personal characteristics. Coby was always the aggressive type, while bigger, fatter Konk was more phlegmatic and less timid. Still they persisted in their attitudes to Joan and myself. Coby was 'my' 'coon, Konk was Joan's and although we could handle them both and we took turns at feeding and bathing them, it was quite plain that each had made his or her choice of human foster parent and decided to stick to it.

Two weeks after Alvin gave them to us the twins were doing so well that they presented now a few problems. I had to buy a wire cage and smuggle it into the apartment, for now they could not be trusted alone in the apartment unless we were sure they were safely under lock and key, which situation was not at all to their liking. They could stand their cage during the day, for they slept through most of the daylight hours, but once night came they did their very best to break out and perforce we had to let them loose and try and control them as they romped over our furniture, climbed the curtains, upset flower pots and stuffed their slender, sensuous hands into the electric toaster.

Raccoon hands and fingers are wonderful things. Rather monkey-like, but much more slender and sensitive, they are used constantly, for these creatures take inordinate delight in feeling, whether it be food, water, themselves, cloth or any one of thousand things. And if there be a small hole somewhere, that's the favourite feeling place, for they seem to play at recognizing objects without looking at them. Often we would see one or the other of our orphans busy feeling, arm outstretched, hand deep in some crack, while the 'coon was looking around the room, bliss shining fully in the quick brown eyes.

Given a bowl of water and a stone or a cork or a piece of bread they would feel and feel and feel, always avoiding their eyes from the object of their attention, never tiring of the game. Some evenings I would run about three inches of water into our bath and I would place their sleeping box in it—it was just wide enough to support itself on both sides of the bath without touching the water—and they would play there, blissfully happy for half an hour and more, batting a champagne cork around in the water,

Our raccoon, Coby, exercising on the window-sill of our city apartment. She and her brother Konk, loved to climb up there and play with the window blinds.

Brother Konk, at large on The Place when about three months old, takes his exercise in manly style, doing some calisthenics on a young white pine.

or feeling some coloured bottle caps we gave them, or just plain feeling the water, working their fingers in it, even feeling the fingers of each hand, or each other's tails.

At last, by summer's close, it became obvious that we could not hope to keep these orphans much longer in our apartment—so we moved out and rented a house! But even a full basement was not enough for Coby and Konk. They just plain hated being under lock and key and each time I thought I had closed every possible exit from their basement quarters, they would find a new one. Nothing seemed to contain them, not even a perfectly smooth concrete wall that would have given trouble to a fly; they climbed this five minutes after I shut the door on them and when I could not hear them trying to get out I became suspicious and returned downstairs to their room and could not find them, until I heard a noise over my head and looked up to see them both crouched between a water-pipe and the ceiling, on their way to explore the rest of the house.

One weekend, towards the end of August, we let them loose at The Place. That was quite a day! At first they played around the cabin, then they gradually went farther afield, climbing trees and having a great time, then they disappeared and Joan's tears started and I had to act like a gruff male and pretend that this was what I wanted for them, which it was, but I was nevertheless sorry to see them go. In the end Joan dried her tears and we spent the rest of the day pretending that neither one of us was at all concerned about the 'coons.

It became bedtime and we settled for the night just as heavy rain started to fall and although we did not speak of it, we were both worried about 'the boys'. And then I heard a raccoon call. They have a peculiar churring call, unmistakable, and this particular call was just as unmistakably made by either Coby or Konk. I was out of bed in a flash and outside, wearing nothing but my shorts, despite the rain I hunted around the cabin and was about to give up when I saw two little whiskered faces peering at me from under the building. Coby and Konk returned to Joan. They were fed and dried and some pine sap was removed, not without a few protests, and they were put into their box for the night.

That Sunday they accompanied us back to the city again, loose in the car, and they spent most of their time climbing over either Joan or myself, which both of us could stand, but at times one or the other of them decided to explore the area around the foot pedals and then I had to get cross before the culprit was hauled out, protesting vigorously, and tossed into the back of the car.

Thus two more weeks went by and we let them loose again and this time they stayed away longer on Saturday, returning late at night; and Sunday morning they wanted to get out again and we let them out and although they visited us that afternoon, they did not come back that night and we left, our twins still out in the bush night, and sadness was heavy upon us because we knew not if we would see them again. But this was the way. It was the teaching of the wilderness, Coby and Konk knew of it, so did we, and we had to abide by the law here.

The next weekend we hoped to see them, but they did not return. They had been back at some time during the week and they had tried to get back into the cabin, a sad, mute tribute from our little bandits, who, while living as they wanted to live, free and unfettered, still missed some part of the humans that had given them life. And, of course, Joan and I missed them too and we wished we could have kept them.

Why did we not keep them? We could have, naturally, and they would have lived longer in our company than they will in the forest; they would have lived well, and become sleek. But they would have lived caged a large part of their life. I would not rob the twins of their heritage, of that vital, subtle substance that shines in the eyes of wild things. So Coby and Konk returned to the forest, old enough now to look after themselves, strong enough to compete in the wilderness. And we hoped that one day, we would see them again.

TEN

ONE BRIGHT, SUNFILLED DAY in early June, before the twins had come to join us, I was clearing away some of the debris of winter on the rock flat behind the fireplace when the fierce buzzing of a bee drew my attention to a partly-rotted pine log that lay with others like it near the outdoor fireplace. The sound was husky, insistent, a heavy buzz too loud for that of an ordinary honey bee. I knew that the noise-maker was a bumble bee, but I did not know where it was or why it sounded so indignant. Cautiously I drew closer to the log and the buzzing became more intent and then I noticed a slight movement within a pile of old grass stems and leaves that had been mounded just inside the hollow of the log.

This mound of grass was the winter nest of a white-footed mouse, built after the first snowfall, when the log was covered in white and its hollow offered shelter and concealment to the mouse. When spring came and the snow melted, the mouse's winter quarters became unsuitable, for now any predator could see at a glance that a white-footed was living in the log. So the mouse moved and left his old nest behind and the bumble bee had appropriated it and was busy fussing with her brood.

I backed away from the log and stood quietly for some minutes and the buzzing ceased and for a time there was stillness in the old mouse nest, until the queen thought that she was again alone. Then movement began anew in the grass as she applied herself to her task and I left her, not wishing to disturb her, and certainly not wishing to enrage her to the point where she would come out fighting. But I was curious about this bee nest, all the same, and I determined to investigate it at the first opportunity.

That afternoon, having almost forgotten the bumble bee, I was passing the pine log when I saw her emerge from the nest and fly off, making for the large, bush-encircled clearing east of our cabin. I watched until I could see her no longer and then I approached her nest. Inside it I found her first brood, each egg encased in its own wax bedroom. Outwardly the waxen nest appeared as a bumpy mass three-and-a-half inches long by three inches in width at its broadest point. It was a rich brown that shone golden when sunlight flashed off the glistening coating of sticky wax with which it was protected. Each bump represented a nest chamber and there were eleven of these, all fully encased in the fibrous, waxy coating.

Nowadays I hate destroying life, yet I felt compelled to open one of those carefully built chambers to see what it contained. Using a scalpel and working cautiously so as not to damage the larva, if the eggs had already hatched, I opened a little trap-door in one chamber. Inside was a white, glistening, roly-poly larva, already well-formed and bearing the outline of head and eyes and sharp body-end that even then showed the undeveloped sting channel at its very tip. After photographing the nest and the larvae I replaced the white grub and put back the lid, using the soft wax to seal it again, and as I was about to put the nest back into its original home, I was struck by a thought. If I put the nest in another location, would the queen be able to find it?

Some twenty feet from the nesting log was another, similar pine stub and, leaving the grasses undisturbed in the mound, I carried the nest to the farther log, laid it inside and pulled some dry grass and covered it. Now all that remained was to watch for the bee on her return from her foraging and see what she would do, and since I needed an excuse to lounge in a deck chair for a while, this enforced idleness seemed like an excellent idea.

For an hour I sat watching the now-deserted log and by this time my stock of patience was getting exhausted and I was itching to be up and doing something more active. As I was about to call the whole thing off and replace the nest on its old site, the queen bumble bee appeared. Straight for her nest she flew, circling the log twice before landing and disappearing into the grass. An instant later she fairly screamed her anger and out she came, obviously furious and, I feared, about to commit assault upon my person. I remained still, the bee continued her angry buzzing and started flying in short circles which gradually increased in their circumference as she evidently engaged herself in a systematic search of the area.

Within five minutes she had found the nest and after a close and careful inspection of the new site she settled down to tending her young. Did she realize the switch, or was she left with the impression that she was losing her mind? I shall never know, for unlike the German zoologist, Professor Karl von Frisch, of Munich, I do not understand bee language, which, this scientist has proved, is an elaborate system of communication made up of buzzing frequencies and body movements.

The presence of only one bee in the log said clearly that the nest I had found was the particular queen's first brood of the year. Bumble bees, unlike honey bees, do not have servants to rear all their young and the first brood are, in fact, the drones who, once they are matured, take over the future young bees produced by their queen, who continues egg-laying through the summer.

Each spring solitary queens, fertilized the year before, set out to look for a suitable nesting site in which to place their nest, for with the exception of these females, all members of last year's colony die in the autumn, leaving their monarch to settle in some sheltered spot where she goes into hibernation until the cold has gone and it is time for her to produce a new colony. After the worker larvae hatch from her first eggs, the queen feeds them a mixture of pollen and honey until, ten days later, they are fully grown and separate from each other to spin silk cocoons and transform themselves into pupae, in which condition they remain for about eighteen days. Then they emerge as fully-developed bumble bees and take over the care of the colony.

Two weeks after my discovery of the bumble bee nest, I ran into violent contact with a paper wasp. I was climbing a tall pine in order to photograph the eyases of the red-shouldered hawk, who were then fluffy youngsters squatting in their stick nest in the poplar. The nest was some forty feet from the ground and in order to get a good view of them I had to get above them, hence my presence in the pine some fifty feet from the ground.

I was wearing an old felt hat, bequeathed to me by Marq de Villiers before he left for Europe. Around my neck was my camera and telephoto lens, a cumbersome machine, and in my right hand was a dry pine limb plentifully furnished with prickly branchlets which was to be my shield if the hawks decided to dive bomb me again. Thus encumbered I climbed slowly, my eyes glued to the hawk's nest and my senses concentrating on the job on hand. Suddenly an angry buzzing reached me. It was similar to that of the bumble bee, but not as husky and at about the same time that I identified it, my eyes, raised upwards, encountered the oval, bag-like, light grey nest suspended from a branch not more than one foot away. Flying in increasing circles just outside of the nest opening, which is always located at the bottom of the paper container, were two wasps, both obviously angry and ready to repel the intruder. It was an impasse. I stopped and remained still while I tried to decide on my next move. I certainly had no intentions of abandoning my quest for hawk pictures, but the smallish nest did pose a problem. Quite suddenly one of the worker wasps zoomed in to the attack. She stung me on the left temple, a sharp, burning sting that almost made me loose my hold on the tree trunk. Now, I thought, the little brute will go away, for I then held to the belief that wasps sting only the once. Not a bit of it. My small attacker zoomed in again (or was it her companion?) and sank her dart two millimetres to the right of the first wound. This time she got action. I flapped wildly, dislodging my hat and dropping my shield branch and, I think, swatting the wasp (or wasps) while I said things uncomplimentary to the genus Dolichovespula maculata, or bald-faced hornet.

While Joan, standing at the bottom of the pine, made suitable noises of sympathy, I massaged my sore temple and waited for the next onslaught, almost deciding to slide down the pine, go back to the cabin and collect my .22-calibre rifle and with it, from terra firma, put to rout the hornet (commonly called paper wasp) and its confounded brood. But nothing more happened. An occasional warning buzz, hollow and echoing, issued from the grey bag suspended above me, nothing more. I settled to my photographs and was allowed to descend the tree in good order.

I had, of course, met *Dolichovespula* before this, on many occasions, and having spent some time observing this creature I soon learned to change my mind about it and its habits. At one time, like so many other people do, I disliked all wasps and feared them not a little and often killed them when opportunity presented, for in my ignorance I believed the foibles of humanity which have succeeded in surrounding the wasp with a reputation for viciousness simply because the insect attempts to protect itself and its nest from the blundering progress of man. Indeed the wasps sting, but only when they are given reason, or when they believe there is reason. Be quiet around them, do not give way to panic or approach their nesting place too closely (as I did in the pine) and the wasps will leave man alone.

In exchange for peace and quiet wasps will consume untold thousands of harmful insects. Mosquitoes, flies, beetles and their larvae and many others are seized and devoured by these creatures and many a time I have watched one of the species pounce on a fly and sit in the sunlight, eating it much like a human gnawing on a cob of corn. But perhaps one of the most fascinating species of wasps belong to the *Pompilidae* family. Commonly known as spider wasps, these creatures nest in burrows in the soil, in cells they make out of mud and in small holes in trees and rocks and even buildings.

Their system of rearing their young is simple and trouble-free. When the female is ready to lay her eggs she seeks out a spider, the bigger the better, it seems, and, having found one, dives in to the attack. The spider tries to evade and even tries to kill the wasp, but *Pompilidae* is usually the winner. With a well-aimed thrust she sinks her stinger into one of the spider's nerve ganglions (a group of key nerves) and paralyses her victim. With the spider's leg and jaw muscles out of action, the insect is helpless and the wasp carried it to her burrow, places it inside and then lays an egg upon its body. Thus, when the wasp egg hatches its young feeds upon the living spider, an ingenious, if cruel system by human standards.

Though this wasp is better known for its love of spiders, it consumes other insects in like fashion, particularly beetles, a fondness for which it shares with the Tiphiid wasps, common enough insects but often unrecognized as wasps. These creatures are mostly small and slender, black and white, or plain black, or black marked with yellow or red, and they are very valuable to man because they are killers of the white grub, the larva of the June beetle that destroys so many kinds of vegetation.

The white grubs, of course, live underground and the Tiphiid must tunnel down also in search of her prey. When she finds one she stings it, rather like the spider wasps, and when it is quiet she massages the lower part of the grub's abdomen with her mouth, 'files' at a crease in the grub's body, between two of its segments, and then lays a single egg in this spot. No doubt made hungry by her excavations and 'filing' she will then likely lop off one of the grub's legs and wind up the proceedings by taking a sip of 'blood' from its body. Later, after she has emerged from underground, she will busy herself around flowers, sipping at nectar.

When the Tiphiid larva hatches, it pierces the skin of the host grub and begins to feed on it and the larva, literally, is eaten alive, as are the victims of the spider wasp, for the grub does not die until the larva is in its last stages of development. By then the body of the grub is almost entirely eaten and the larva spins a cocoon and pupates in the soil, later to emerge as a wasp.

There are thousands of insects on The Place, all of them with a destiny to fulfill, with a duty to the land. Some are 'pests' by the standards of man, some are 'good' by this measure, some are large, others so small they cannot be seen by the naked eye, some common and well-known, others common but known not, yet others uncommon and little known and still more that are completely unknown, that are waiting to be discovered by man, named, studied, catalogued and placed on the record.

Between them they control the destiny of The Place, for they give life to many creatures, they propagate vegetation, they 'cultivate' the soil. Some are there for control purposes, to stop certain species from over-populating and becoming truly harmful to the land; others are there to be of direct benefit to the trees and the grasses and flowers and shrubs; still others are there to feed birds and other insects and mammals. There is not one of these small creatures that does not, in some way, contribute of itself to the earth and that which grows under it, upon it and out of it, and even in death, these tiny decaying bodies are of value, for they feed the very soil and it digests them and turns their meagre scraps into usable energy and the land and all that is in it live on.

Once, a number of years ago, I asked myself: What is earth? It seemed a silly question. Everybody knows what earth is. But do they? We call it dirt, and mould, and humus, and soil, and mud, and clay; we all know it and what it looks like; some of us know what it smells like and what it tastes like. The farmer knows it is living matter, so does the scientist; living, creating matter that goes on and on and has become so familiar that we despise it, we scuff it and kick it and litter it and kill it, and we do not know that we are also killing a part of ourselves.

Soil, the moist dark womb of humanity, of the world; the simple element that is yet so complex, the origin of life. As I stood upon the soil of The Place one fine summer evening I gazed at a handful of it that I had picked up from under a rock. I searched its particles and I asked questions and a thousand thoughts coursed through my mind. I smelled this damp earth. Acid entered my nostrils, pungent and smoky, a strange scent composed of a dozen aromas, suggestive of mushrooms, and rot, and rain, and new-cut grass; and war. I remembered the first time I had really smelled soil. The earth had been slashed and I was inside it, mouldering in it, a part of it, for it was a part of me; it was on my clothing and on my hands and on my face. It was in my nostrils and in my mouth and I tasted it and it was bitter and its strange smell was a new thing to me then and it was pleasant for it did not hold the odour of death as all other things around me seemed to do. I lay inside the earth and I breathed of it and I felt it shake, shiver, like some giant monster suddenly and cruelly assailed. It cushioned me, protected me, and its smell lingered in my nostrils for years after, until time and other smells replaced it.

These things came to me as I looked at a handful of red-brown soil picked up at random on The Place. The sun had put warmth into the rock that had sheltered that patch of soil, but the clinging particles in my hand were cold, for the heat had not been able to reach down through the granite. I squeezed my hand shut over the mound and some of it squirted through between my fingers and fell in little clumps on to the ground. I opened my hand again and the impression of my fingers was left in the earth and I saw a tiny red spider erupt suddenly from out of it, a minute carmine thing that had been hidden by the soil. It shook the earth in my hand, an infinitesimal caricature of the bomb bursts that had showered me with earth one morning in a French field and it reminded me of myself as I must have appeared as I heaved and struggled to extricate myself from the mould that encased me. The little red spider cracked the soil I had compacted with the pressure of my fingers; nearly-microscopic fissures appeared upon its surface and a little bump of loosely-packed earth arose after the cracks. I saw a tendril of leg as it eased its needle-point tip through a crack; another leg appeared, and another and a red-black spider's face, a miniature gargoyle mask, followed the legs and the delicate red of its body began to show and soon the insect was free and began scurrying over the cupped earth. Gently I replaced the soil in its bed, taking care not to cover the spider and I watched the tiny creature scuttle away to hide itself in a crack.

For some time more I stared at the soil and I thought about it and pondered over its formation, over the need we have for it. Soil, I mused, is perhaps one of Creation's most cleverly-constructed substances. Today it is made largely from the rot of plants and insects and bacteria, helped along on its course by minute fungus growth that is hidden within it and active, always-searching bacteria that do their job, breed and multiply and die and furnish more substance with their rotting selves. Some of these micro-organisms are found in the soil itself, others grow only on the roots of plants. But how did it all start?

Once, in the darkness of time, the earth was a mass of great craggy rocks. Hardness and coldness and nothing but rock; this was the earth once. There was no soil; no plants greened in the surface of this planet. The hardness of stone dominated in the high places, but in the hollows there was water, great lakes and seas, some fresh, some salt, swirled and boiled by winds, shrouded by great sluggish mists, cleaved by spears of lightning, concussed by rolling thunder. This was earth, a bare, lifeless, rock-studded, water-engulfed ball that twisted slowly upon itself, a stone orange adrift in an abyss.

Then the miracle. Life. Primitive, shrivelled, insignificant life sent out sinuous white tendrils into the water. Still the high land remained naked, soil-less, a place where not even death could find a foothold, for to have death we must first have life. The ancient storms still roared and swept over the clean rocks and cleaved the seas and the lakes and somehow, out of one of these places of water, a bit of its life was swept upon a rock, buffeted by the wind, left there to die. But it would not die. It clung to its rock and it had the will to survive and it found ways of extracting life from its host. Time travelled while the earth aged and the green life upon the rock grew strong and slowly adapted itself to its new place and it changed its shape and now we recognize it by a name—lichen. Today it grows in many forms; irregular, leathery patches on rocks, hanging feathery from the dead branches of trees, in clusters on the ground. But there is one kind that still finds and extracts life from bare rocks, that actually makes soil from its host. It is demure and inconspicuous, more like a darkish green stain than a plant as it presses itself tightly against a rock, seeming to be a part of it. This lichen is not just one plant. It is a colony of tiny plants, composed of two different species, one dependent upon the other. It is a fungus and an algae. The algae supplies nourishment for itself and its fungus partner, without which it cannot exist.

Between them, these two primitive, soft, helpless growths are able to break the rock that offers them shelter. The lichen first leaks an acid that leaches into the rock, where it loosens the surface of its cement. Then, affected by wet weather and by dry atmosphere, the lichen contracts and expands itself and as it is sticking hard to the rock surface, its movements back and forth break off tiny pieces of the rock. This is soil-making. The weather, rain and snow and sun and frost further break down the rock attacked by the lichen and as this creature of the past gathers to itself more and more minute particles of the rock, and as part of the lichen dies and rots and mixes with these atoms of granite, soil evolves from the mixture. This is poor, starved soil, yet it can offer life to other, slightly higher forms of plant life which in turn, by dying, add of their own bodies to the bits that gave them life and gradually enrich the soil and now it is suitable for plants higher still in the scale of evolution and the process continues, even today, so that where once there was but bare rock, now there are bushes and even trees, their matrixes amounts of rock dust that have been patiently fed by the bodies of decaying plant matter so that humus, life-giving, rich soil, has formed.

This process started it all and though today there are so many creatures and plants on this planet that soil continues forming without the need of the primitive lichens, the same process still continues in places, adding its own little bit of soil to the world's total, creating gardens where once there was only rock, small gardens perhaps, but enough of these creative little patches add up to one big garden, a natural garden, a forest. It was a patient, cumulative process, now it is a boundless, tireless one. It is life. In the forests of Canada the centuries have cultivated rich layers of humus. Trees grew and dropped their leaves and the leaves were attacked by insects and some of their green body was eaten and some was left to rot, to ferment and supply substance to the soil by forming an area of leaf-mould which is itself a place of chemicals, a veritable factory in which labour vast, yet microscopic, armies of insects, and bacteria, and fungus, and worms, and grubs, and small animals; these workers of soil convert the rot of the fallen leaves, turn it into humus.

Plants grow here, their seeds blown or dropped by bird or animal and their roots reach downwards, seeking nourishment from the soil and in reaching down these sinuous tendrils bring up hidden minerals from the earth, sucking at these life-giving substances and pushing them upwards with their sap to feed the leaves, helping this in their quest for life, giving them the strength to take water and invisible gases from the very air until they are mature and the plant or trees of which they are a part gives birth to blossom and the blossom gives birth to fruit and the fruit produces more life, for some of its is eaten and some of it falls to the earth and from this more plants grow and more mulch is left upon the earth and then the leaves die and they, too, fall and the process begins again. This is infinity. It is earth, soil, the humble element that gave birth to man.

Soil provides the foundation to all things. It is at once solid yet it is soft enough to allow tender rootlets to dig into it and to anchor their bodies in it. It can hold up a small bush or a mighty tree with equal facility. It serves as a reservoir for water and as a storehouse for the minerals needed by the plants. Many of these minerals are needed by every plant, and other substances, too, such as carbon, and hydrogen, and oxygen, and nitrogen; these are gases, they are the partners of the minerals, of calcium, and iron, and magnesium, and potassium, and phosphorus, and sulphur, and elements such as boron, copper, cobalt, manganese, and zinc. All these are needed to give life to a plant. And in addition, to be productive, the soil must contain humus, the rotting remains of plants and animals, which gives soil its colour, making it brown, or black, or, by mixing with high contents of minerals, making it yellow or red. Humus also provides the earth's pores, allowing proper drainage and allowing air into the soil, for even the very earth must breathe.

Soil is also the home of an insignificant creature, a thing that causes some humans to shudder and turn away from in disgust, a creature that is man's symbol of ridicule, of weakness, of cowardice, and yet is none of these things and is, instead, an important part of our earth, for it is a true farmer, one of the most efficient workers in the darkness of earth. This is the earthworm. The pink, slimy wriggling thing that is the bait for fishermen, some fifty thousand of which tunnel and slide through one acre of soil and, between them, during but one growing season will gorge themselves on eighteen tons of earth, take nourishment from it and squeeze its remains through their tubular bodies to deposit it in little brown, damp mounds upon the surface of the earth. Through its burrowing, swallowing, digesting and excretions the humble worm keeps turning the soil and mixing into it organic matter, thereby enriching it.

Once I looked closely at the earthworm. I looked long and with deep interest, until I became so familiar with this humble, yet complex creature, that I could visualize him crawling through his small tunnels under the earth and I could almost place myself in his situation and feel his body and know what it contained and how it moved and what it lived on and how it digested its food and how it reproduced of its own kind. And since that day the earthworm has meant more to me than just a slimy little creature of pink pulp good only for baiting a fish hook. I learned then that the humble worm can feel pain, and recognize danger, that it has a brain and no less than five hearts and that it has 'hair', and a mouth, and nerves.

It is 410 million years since air-breathing insect life left the waters that spawned it and took up residence upon dry land, and during that gargantuan span of time, so the fossil record tells us, strange, ancestral scorpions had to learn to defeat one great enemy—the sun. This was a problem common to all forms of terrestrial life, encountered by plants and animals alike, for if today the sun produces life, it did not, in those mysterious ages, offer its help to the earth. It was, in fact, an enemy. A powerful hurtful force that threatened to dry up, to dehydrate all land creatures until these learned how to take moisture from the earth, store it in their bodies and use it not only to defeat their enemy but to harness its wonderful energy for their own use; and no sooner was this challenge overcome, than a second, equally serious danger faced life. Water had provided the perfect medium of protection to the offspring of those primitive things, which, by the simple process of releasing their sperm into the liquid of their environment, were enabled to create new beings like themselves when male sperm and female ovum met and joined within the vast liquid cushion that housed them.

This system would not serve on land; cold and heat and wind and the rough hardness of rock threatened always to destroy the delicate organisms of birth and a new way in fact, many new ways, had to be found. The plants solved their reproduction problems by learning how to manufacture dry, light pollen to transfer the sperm to the egg, using first the sun to dry the sperm pods and ripen them, then the wind and birds and insects to carry them to union with their female partners, where the delicate embryos received protection from the tissues of their mothers or by the coverings of their seeds. Other creatures, unable to find safe ways for breeding on land, settled for a compromise, returning to the water to give birth; thus were the amphibians created. Still others, insects, snails, reptiles, birds, mammals, and earthworms, learned to transfer the male seed to the body of the female by copulation and then, within the body of the mothers of each species the sperm and the eggs were surrounded and protected by a water medium and further safeguarded by an elastic, tough shell. Thus, it would seem, that the old riddle of the chicken and the egg is answered; the chicken came first, arriving from the water to set up is claim to land; and undoubtedly many, many 'chickens' came from the water, one at a time or by their dozens, tried to breed on land and failed until one day came a 'chicken' whose body has mastered the art of egg-making and the first ovum was laid.

From the waters of prehistory came the earthworm, a humble, slow creature which yet had a definite purpose ahead of it, for, like all creatures upon earth, while it took nourishment and found shelter in the soil, it returned to Creation a new product—the organic wastes from its body—and it used its soft self to provide a vital function, the turning over of the soil.

As its Latin name, *Annelida,* suggests, the earthworm is made or rings, its body consisting of two tubes, one inside the other, each of which is segmented; each worm being composed of some 100 different rings inside of which are either one or two organs belonging to one or the other of the tubes. Separating each segment are 'up-and-down' bulkheads, or seals, for each ring is a separate sub-unit of the body and each is likely to carry out a specialized job. Centuries ago the earthworm settled its quarrel with the sun by first going underground when it came out of the water and then developing an outer layer of thin, tough skin which is kept moist and slippery by a mucous solution manufactured by special cells located within the creature's proper skin.

Often I have watched the progress of a worm and wondered at it. Now I wonder no more for I know that the creature owns two sets of muscles, each working independently, that contract and stretch the body, allowing it to travel in 'waves'. These muscles are housed in the body wall, the outside tube, as it were. One set is circular, the other runs along the length of the animal's body. Also, each body ring is endowed with four pairs of bristles, each of which has its own small muscles that can move it in and out. When the worm contracts its circular muscles, the pressure that these place upon the tube body stretches it, makes it longer, rather like a piece of elastic that is stretched. The bristles at the front half then cling to the surface of the worm's burrow and when the worm relaxes its ring muscles and in turn contracts its longitudinal muscles, these have an opposite action, they shrink the body, making it short and fat and since the front bristles are hanging on, the back end of the worm comes forward; thus it moves ahead for half its length. By repeating this process over and over the earthworm makes progress along its underground burrows.

Earthworms eat, and swallow, and digest their food. They have a mouth which intakes green stuff and quite a wide throat for swallowing, and a crop, and a gizzard, and, lastly, intestines. The crop stores the food; a sort of cupboard which passes supplies as they are needed to the gizzard, which is nothing more nor less than a crushing mill. Here the worm's food is ground to bits before its wastes are passed along into the intestines and finally excreted back into the soil, mixed with other body wastes. The worm's blood supply is pumped by five hearts which are composed of five pairs of muscular pumps that drive the blood at command from the creature's brain.

This is the earthworm, the humble thing despised and avoided and carelessly destroyed by man. It is still a primitive being, puny, and insignificant bit of Creation. Yet these creatures, it is estimated, are collectively responsible every ten years for turning over enough soil to cover the entire land surface of the earth with a layer of 'dirt' two inches deep.

There are times when it is left to the humble creatures of this world to teach man a lesson in humility. There have been many such times for me on The Place, occasions when I pause to look at some object, casually, more out of habit than curiosity, and I am suddenly engrossed by what I see. It happened thus with the big anthill at the beginning of our road, a mound of fine, well-worked soil that rises for some two feet from the ground. Small, red-black ants inhabit the interior of this mound and there must be literally thousands of these mites housed in their earthen stronghold.

I know not how long the hill has been there, for the insects had already constructed it when Joan and I came to The Place, but although I had seen it every time I drove or walked up or down our road I had but glanced at it incuriously, noting its presence, noting also the creatures that made it, for there were always numbers of them crawling over it, but never really pausing to look at it, to actually see it. Then one morning early, as I was starting out for a walk, I stopped by the anthill and looked upon it. At first I was merely curious, then, seeing a dead June beetle lying

What is it? I call it an unidentified flying object. It is a night insect and unknown to me; perhaps it is one of the million or so insects still awaiting identification?

Metallic wood-borer beetles lay their eggs on downed trees and their larvae eat their way into the timber, pass the winter there, pupate and emerge as adult beetles. They are eagerly sought by the woodpeckers.

Large carpenter ant larvae,mixed with the larvae of the small aggressive ants which raid the nests of the black ants and steal their larvae, which are taken to the nests of the small ants and used as slaves.

near me on the road, I reached for it and tossed it upon the anthill. At once a dozen or more of the tiny creatures surrounded the great beetle and began the task of moving it towards one of their subterranean entrances. It made me think of the building of the great pyramids of Egypt. The beetle bulked greater than 100 of those ants, yet a mere sprinkling of them were engaged in moving it, infinitely slowly, patiently, with a strength that was astonishing.

I continued to watch and presently help came. At the response of some mysterious signal, hundreds of ants scurried out of their little tunnels in the mound and fell upon the beetle and soon the big insect was dismembered, chopped up and carried away, down the tunnels into the underground store-rooms. Now I was fascinated. I wondered what would happen if I disturbed the hill slightly and I broke off a small twig and dug it into the mound, piercing the loose soil for a distance of about one inch and then moving the stick from side to side, making a funnel-like depression. Immediately ants boiled out. They came from the depression I had made, they came from tunnels in other parts, hundreds of them, and at first they scurried around madly, obviously seeking the enemy at their door. But I had removed the stick and I stood still and there was no enemy on the mound and soon the ants settled into an inspection of the damage to their fortress. Perhaps I imagined it, but it seemed to me that a number of the ants were left with the job of surveying the damage, for while the greater number of them milled about, a few crawled into the depression and moved slowly around it, as though assessing the problem. Presently these 'engineers' crawled out of the crater and then all the ants set to, fetching and carrying and digging, repairing the damage, filling in the depression so quickly and effectively that inside of ten minutes there was no sign of the hole that I had made.

Activity on the hill became normal when the co-operative construction job was completed and as I was about to turn away I was struck by the grass that grew upon the mound. I was not sure at first what it was that drew my attention to it and I looked for some time, knowing that there was something different about this grass, yet not being able to discover what it was. The growth was fresh, green, tender. It stood three and four inches tall and, I thought idly, resembled more a planted crop than a haphazardly seeded growth. It was that apparently inconsequential thought that made me realize what it was about the grass that first drew my attention to it. It did, indeed, resemble a crop, and a well-tended one at that. It was as though I stood before a Lilliputian farm plot. Only spears of that tender young grass grew upon the mound, nothing else. On any other part of The Place grass and many other weeds grow side by side. Here no weeds grew, instead there was just grass, each plant well spaced, the earth around it worked until it resembled the most carefully cultivated of human farms.

Here was a riddle for me. Did those little ants knowingly cultivate the grass for feed? Or was this merely an accident brought about by a series of circumstances that prevented other things from growing but did not molest the grass? It could be, I said to myself, that other seeds were not allowed to take root on the hill because as soon as they were blown there a host of ants seized them and carried them to their larder, food for later days. This was a possible explanation. Then I noticed that numerous grass stems had been cut down, for only short stubs protruded from the earth. Did the ants do this? Did they use the grass for food? A little later I realized that only fresh grass grew on the mound; not a stem of old, dark-green grass was there to be seen and not a trace of old, dry grass was left. And as I watched I saw five ants attack a grass stem, working on it until it toppled over, like some miniature tree cleaved by the woodsman's axe. The stem was trundled away and taken below ground.

Scientists, those hard-headed men and women who study the mysterious and the impossible, do not ever jump to conclusions; they see and they doubt and they experiment and they have invented a term, coined from the Greek, which they apply to certain kinds of knowledge—empiricism; meaning experience and observation. Well, on that day I had observed, but I lacked the experience, so I proposed to be as empirical as possible about those ants and their grass and I watched them and I am still watching them. Nothing has occurred to date to change my view: added to their many other interesting and ingenious ways ants, at least the ones that inhabit the hill on The Place, are farmers who harvest a variety of wild grass that is always 'mowed' when young, picked when ripe, as it were, and probably provides them with needed vegetable nourishment. Mind you, I am not *sure* of this, not yet, anyway, but it is an intriguing idea. And why not? Ants are already notorious for many incredible things, especially their highly organized 'civilization', a form of pure Communism, where every member of the colony works for the good of all.

The small ants harvest the tender stalks of young grasses, which they use for food. Photo shows areas that have been 'mowed' by the ants.

Ants are equipped with minute scent glands that are apparently able to produce at least two different types of odour; the one is used for alarm purposes and the merest whiff of the stuff is enough to bring out the fighting men of the colony who charge about wildly, furiously, ready to repel any attack. Another scent is used to mark their trail, so that when one or two ants locate a good supply of food they discharge their trail scent on the return to their hill or burrow with their first load of the food. This not only allows the scout to find his own way back, but also permits his fellow workers to join the procession.

Ants are also able to 'tell time'. In fact, like so many other creatures, including man, ants have a clock built into their bodies, invisible, still mysterious, but none the less most effective once it has been 'set'. Sometimes this setting process has to be done several times in the lifetime of each ant, at other times it is only done once, shortly after the birth of the ant. It happens this way. The creatures are born in the dark, their clocks rely on the sun for time sense. At first these clocks are running slow or fast and the young ant literally does not know the time. But once they emerge from the darkness the sun penetrates the armour-plating of their heads and reacts upon light-sensitive areas of the brain. Thus a young ant will sit for three or four hours in the sunlight, intently watching the course of the sun, 'setting' its clock by it. Once this is done, the creature is able to navigate with the aid of the sun. In this way, too, adult ants who have been confined to the darkness of their burrows, hills, or in the cavities of trees during winter must set their sun compass upon emerging into daylight in the spring. It is this hidden, invisible, unexplainable clock that tells the ant when to do what.

In the same way do plants govern their daily actions, for they, too, own such 'clocks'. These work a little differently, though. The sunlight enters the plant and invades its chlorophyll—and the way in which this is done has not yet been explained—and sets the plant's clock so that it controls the timing mechanism. The full cycle of the plant's life is controlled by this means from the 'running' of the sap to the lifting and dropping of petals and leaves.

ELEVEN

ONE DAY RECENTLY I looked at the sky and saw flashing against the azure and white of the heavens a shape of rare sleekness. The bird was all white but for a shading of black at its wing tips. At a quick glance it could have been mistaken for a large gull, but a second look disclosed the unmistakable lines of a bird of prey. This was a gyrfalcon that was planing so effortlessly in the sky over The Place and it was the first of its kind I had seen this far south of their northland breeding grounds. Migratory in habit, I judged this one was heading north, dallying in hopes of a meal over the pines of The Pace.

Once it flapped its pointed wings, then it played with the air currents, steering gently with its tail so that it moved in lazy circles gaining height at the end of each spiral. I had my movie camera and I was able to capture the gyr on film, briefly, but lastingly. Through the view-finder I watched it become smaller and smaller, always planing and circling, never flapping its wings, until at last it was gone; and for a time it took my mind with it to the ancestral nesting grounds in the Arctic, where I had first seen and recognized its species.

On The Place it was early May and if the weather was yet chill and the nights were pestered by frost, I knew that the white falcon was soon to be in a land where ice still dominated the scene. But this would not hinder the gyr. On some ice-crusted ledge it would alight, its mate close by, and it would begin again the work of clearing the old nest, making it ready to receive the four creamy eggs that would soon be laid in it. The nest would be large, a great mound of sticks in which would be mixed the bones of creatures hunted in past seasons, and whitish pellets, made fluffy by time and weather; old pellets, composed of waste matters which the bird and its ancestors had been unable to digest and which they had coughed up, or cast, as this practice has been named, in the form of balls, some bigger, some smaller, irregular of shape, containing bits of bone and mangled feathers and fur.

There is infinite grace in the movements of birds of prey. Of all creatures that fly, theirs is the most perfect command of the air, perfect and awesome to watch, for their sure, seemingly-lazy motion reflects their powerful rapacity, draws in the sky a picture of waiting death; yet so perfectly is this depicted that a watcher must be struck by the artistry of these feathered killers, by the supreme confidence they show as they dare one of Creation's mightiest elements, the wind. They own the skies, these hunting birds, playing in them, frolicking with the wind, using it, moulding it to their will, all the while making their actions look simple.

Always I must stop to watch them as they glide effortlessly across the skies of The Place and always I am divided by my admiration for them and by my fear of them; fear that is not for myself but for the small creatures that they hunt, my friends, and Joan's, the Beau Brummells of our woods, and the Nutsies. Yet I will not stop them. In my wilderness I do not make the laws, Creation made them long ago and if I am to be a part of this fascinating, ever-changing scene, my human emotions must be subservient to rules that were slowly, painfully etched by the evolution of time and the species. The wilderness laws are good laws; without them there would be no wilderness.

It is the law of the wilderness that drives the turkey vulture to the scene of death, for it is this great black bird's duty to clean up the forest and if some find this red-headed scavenger repulsive, it is probably because they have not seen him in his own environment; a vulture in a zoo is not a vulture, for he is earth-bound, captive, and these magnificent birds are only truly alive when they glide tirelessly through the skies on wings that hardly move. These are several pairs of vultures living around the area of The Place and one of them nests in the vicinity of the beaver lake and one day I shall discover their nesting site.

They are the size of an eagle, black mainly, their wings two-toned on the undersides, black in the front and grey at the rear, their reach spanning six feet, their tips, finger-like, curving upwards as the big birds seem to sway in the air. If they are flying a hundred feet or so above the treetops their bare heads, wrinkled and small and red with a white tip at the beak can be clearly seen, giving the impression that the creature has just dipped itself in fresh blood. For hours they will plane as they patiently scan the ground and work their intricate olfactory organs as they probe for the smell of carrion, for these birds use both their eyes and their nostrils to locate food, probably relying on their acute vision when they are soaring high, and using both their nostrils and their eyes when they are gliding through the low reaches of air.

Creation, ever careful, designed these birds so that they have little choice of food. At one time it was thought that vultures ate only decaying meat as a matter of choice, out of liking, but more careful observation has shown that they probably have no alternative. Their feet are not made for grasping, as are the talons of eagle or hawk or owl, and their beaks are relatively weak. Unable to hold their food with their feet, and owning a beak that is not capable of ripping healthy flesh, the birds must wait until decay has softened their food, allowing them to dip their beaks into it easily, and it is for this reason also that their heads are bare of feathers. Alighting at a rotting carcass the birds peck away until they have made a hole in the dead creature, then they dip into it, sinking their heads into the putrefying, slimy-moist interior and if they grew feathers on their heads these would be constantly caked with decay, so apart from short, fuzzy 'eyebrows', evolution changed their heads, giving them instead their wrinkled red skin covering.

I have seen these birds on the ground, often at close range, and have always found them interesting. They smell, I must admit, but I have learned to accept the odours of the wilderness for they are an essential part of it and can teach you much about it and its creatures. So, smell and all, I like to sneak up on them if I can to watch them on the ground, but it is their performance in the air that truly interests me. Their flight is wonderful to watch. They can hang in the air, motionless but for a slight rocking of their wings and bodies and a tiny rippling of their 'fingertips'. Then, without flapping once, they can rise in circular sweeps right out of human sight. Their great pinions spread, they glide in huge, climbing spirals, their bare heads always on the move, shifting quickly from left to right, from right to left, as they search the ground for food. Now and then, when going to and from their nesting area, they fly low over The Place and then, apparently intent on getting to wherever they are bound for, they flap their wings, lazily, one flap every so often, using just enough energy to keep themselves moving, the sanitary inspectors of the forest on their way to or from a job.

In daytime the hawks and the vultures; at night the owls, ghostly hunters of darkness who drop to kill, powered by silent pinions; big owls, like the great grey and the horned owl, the greatest killer of them all; small owls, like the saw-whet and the screech, birds that have been credited with sagacity, the wise ones who have been invested with powers they do not hold because man has ever been struck by their great eyes and sage expressions and by the mystery of their voices in the dark on night. They are not stupid, of course, but neither are they symbols of wisdom that legend would have us believe; this was created by the Greeks who, in ancient times, regarded a little European owl as the companion of the goddess Athene, or Minerva, as she was also called, who was the patroness of wisdom and leaning. From this mythological belief has sprung the owl's reputation and, because of that little creature worshipped by the ancient Greeks, all his relations bask today in the sunshine of knowledge.

Owls vary in shape, size, colour and in many other respects but they all have certain characteristics in common. They live a long time (one kept in captivity celebrated 68 birthdays at the zoo), their eyes, like those of hunting cats, absorb much light, giving them amazingly keen night vision. In flight they are all silent and this is because the edges of their wings are soft, fluffy, allowing them to flap and glide stealthily through the forest night while their great eyes and very sensitive ears probe the darkness for prey. Unlike most creatures, the eyes of an owl are immovable. They look straight ahead and if the bird wants to see to left or right, it must turn its squat, broad head, so that when it is flying it is constantly scanning its whereabouts, rather like the turkey vulture, and if it is stationary on a tree branch and wants to follow movement, it does so with a slow turning of the head, keeping pace with its visual target until it would seem that its head is going to twist right off. In fact, if you watch an owl doing this, you would swear that it is able to twist its head a full circle, but this illusion is brought about by the great speed with which the bird moves its head if that which it is watching passes around it. If, say, a man approaches a sitting owl from the left and continues walking towards the right, the bird's head swivels slowly as its eyes follow the man. But if the man turns at right angles and starts walking behind the owl, the moment that the bird feels it is losing sight of its target, it quickly flips its head to the left, twisting its neck to the fullest and picking up its target where it left off. It does this so swiftly that one would think its head is on a swivel.

The food habits of the owls vary with the species, though they all are meat eaters and all prey on small rodents, such as mice and moles and shrews, but the bigger the owl, the bigger its prey and the greatest and fiercest killer of them all is the great horned owl. This bird, a veritable tiger of the skies, has even been known to strike down a good-sized dog. It is precise, deadly, as it swoops on muffled wings at its victim. In flight, its horns, feathery projections resembling ears, are not readily visible, for they blend with the owl's body, but when it is sitting on a branch, these tufts stand out, giving the big bird (two feet and more in length with wings that span more than four feet) a military appearance.

Like its other relatives the great horned owl swallows small creatures whole, digesting the flesh and other body-building substances of the victim while its crop gathers together the bones, fur or feathers of its victim into tightly-packed pellets which, like the gyrfalcon, the owl later regurgitates. A keen-eyed woodsman can often find an owl's daytime roost in the forest by spotting the pellets cast by the bird.

The voices of the owls fill the forest around The Place at night. Raucous, hoarse, their cries blend with the other noises of darkness to form the bass accompaniment of the night concert of the wilderness: hoo, *hoohoo, hoo, hoo,* the great horned owl launches its five ghostly notes, his voice deep and resonant, now and again varying his repertoire by hooting six times, or only three. From another place in the forest a great grey owl seems to answer his relative: *whoo...oo...oo...oo,* chants the big bird at regular intervals, its pitch deep, at times its cadences rising until they fill the wilderness with a soft booming sound. Down in the ravine to the south of our cabin nest a pair of barred owls and their voices are easily detected amongst the medley of calls and shrieks and whistles that fill the night: *hoo-hoo hoo-hoo hoo-hoo-awgh*, yells the barred, sounding almost as though he had choked over the last syllable of his call. Now and then a screech owl bursts its voice upon us, a maniac's howl, tremulous whinny that often starts out high and gradually runs down in scale until it tails off in the darkness. One of these fellows almost made me jump out of my skin one late evening when I was returning from the lake. I was walking through the darkish quiet of the forest when he launched his insane cackle at me from his perch high in a pine and, believe me, I nearly took to my heels. The call was so unexpected and so close and so very, very weird and I was not thinking about owls but about how best to plan the year's hunt for the vulture's nest. The effects upon me were brief, though startling at the time, and when I realized what it was that had made that frightful row, I stopped and tried to find the bird. Perversely, the creature did not utter another sound and it took me a good ten minutes to spot his shadowy outline against a paling skyline that was trellised by the pine's evergreen boughs.

One night, two winters ago, when Joan and I were returning to our cabin after visiting the Adams family, we spotted a strange little upright shape sitting on a pine branch just outside the cabin door. The gnome-like figure stared at us with its unblinking yellow eyes, for all the world like some tiny, ageing, infinitely wise professor. This was the first time we had seen a saw-whet owl upon The Place and it was ridiculously tame, perching there in the glare of my flashlight as innocent-looking as a babe. For a time he allowed us to inspect him, seeming to be posturing for us, then he flitted away into the darkness and presently his mellow whistle reached us. This owl has been named because its call is likened to the sharpening of a saw and although it is a reasonable enough analogy, I doubt that there are many people today who would readily recognize the noise, for saw-sharpening is no longer the enterprise that it used to be. In any event, this little bird's call reminds me more of a miniature train whistling melodiously in the night. It seems endless, its call being repeated a hundred or a hundred and thirty times in succession, a bell-like *too, too, too, too, too,* which appears to go on and on.

In the spring, when the wilderness is vibrant with the voices of frogs and the monotonous chant of the whip-poor-wills, one can miss the calls of the owls if they are some distance away, but in winter, when the forest is silent, wrapped in its shroud of snow, when the only sounds are the occasional frost-crack of a tree or the distant, mournful howl of a wolf, the voices of the owls fill the bushland with sound. Sometimes they come close to our cabin and hoot repeatedly for an hour or more, their muffled calls penetrating through the wooden walls, ghostly sounds that have lulled me to sleep on many a night.

The ways of birds are endless. Many of their habits are still unknown to us and no one man in his lifetime will be able to master all the secrets of all the birds. Of intriguing interest to me is a strange habit shared by some hundred and fifty different species of birds, a habit that is at once fascinating and mysterious and which has puzzled naturalists for many years and remains as shrouded today as it was when it was first observed. For want of a better name, this puzzler has been called 'anting', and it involves the capture of a cluster, or brush, as it is called, of live ants, perhaps six or seven, perhaps only one, which the birds rub upon their outstretched wing feathers, the while showing every sign of blissful exaltation.

I have watched a number of birds do this, but the first time I saw it happen, quite a number of years ago, I did not really take it in, not realizing what the bird was doing. More recently, on The Place, I watched a blue jay indulge in the ritual. The bird was hopping along the ground when I first saw it, stopping now and then to peck at something from the grass, and after its third such stop I realized it was collecting a brush of carpenter ants. When it had collected seven of these insects, which it held lightly at the very tip of its beak, evidently careful not to kill them with pressure, it stopped by a small bush. From the somewhat silly look that came over its countenance I knew what it was about to do and, sure enough, in another moment it had begun its antics. First it spread its wings wide, showing off its primary feathers like some lady of old skillfully manipulating a fan; then it hopped lightly and its tail flicked downwards and after a struggle or two this was forced between its legs, so that the bird looked as though he was sitting on it. By now its eyes were glazed and it began to run the bush of ants up and down its feathers, half shutting its eyes and stumbling slightly in a veritable paroxysm of ecstasy. For about three or four minutes it kept up this seemingly-senseless performance, then it straightened up, shook its feathers into place and carefully swallowed the still wriggling ants. At last it shook itself again, rattling and puffing its feathers before flying off into the forest.

Why do birds indulge in this strange habit? There are many guesses, but so far no one knows the correct answer and the strangest part of all is that birds will perform similar antics while gripping a mothball between their beaks (but they do not eat these) or smelling smoke and even onions and once I saw a robin performing with a ripe wintergreen berry held between its beak. It has been suggested that anting is done because the birds enjoy the feel on their feathers of the formic acid discharged by the struggling ants; another guess is that this acid helps rid the birds of the lice they carry and it has even been said that the acid provides some sort of needed chemical that helps the birds keep their feathers in good condition. I certainly do not know the answer, and neither does anyone else that I am

A nuthbhatch dining on fat from a wire-net dispenser. Nuthatches eat upside down!

aware of, but I rather feel that none of these guesses is too close to the true reason. We may learn the answer to this riddle one day, in the meantime we can only keep on watching, and guessing.

Can animals talk? If this question seeks to know whether animals, birds and insects have an academic language such as those employed for communication by man, then the answer must be in the negative. But many creatures other than man do, nevertheless, talk, in that they use sounds, and sometimes actions, to communicate with each other; and in some cases the degree of communication is surprisingly great. In fact, almost all creatures that have either vocal chords or the means of making noise have some system of communication. The angry chatter of a red squirrel, for instance, has varying tones and notes, their frequency depending upon the little animal's degree of irritation, and the nearness of the cause of his anger. In the same way squirrels warn each other of danger and over the centuries many other creatures of the forest have learned to interpret the warning of the squirrels and often escape with their lives because of this.

In exchange many birds issue warning notes that alert the squirrels and other animals, so that, in a way, there is in existence a limited 'international language' in the wilderness. But apart from this, naturalists have discovered that at least some creatures have a definite language with which they can talk freely to one another. Crows have such a language, composed entirely of sounds, so do geese, and bees, though these insects use sound, body movements and vibrations to tell their stories.

Perhaps the most advanced—in so far as we know, for there may be others equally or more proficient—are the crows, amongst whom, so far, some 300 different sounds have been identified by scientists, though the majority of them have as yet no meaning to man. All that we know just now is that these birds have the ability to utter different calls and that at least a proportion of these calls have a definite meaning to those of their own kind. One of these, for instance, is a long, uninterrupted caw, which, by dint of patient observation naturalists have been able to interpret. Such a call is a summons. Upon its sounding, all birds in the flock come to the meeting.

I watched this happen recently in the ravine behind the cabin. I was watching for the red-shouldered hawk when two crows landed in a pine not far from where I stood. At once, as though by previous arrangement, they both began to make the 'emergency meeting' call. Presently one more crow came and joined the two in the cawing; two more flew in and added their voices to the racket and after about two minutes 18 crows were perched in the tree. With the arrival of birds number 17 and 18 there was silence and the last two, as far as I was able to notice, did not utter a single caw. Which makes me ask, can crows also count? How did the flock know that all its members had gathered at the summons? How did the last two birds know that the were the last two birds? Or did they? Was the silence coincidental? A lot of questions, these, and I am afraid I cannot supply the answers to them.

At any rate, when the gathering was apparently completed, and after about a half a minute of silence, a veritable babel of cawing broke out among the 18 birds. But now it was different. Too rapid for me to decipher, yet I was able to notice that the birds were cawing in ones and twos, seemingly 'discussing' some mutual problem. Five minutes later they all flew off, keeping together and making for the deep part of the forest, as though something of importance had been decided upon. I did not see them around the cabin for the rest of that day.

It is significant that this 'language' of the creatures is not universally the same within the species. Crows from Canada, for instance, do not understand crows from Europe, each kind, while 'talking' a similar language, having developed their own 'dialect'. In the same way the songs of many birds of the same species vary according to areas to such a surprising degree that humans familiar with the call of, say, the wood thrush of northern Canada, may fail to recognize the call of a wood thrush in Louisiana, though I do not know if the birds themselves would understand each other's song; and, to bear this out further, the call of the red-shouldered hawks that nest on The Place is quite different to the call of one of its relatives from the United States. This bird, its voice captured by a recorder, confused me so much that at one time I began to doubt the hawks on The Place wondering if I had identified them incorrectly. The call was similar, of course, but its inflections were different.

Undoubtedly, call it what you will, animals and birds and insects have the ability to communicate with each other, usually within the species, often, to a more limited degree, between the species, rather as man has learned to communicate with his neighbours in other nations.

And not a few men have learned animal 'talk' to the extent that they are able to understand the language of certain creatures and are even able to communicate with these creatures in their own language.

The German naturalist Konrad Lorenz learned the language of geese and was able to communicate with them despite the difficulty which he had in imitating their hoarse sounds; while a colleague of his, Karl von Frisch, of Munich, spent a lifetime studying the language of honey bees and became so proficient in his understanding that he was actually able to listen to their 'talk' and know where they were going and what they were going for. In a far more limited way I am beginning to understand the language of the red and black squirrels on The Place, knowing from their calls the mood which holds them at the moment and, in some cases, knowing which squirrel is calling though the creature may be invisible to me. I understand, too, some of the calls of the birds on The Place, though to a lesser degree, and after our experience with Coby and Konk, Joan and I picked up a smattering of raccoon 'talk', in particular the panic call, a short, twice-repeated monosyllable formed (in my case, at any rate) at the very back of the throat, hoarse and staccato and impossible to capture in prose but sounding rather like the noise emitted by a person suffering from whooping cough. This call, when emitted by one of the young 'coons, immediately brought the other to the rescue and when sounded by me sent them both scurrying for shelter.

Often, when I sit on some downed log within the wilderness of The Place, I wonder about the 'language' of the forest, aware now that each piece of bushland has its own means of communication, a broad, international idiom, as it were, intelligible to the creatures that inhabit the area. Each time I visit The Place I learn the meaning of some new, small sound and slowly, very, very slowly, I am learning to 'talk' to the forest and, more important, understand something of what it says. But at one time the sounds of the wilderness represented only a cacophony of noise that held no meaning to me. There are countless sounds in the wilderness, yet each of them has its own meaning. A northing wind, weak yet and high in the atmosphere, comes to pluck at the heads of the trees; to man this is meaningless, just another rustle of leaves; to the creatures of the forest this sound, coupled with a new feeling in the air, carries warnings of an approaching storm. Suddenly, on the heels of the faint rustling, silence invades the forest as each creature seeks shelter from the oncoming weather.

Such occasions make me feel humble, for I realize how infinitely small is the sum total of my knowledge of the wilderness, and I smile now and then when I think of that supposedly-humorous and much abused reference to the 'birds and the bees', seldom seriously used, but prudishly intended to convey the meaning of life to small children. I smile because it seems incongruous to me that man has for so long shrouded in secrecy and evil the very natural way in which man and his fellow animals procreate.

Yet I would like to be old-fashioned here and explore at least a part of that expression. How *do* birds ensure the continuation of their species? Everybody, of course, knows that small birds are born from the eggs laid by the females of their species; but how exactly? Let us go and find out. We'll take a journey to The Place and watch a pair of blue jays.

Spring has arrived on The Place. As yet it is in a capricious mood and threatens daily to retreat, allowing winter one more foray through the wilderness. Patches of snow still cling to the shadows cast by the evergreens and there is frost rimming the waterholes and the lake each morning and each evening; but there is that new feeling in the air and the hardier birds are beginning to arrive from their wintering territories. Around our cabin the flock of blue jays that has dared the harshness of a Canadian winter becomes suddenly restless. Fights break out amongst the males and the birds do not gather in friendly groups as they did during the cold months.

Soon the fighting and the pairing has taken place and now the raucous screams of the birds are less frequent and instead soft, sweet cooing noises issue from their throats as males court their females in between pauses in the claiming of their nesting territories. Occasionally, fresh fights break out as birds defend their chosen home sites from intruders, but at last the disputes are over and the males mate with the females, depositing within the bodies of their mates the seed of life. The hens begin to build their nests, the while pausing in their task to accept some morsel brought to them by the cock birds, then the home-building continues and by the time the nest is finished the female is ready to lay her first egg.

The female has two ovaries—those factories which are responsible for egg production—but with a few exceptions, it is only the left one that is productive in birds and then only during the breeding season. When egg-laying time arrives the ovary becomes much larger as the eggs develop inside it and, could it be seen, it would look rather like a strange bunch of grapes, the berries of which are in various stages of development, some tiny, others of medium size, yet a few almost ready to start on the second stage of their journey to life. Now these almost-eggs are yellowish and streaked with red veins as each is stimulated by a growth substance, called a hormone, discharged from the pituitary gland of the female bird, each being regulated, made ready, for its individual appointment with the outside world.

In reality the egg is a single, large cell, a 'room' full of the vital needs of life, which is composed mostly of yolk. As each egg reaches its last stages of development it is moved to the entrance of the oviduct (the egg channel) and it is there that it is joined and fertilized by the male sperm. Thus, in birds as in humans, the same basic principles have taken place. But now the spark of life inside a bird takes a journey different to that of its counterpart inside a female of the human species, for, instead of remaining in the shelter of its mother, the egg (or embryo) begins its journey towards the outside. Through a narrow, moist passageway it is pushed, and as it travels it receives a layer of albumen, the 'white' of the egg, from glands concealed in the walls of the oviduct; and as it continues its journey it is further coated with membranes which will later become the lining on the inside of the shell, this last coating being formed by the lime manufactured by the bird which hardens to form the shell. Now the egg is ready and it is laid by the bird big end first, as a rule.

One pair of jays interests us more than the others. The female has built her nest in the thick of a young spruce and inside it she has laid three eggs. One more egg is now journeying towards daylight and when this is laid the female will begin to incubate, or hatch, her brood, for most birds do not incubate their eggs until all have been laid, thus making sure that the young will be born at about the same time and allowing them to devote equal attention to all the young ones. The eggs we are watching in the spruce are a very pale greenish colour, almost buff, speckled by irregular brown flecks.

The nest, built with great care by both birds, rests on a platform of twigs and grass and bark upon which a bed of mud has been laid. On top of this was built the cup, made of fine rootlets and discarded feathers and bits of moss. In this container sit the eggs and now the female jay is upon them, warming them with her body, turning them when needed while her brood patches, places on the soft stomach that are bare of feathers when the bird becomes 'broody', become lined with a fine network of blood vessels that are very near the surface of the skin and supply the extra warmth needed to keep the eggs at their incubating temperature of 93 degrees Fahrenheit, more or less.

Inside each egg the minute embryo that began to grow when the male bird's sperm joined the newly-shaped ovum, grows on top of the yolk and is fed by it and by the white, or albumen, which also cushions any shock to the embryo. Through the porous shell air reaches the developing bird and harmful waste gases from its small body escape to the outside, and, at last, placed at the blunt end of the egg is a sack containing air, put there so that the fully developed bird can breathe of it just before it cracks the shell with a tiny horn, known as the egg tooth, which it has at the tip of its beak. Once the young bird has cracked the shell it struggles until it manages to break it in two, and two or three days later the little tool given it by Creation dries and drops off the beak.

Some seventeen days after the female jay laid her last egg the first of her brood pips the shell of its egg. Faint cheeping sounds are heard as the little bird struggles to freedom and soon the other three chicks have followed. Now four blind, nearly-naked little creatures with long, wrinkled necks and grotesquely large heads are nestled under their mother, too weak to feed yet and in no need of nourishment, for their cold-blooded bodies are still supplied with food they have absorbed from the yolk. Their first two or three days are the most critical. Being cold-blooded yet (creatures that are popularly termed cold-blooded are not, really; they are merely unable to control their own body heat and absorb heat or cold from their surroundings), the mother bird must protect them from the heat of the sun and the chill of the night, but if they survive this time of trial their blood-circulating systems begin to function, their downy feathers begin to grow and they are no longer as delicate. Now they spend most of their time gaping for food, the inside of their mouths 'painted' a vivid reddish colour which acts both as an aiming mark for the parent birds and a stimulus for them to feed the babies, for it seems that adult birds cannot resist a desire to stuff food into these coloured cavities whenever they see them and birds have been fooled into feeding crude wooden dummies that have been fashioned to look something like young birds provided the dummy mouth was brightly coloured.

Canada's blue jays are noisy comics who delight in imitating other birds. They soon learn to come to winter feeders and even a whole peanut does not present problems for them.

About five or six days after birth the nestling's feathers begin to grow rapidly, coming at first as bluish, tube-like containers at the ends of which are little tufts of feathers which continue to grow out of their sheaths until, three or four days later, the baby is quite well covered. Now the babies are getting frequent meals of insects and berries and seeds, all of which have first been swallowed by the adult birds, pre-digested and then regurgitated into the gaping mouths of the nestlings; and after each baby has been fed he or she promptly defecates, discharging a tidy little sack of excrement which the adult bird swallows or removes from the nest, keeping the youngsters clean at all times. At this stage the babies have their eyes open and, thought still wobbly when they raise their big heads for a feed, they are active and noisy when they hear or see their parents, each competing lustily for the food they know is coming. Two weeks later the youngsters are fully dressed in their blue and white and black plumage and shortly after this they make their first flight, though drop would be a better word for the feat of acrobatics they indulge in as they try to find their wings and usually manage nothing more than a windmill-like tumble to the ground or to the nearest tree branch. But after a few more tries and some encouragement from mother, the babies learn to fly. Four more birds have been born on The Place, four more screaming, squawking, friendly voices have been added to our flock.

Twelve

His first world was made of darkness; moist and silent. Inside this damp envelop his eyes, which had opened at the moment of his birth, were useless things and he felt a great fear take hold of his small black body. And he cried. It was thin and insignificant, that baby wail of his, but it was the only thing that he knew how to do. He was wet; warm-wet at first, and sticky. And his nose and mouth were pressed hard into a cold, suffocating mattress, and his ears were attuned to slow movements above him and a new noise, a soft, mumbling sound, reached them. Where was he? His newly-awakened senses cried silently inside his brain. What was he? The voice of instinct within him whispered again. Then another thing like him tumbled down from somewhere and a small wail, akin to his own, reached his ears and some of the fear left him, because he was not alone.

Still he knew not what manner of being lived within the ball-like, furry body. How could a small animal-creature only heart beats old know such things? And yet his brain was quick, his senses alert. He recognized at once the contours of his limited world and his great fear shrank, became a small worry and at last was gone as the warm harsh tongue of his mother stroked away the wet stickiness of his birth. He knew it was his mother, for he could smell that part of her that was also in him and although he could see her not and knew not what she was or what she looked like, there was inside of him an instinct that told of comfort and safety and nourishment that was to be had from the thing that pawed him and mumbled over him and licked him with that warm tongue. And when she had finished licking and turned away from him to comfort the other that was there, his nostrils captured a sweet smell and followed it, pulling his body towards the moving being that was mother. Under her, amid warmth and softness, his questing lips found a milk dug and he sucked. Life came to him quickly through the veins and glands that ended in the pointed nipple. And warmth and awareness.

This creature, born in subterranean darkness upon the lake on The Place, was a beaver. His birth place was inside the big lodge of sticks and mud that sits against one side of the rock island on the lake. His birth was several seasons ago, and I wonder if today he still remembers the delicious sensations that filled him and caused him to mumble as did his mother; caused him, too, to nuzzle into her softness and smell of her and to sleep to dream of the sweet, musky odour of her. Now this child of the swamp lands is a hoary old male weighing some fifty pounds as he swims in a leisurely manner up-lake, into the ancient beaver canal to wade in summer among catkins and lotus roots and take his feed from them. Joan and I watch him now and then and it was during one of these times that I began to wonder about him and to reconstruct his birth and his life. I wondered, too, about the newness of life in a wild creature and slowly, bit by bit, I began to capture, as best as man can, the sensations and emotions of a new-born wildling. And so, for a short time, I am going to let my mind wander beneath the murky lake waters and into the life of a young female beaver...

She was sleek and fat, her glossy coat shining a deep chestnut in the sunshine and she awoke a great urge within the being of a big male who saw her, one cold January day, sitting beside her ice hole. She was eating the bark from a hazel branch which she had cut near the shore and carried between her big, yellowed teeth to where she could eat it in safety. She still had plenty of food stored beneath the ice that surrounded her lodge, but there had been a need in her when she awoke that morning, a need which she had not experienced before and which drove her away from the safety of her lodge and up through the ice hole. At first she had thought she was hungry and so she had cut the hazel branch, but while her chisel teeth peeled the bark off the wood, she realized that this was not what she wanted; the food tasted flat and her need was still within her forty-pound body.

The beaver had never been mated. She was almost three years old and had been turned out of her lodge the previous spring when her mother became birth-big with a new litter. The breeding time was then past and so she refused the males that came to her and she began instead to build a lodge, feeding in between her work on water lily roots and other vegetation that she found in or near the lake. And on that January morning she did not hiss spitefully at the male beaver that came to her across the snow-covered ice. She stopped eating and watched him as he waddled at his best speed, and she admired him, for he was old and hoar-rimmed and he had long, almost-black fur and magnificent whiskers. He mumbled as he ran, a strange, low sort of noise smelling each other, inhaling the wonderful musk aroma and knowing that they would soon mate and stay together while life remained in both of them. Thus, a little less than four human months later, the beaver and his sister were born in the lodge which the she had enlarged on a bed that was lined with grass and leaves and shredded wood and fine roots, which the babies were to eat some days later, when they began to try their teeth.

Came the day when the youngsters were old enough to leave their lodge for the first time and the mother led them out of the darkness and up through the grey water and into the daylight of a new, frightening and unknown world. It was a soft, placid morning in late May, one of those mild, lazy days when the skies are clear blue and high; lofty caverns of space that deceive when looked at, for they hide the greatness of the universe. The flying insects had come to The Place, but they idled, hiding under green, newly-opened leaves, and in the grasses and within the curling cracks of tree bark.

Our lake is small and holds only four lodges, but the young beavers know this not as they popped up to the surface of the water and they were afraid at first and their father, swimming a circle around them, seemed to become impatient, for he hissed at them, the sound of anger of the beaver, and immediately the she beaver charged the buck and hissed back at him and she led her young up the sides of the lodge. Sitting in the sun on top of the lodge the young beavers grew brave. The little male sat upright, allowing the weight of his body to rest upon his flat tail. He looked around, greatly intrigued by the newness and his eyes caught movement in the water. A grey muskrat was paddling away from the mud and sticks of the dam; and on the south bank of the lake a blue heron, big, ungainly bird, stood on its stilt legs and stared into the murky water, his long neck held sideways so that the fine twin plumes on his head were thrust backwards at an angle. The heron was looking for a frog. He had spotted a leopard frog as he stilted clumsily along the shore line and he had tried to stab the amphibian with his long beak; but the frog had moved too quickly and now the old heron was searching for it.

The frog was only inches away from the bird's feet and around the heron's bony toes, immersed in six inches of water, the lake ooze, dis-

A small leopard frog lies immobile, waiting for insect prey, in a quiet backwater of our lake.

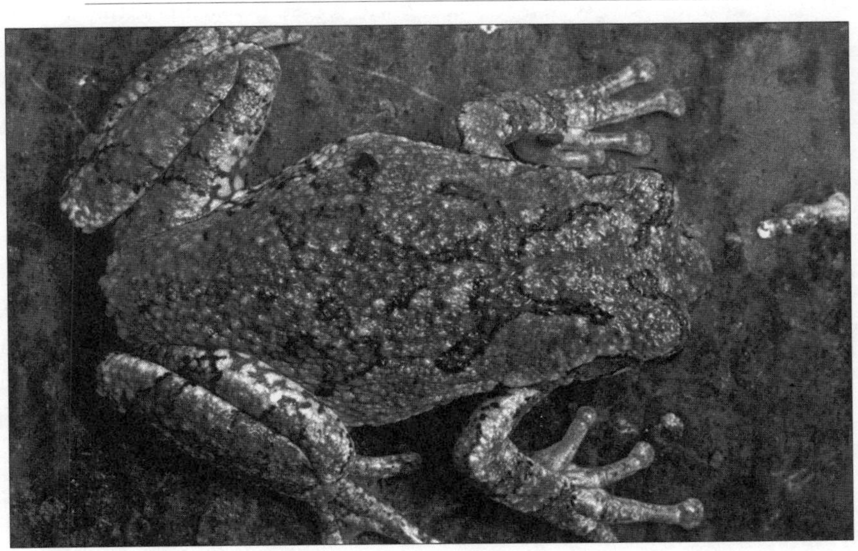

A tree frog, one of the many on The Place whose voices serenade us during summer nights. Equipped with round sucker pads on their toes, these frogs spend most of their adult life moving about in the trees, feeding on insects.

turbed when the bird walked, had settled and now partly concealed the outline of the frog. The heron kept looking, using first one eye to peer into the water, then the other one, each time moving his snake-like head slowly, carefully, as though he was afraid that it would snap off it he moved suddenly. The frog remained statue-still, its green and brown body blending with the algae and the mud of the lake bottom, its shape further concealed by flecks of diluted ooze that had settled upon it. The heron was hungry and determined to spear the frog. The frog knew this in his tiny, cold brain and took refuge in stillness and camouflage.

The young beaver was so interested in the heron that at first he did not hear his mother call. His sister had left his side and was already in the water when the she hissed sharply and the small male moved to follow her. He dropped down on four paws and slid and fell down the sloping sides of the lodge, passing his mother and landing with a flop in the water. Down he went, and for a moment panic seized him, but instinct came to the rescue, for all beavers can swim shortly after the moment of their birth. He used his flat tail and his webbed back feet and soon he was swimming under the water and could see the shape of his father and his sister above. Then the mother came to him and swam next to him and he knew at once that she wanted him to swim upwards. But the youngster wanted to play and he tried to swim away from the she and she chased him and caught him quickly and her big teeth nipped him, not hard, but with just enough anger in the bite to warn him, and he kicked down with his back feet and curved his tail, and upwards he slid, until his sleek black head broke through the water.

The young beavers were two weeks old on that day and although this was the first time they had been taken away from the lodge by the adults, the small male had been out of it before, on the first day of his birth, when, crawling unsteadily across its wet, earthen floor he tumbled out of one of the exit holes. Gripped by the dark water he had cried, a pitiful, child-like wail, muffled to almost total silence by the water, his throat choking with fluid, and if the she had not reached him death would have claimed him quickly. Then darkness had been his companion, a great velvet black that was broken only by two faint round patches of lesser dark, one at each end of the lodge where the slide holes were. But on the day of their first outing, the beavers frolicked happily, their vision functioning upon sunny daylight for the first time. Ahead of them lay a future unknown and uncertain, a short pace behind them was their youth, those few days of carefree play that Creation has allowed the beaver, a creature characterized by patient, plodding solemnity for nine-tenths of its life.

Humans, who often look upon beavers greedily, who kill them for their fur and their meat, do not often pause to try and understand their ways. And yet their life is many things. It is work; great, patient, clever work. And it is danger; mortal peril that stalks them and makes their wits sharp and lends tone to their ears and image to their eyes. It is water in spring, and summer and autumn, and it is the cold ice of winter. It is darkness and light, and mud and grass. It is feeling; quick, sensitive feeling: feeling for things and feeling for smells and sounds and sights, and these give them knowledge, teach them and make them wary, for they cannot learn through reason as quickly and easily as humans do. And all these things that make up the life of a beaver were taught early to the young born on the lake on The Place. Some lessons were given by the father, others were taught by the mother; all were quickly received by the two young ones.

On that first day in his second world—his first was the darkness and fear born with him in the lodge—the small male beaver began learning his many lessons of survival, but he did not know he was being taught as he played in the water beside his mother, or watched as his father and his sister swam quietly a little distance ahead. He was carefree, active and seized by an awareness that flooded every sensory part of his body. Of course, he was ignorant. With the exception of his family, not one thing that his eyes beheld that day was familiar to him and despite his careless playing and lack of attention to the example lessons of his father, his brain was being filled with knowledge.

Overhead the sky was pale blue and the sun, still a half disc of orange and red showing above the tree-tops, dazzled him as he gazed into its flaming face. He moved his eyes from it and they stopped watering and he found he could see other things again. Once more he looked into the sun. Water came to blur his vision and his eyes smarted anew. Thus he learned that there is power to hurt in that redness in the sky and he avoided looking directly at it, even when he was its twin hiding in the water of the lake. At first he was puzzled by the second sun that danced and shimmered with the movement of the water, but he was curious, too, and he swam towards it, and it disappeared, and in another moment it reappeared elsewhere and he tried to reach it and it eluded him again, only to move to a different place and shine fluidly, seeming to mock his attempts to find it. Then, after a time, he understood. He knew not how this thing happened, but he realized that somehow the sun in the water was not the real one that hung in the sky and had power to hurt his eyes. And this discovery helped him understand other reflections that he discovered dancing upon the quiet waters of the lake.

Through the first month of his first summer he swam with his parents and his sister, slowly becoming intimate with his narrow world. He explored the lake upon its surface, now and then climbing out and waddling up its banks, or clambering on a muskrat house, small, meagre dwellings after the spacious lodge that housed him. He explored the lake, too, under its surface, discovering the dead, water-soaked logs that many seasons earlier had given up their places in the world above to sink slowly, one end first, to the bottom of the lake. Now they lay rigid and stiff, great black shadows encrusted with weeds and slime and holed by water insects, and small fish, and crayfish, and they were wonderful places over which to play. At this time the water lilies were growing tall, shooting their thick, dark green tendrils from out of the tuberous roots that housed them, and these roots, the life-system of the plants equipped with the same geotropic force as the tiny seed which I found one day under a rock, also supplied food for the beaver and his family; and the ghostly curtain of stems that responded to the mysterious growth stimulus and rose upwards to reach sunlight and oxygen, offered new excitement to the beaver who would at times follow one of them upwards and pounce upon its great, shiny leaves. At other times the young beaver and his sister would race through this floating curtain, parting the stems with their bodies, pulling at them and watching the big leaves bob down into the water and pop up again when they were released, and this game was another lesson for the beaver, who, later, would need to keep swim channels open through these tenacious stems, thus leaving their mark upon the surface of the lake, a visible passage that denotes the travel pattern of the beaver, who live extensively in summer on the lotus, eating first the stems and leaves and then digging up the roots from the lake mud, great clusters of pale tubers that are often taken ashore, their remains left there.

Sometimes the beaver watched the fish. There were bass, big, husky, dark and mottled, with great gaping mouths that opened and shut slowly when the fish rested in the shadows made by a patch of lilies; and there were pike, long, slimy fish with fierce heads and rows of shining, sharp teeth and baleful, seemingly hate-filled eyes, and some of these were big and shiny like a pale sky underneath and white under their jaws and they looked at the small beaver and his sister and would have taken them if the adult beaver had not been near. The beaver watched the fish hunt. The bass sometimes hung motionless in the water, waiting. Then a small fish would come near and there would be a sudden swirl and the oval body of the bass moved with great speed and the little fish would disappear into its mouth and the hunter's jaws would move two or three times and suddenly a cloud of small, shiny waste particles were forced out of its gill slits and these moved away backwards, fanned by the water that the bass took into his mouth and pushed out through his gills as it chewed its prey and at the same time extracted oxygen from the turgid lake water. Those little shining particles were all that remained of the small fish taken by the hunter, ejected backwards by force, so that they would not cloud the water in front of the hunter's eyes, blinding him to more prey or to the coming of a bigger fish that would itself feed upon the hunter.

Some days the beaver watched as the fish lay quietly, almost on the bottom of the lake, eyeing the water above. The bass looked for flying things, insects, or frogs swimming across the surface of the water, and when these appeared they would streak towards them, streamlined and quick, and their big mouths would fasten on the prey and they would swim down again, leaving a ring on the water surface that grew bigger until it disappeared against the shoreline. The pike, too, took flying things, and frogs, but they hunted other creatures mostly; fish and water shrews, and ducklings and birds that fluttered down to drink.

Sometimes strange, black creatures, soft and slimy and small attacked the young beaver, stealthily fastening sucker mouths upon their flesh and seeking the warm blood of the young ones. These were the leeches of the lake, ribbon-like, darker on the top than on their lined abdomens, seemingly-helpless as they floated about in the water in aimless manner, but painful when they sucked, and the youngsters would flee with them to the mother who gripped the noisome creatures with her sharp teeth and wrenched them free, grinding them after between her molars and swallowing them and the blood of her offspring that they had stolen.

Food for a young beaver recently weaned is almost limitless. During its first winter it must get along with the bark of poplar, willows, cherry and birch and a few water plants that manage to survive the cold, but in summer, the woods and the lakeshores are crammed with edibles. Quickly our youngster and his sister learned of these foods. Duckweed, eelgrass, lily roots, were fare taken from the water. On land, grasses and herbs, young shoots and tender rootlets, buds and even leaves of small plants; while, for a rare treat, a few wild raspberry canes provided temptation.

Now and then in summer a beaver may cut down a tree, perhaps out of habit or for a change of diet, but as a rule their tree-cutting activities are confined to the fall, when they are stocking their underwater larders for the advent of the big cold. Yet there are days when the sun shines warm first thing and young beavers are tempted to go out and cut themselves a tree.

Such a day dawned for our young beaver. It was still dark when he slipped out of the lodge and into the water and began a slow circle on the surface of the lake. Behind him came his sister, and his mother followed, and lastly came his father and the family cruised in leisurely manner, inspecting their world, probing it with their noses and ears and even with their eyes for the sounds or sights or smells of predators, and by the time that the father felt it was safe to make for the shoreline, the first rays of sun began tinting the east and young daylight turned the dark into a hazy, blued light that cast long shadows and coaxed song from the birds of the lake. A red-winged blackbird was the first to raise his voice that morning. He was followed by the nasal chant of a nuthatch. One by one the voices of the birds of lake and marsh filled the early day and the forest began to awake. A mother raccoon and her four ring-tailed, fluffy babies turned their backs on the lake, replete with the snails and crayfish and freshwater mussels they had fed on. A red fox slunk away towards his burrow, startled by the churring call of a red squirrel. Out amongst the reeds the ducks were talking and the blue heron made his hoarse call as he stepped out in search of frogs. It was a typical bush morning in summer, typical, but always magical to man and beast alike, a slowly changing panorama of life occurring once again after a million, million days of Creation.

The beaver family swam along the lake until they reached their north feeding canal, cut by unknown beavers. Up-channel led the father followed by the young male, his sister and their mother and soon they reached the place of exit on to land, a small, muddy, sloping section of shoreline that was smooth from use and bore many imprints left by the webbed feet of the beavers. This place is familiar to Joan and me and near it we have spanned the canal with dead-fall trees which are now our foot-bridge to the other side, and a little north of our bridge is a feeding station and bedding dump of a muskrat, a small mound of debris that has accumulated as the rat, an habitual creature, sits there nibbling some titbit or swims there clutching his old bedding, soaked and mildewed, which he dumps on the mound before gathering a fresh supply with which to line his bank den.

Past this place led the beaver male, waddling clumsily up a slight slope and following a game trail towards a clearing where new grass made verdant the forest. Here the family settled to feed and after a time the small male edged back towards the fringe of trees that shelters the marsh-land at this point. Straight for a young poplar he went, careless, forgetting in his excitement the caution he normally used when travelling on land; but there was nothing to fear this morning and the younger reached his tree and sniffed at it, moving slowly around it, now and then taking a tentative nip at its bark and savouring the clean new taste of it. He stopped suddenly and raised his body to the upright, his paddle tail set firmly-flat behind and acting as a support. Now he bit at the tree, his young teeth cutting a thin groove in the bark as he pulled his head back with the wrenching movement. Again he bit, and again, and slowly a notch appeared in the tree trunk, shoulder-level with the beaver. Now he reached higher and began a new attack on the tree and repeated the process until a second notch was cut about three inches above the first. He paused, as if to inspect his work, then, reaching forward, his shoulders hunched slightly, he opened his mouth wide and grasped the portion of wood remaining between the two notches. He bit deeply, relaxed his already-powerful muscles for a moment, then bit again, and as his sharp cutting teeth became firmly fixed to the wood, he wrenched backwards and the piece of tree came away in his mouth.

Now he moved slightly and began again to cut a new notch and thus he progressed, cutting twin notches, biting at the wood in between and wrenching it free, until he had cut a circle around the trunk which was about an inch and a half deep, wider at the outside than it was inside. When the tree had been girdled he began biting more notches inside the new-cut wound and repeated his little wrenching movements, pulling out more and more tree-wood until the young trunk began to resemble two

A beaver has been at work here. This poplar was felled by a beaver who towed its tender, upper branches to his lodge area. Note the clean cuts left by the great chopping teeth.

pencils joined point to point. At last, with one final, giant heave, he removed a bigger mouthful of wood and the tree began to lean towards the clearing. The young beaver stopped and backed away from the tree and he watched its slow progress towards the ground. For a moment or two it seemed to hang suspended in the air, its downward progress arrested, then it moved again, faster. With a last rush it swooped and lay trembling upon the grass. The small male waddled happily to the tender top leaves and began to eat of them and presently he was joined by his sister and his mother and soon the tree was stripped of its leaves and small branches and the father beaver came and began peeling the bark off the trunk.

Suddenly the mother looked up and hissed and the father stopped chewing. The family paused, immobile, listening, then they turned as though at a signal and waddled as fast as their short legs would take them. The female had heard the coming of man. My coming, for I was walking slowly towards them trying to get in position to photograph them. Again I failed in this, but again I was privileged to see the family, only briefly, as it dived into the canal and I noted the growth change in the young ones since I had seen them last, two weeks earlier. Now, I said to myself, the youngsters will survive. They were well-grown and sturdy and fast approaching the time when they would be able to take care of themselves in the forest and the lake.

By that autumn, the first in the life of the young beaver, I could hardly tell them apart from the adults. They were smaller, of course, weighing then, I estimate, about twenty-five pounds, but seen alone, or swimming with their parents, they were difficult to separate. Only on land, when the difference in size was noticeable, could I recognize them. Now, of course, both those young things are mature and impossible to know, though occasionally, when I see the old fat fellow plodding about at the edge of the marsh, I like to think he is the youngster I watched grow. Certainly he is getting quite used to my presence around his domain and will even swim close to where I am standing on the bank to get a better look at me, but he is still cautious. If he is the one, when he is on land I have not yet been able to photograph him. Once, when Joan and I were out for a walk and we paused on a rock height that overlooks the northern end of the marsh, I could have got several photographs of him for he was swimming quietly in shallow water, occasionally having to walk over some log or rise of marsh bottom, but on that evening I had left my cameras in the cabin, so Joan and I watched him instead. After a time he left the water and disappeared among a veritable sea of catkins and, try as I might, I could not find him, even though I had field-glasses and searched the catkin forest with them. He simply disappeared, undoubtedly in some quiet patch where he very likely settled to an early snack.

Sometimes I stand and watch beaver as they swim under-water. Now and then I am rewarded by a glimpse of their sleek bodies as they rise closer to the surface, more often than not all that I can see of them are the air bubbles which they release once in a while or the riffle in the water caused by their passage. If I am patient enough and the bubbles are rising in clear water, I see them when they come up for fresh supplies of air, for come up they must, at ten or fifteen-minute intervals, to take a quick breath, if they are intent on further under-water exploring, or to stay on the surface if idly ambling through their kingdom.

One late afternoon in September three years ago I broached a small hole in their dam and waited for them to come and repair it. I had driven in, using the old logging trail that leads to the lake and since I happened to have my logging axe in the back of the car I got the idea of chopping a hole in the dam. It was an idle thought, one of the many that come to me when I am browsing through The Place, but if the axe had not been in the car the deed would not have been born. Beaver dams are well-knit, incredibly-tough feats of engineering, and to clear one out completely, dynamite is needed. Using only his hands a man would find it impossible to remove more than a few surface sticks. Even with an axe, the job is such that after a very small section has been cleared a human is glad to give up, as I was when I had chopped a hole into the lip of the dam that was about two feet wide by barely one foot deep. Still this was enough for my purposes. The water immediately rushed to this low spot and accelerated its run-off rate and, as I had hoped, this difference of flow was noted by the beavers.

I had been there about twenty minutes, concealed by some willow scrub near by, when I saw the first dark, shaggy head appear on the surface of the water some thirty yards from the dam. Cautiously a fat old male (to judge from his size) swam close to the break, paused about ten feet from it and then swam parallel to the dam, quite evidently inspecting it along its entire length. Satisfied that there was only one break in its walls he returned to the hole I had chopped and swam in close, almost touching the break with his nose. Then he scrambled out of the water and seemed to be inspecting the damage. Within two minutes he returned to the water, swam out a little way and submerged and was gone for eighteen minutes by my watch. When next I saw movement on the surface of the water there were five heads, the old fellow's in the lead and four more and three of these were smaller than the others. The father led his family to the break and they began to rebuild.

First old sticks were towed and thrust into the break, anchored there one by one as they were forced into the mud. Now and then one stick would break free and disappear over the rim, but another was pushed into its place until a trellis of peeled branches, some newly gnawed, others old and rotten, filled the gap I had chopped. Then mud was used, and plants the animals dug up from the bottom and some of these were washed away, too, but more were added, each animal returning to the hole carrying mud or plants in its two front paws, walking clumsily on their hind legs and dumping their load, patting it in place before going off for more. Stones, too, were fished up from the bottom and wedged in place and soon the water was slowed. Now the job was easier and, unless I imagined it, the pace relaxed a little and the father remained at the break, patting and pulling and pushing, while his helpers ferried supplies. It took that family barely half an hour (28 minutes, to be precise) to close the hole that had taken me and hour to make. Once it was done, the mother and the three youngsters slipped back into the water, while the father hung back a moment or two, as through admiring his handiwork, or perhaps just checking to see that the hole had been properly plugged.

When they were gone I stepped out and went to take a look. If I had not known exactly where I had made the hole I could not have found the place. Except for a profusion of tracks in the mud and some of the wood chips left by my axe, the repaired section of the dam was identical with the rest of the lip and I marvelled at the technique of these seemingly-clumsy creatures, at the skill that nature has given them, so that, in creating for themselves a place of refuge and a place in which to grow much of their food, these beavers of Canada also serve by holding back, storing, water that is needed by the wilderness during the hot, dry months of summer. Without the beaver many areas of Canada's wilderness would be barren places, a development discovered by the early fur trappers who wiped out beaver populations in some areas and found that when the dams crumbled and washed away, the forest died and the creatures that took shelter in it moved away, if they did not first perish also, and all that was left was a triangle of impassable terrain incapable of sustaining life. In later years some of these areas were reclaimed by patient men who restocked beaver during good, wet years. The beaver did the rest and today, thanks to the industry of these strange creatures, new life pulses again in those old barrens.

At times beaver flood farmlands and appear to be devastating the forest with their tree cutting and their dam building, but on the whole these creatures give far more to the land than they take from it. Of course, they cannot get along with people. In settled farm areas they must be kept down by trapping or, in severe cases, removed entirely from the area and, in this instance, government experts live-trap them and move them to another, wilder area, there to be released to continue benefiting the land that gave them life, for Canada and the beaver have gone hand in hand since the beginning of this continent and no other animal has done so much for the land. It was the beaver that brought civilization to this nation, for men came here lured by the creature's fur and the great, romantic days of the fur trade spawned the pathfinders, men like Pierre Espirit Radisson and his partner, Medard Chouart des Groseilliers, native Frenchmen who came to Canada in their youth and who, about 1860, made two expeditions to the west of Lake Superior (almost totally unknown at the time) and passed beyond to the rolling prairies and there saw the huge herds of bison. This they did, and more, because of fur, beaver fur, which led them on and on to areas never before trodden by the white man and on their heels came others like them, all thirsting for fur, and Canada, as a nation, began to take shape.

Romantic days, those, believed by many in this enormous land to be gone forever. But are they? Not really. This is a land that still offers room; room for the expansion of individual man, room for the expansion of the soul; room for exploration and discovery. There is romance here yet, lots of it, for those willing to come here and seek it. Imagine the vastness of this land of ours; a nation of eighteen million people with room for more than a hundred times that number, with vast areas that are still to be fully explored; great sections that are yet to feel the tread of man. Think about this; think also of The Place, a piece of forest within one hundred miles of a city that houses two million people, Toronto. Where else will you find such rich wilderness? Here on The Place, within two hours' drive of the

A muskrat lodge on the lake. These little houses are similar to those of the beaver, but much smaller; when winter freezes the mud that has been packed into them, the rats are secure in their fortresses.

'big city' lies an area untouched, hardly, by humanity; an area in which the wildlings know not the ways of man and, ignorant of these ways, trust him, so that they come to us, to Joan and me, expecting and receiving security, finding only at our hands understanding, so that their wild spirits commune with ours. Is this Eden before the apple? I know not, for the original paradise is a segment of ancient mythology. Yet, if I were to describe Eden of ancient times, I would describe The Place.

How can I explain this? Have I, in the preceding pages of this narrative, been successful in depicting life upon The Place? Do you believe that man in this century can find such complete fulfillment upon a virgin tract of land, find a oneness with the beasts and birds of Creation? There is trust here, for man has been accepted by the forest and by its creatures. At present I can ask for no more, yet I would spread my understanding of the wilderness, for it has brought me peace and pleasure, two commodities which are today in quite short supply.

THIRTEEN

SPRING WAS LATE ARRIVING when Coby and Konk chose to return to us one blustery, cold April night. I had fixed a platform feeder on the south window of the cabin and we were in bed, Joan asleep, I reading in gaslight, when movement at the window attracted my attention. Peering in at me was Konk, one glance at the white-tipped ears and the light face was enough to identify him. But he was a much bigger Konk than the little fellow who had gone scampering off into the autumn forest almost seven months before, and he was timid yet, for while his brain undoubtedly connected our cabin with faint echoes of food and safety, his wild instincts cautioned him against the presence of man. I woke Joan and we both watched our raccoon while he fished about amongst the seeds on the feeder, his fingers as busy as ever, his inquisitive eyes focused on every move we made.

I wondered if he would stay at the window if I got up to find him some titbits, but as soon as I rose from the bed he backed away, returning to ground by means of a step-ladder we had left outside the window. By the time I looked out he had disappeared under the house, so I put up some raisin bread (we remembered that he always had owned a sweet tooth) on the feeder and a few other food items and we waited. Presently he returned and accepted the offerings and it was then that it occurred to us to look for Coby. Again I got up and this time Konk just backed away from the glass while I shone my flashlight through the window and focused it on the feeder we have affixed to a pine outside the cabin door, the feeder in which both the young 'coons used to play before we released them. Sure enough, there was Coby, her own features as quickly recognized as Konk's, for she has darker markings, each with its own characteristic. Here again was a much larger raccoon, but still in all, 'our boys' as Joan still refers to them, had both returned home.

From that evening on, our renewal of friendship with our twins developed each weekend. Coby, we discovered, was pregnant, and less inclined to our company, though she invariably came for her food and, strangely enough, was much less nervous than Konk. She was not afraid of us, this much she made obvious; just cautious, and I remembered that she had been the fighter of the two, the more inclined to snarl when Alvin Adams found them and when I picked them up. She had changed little. Her brother, on the other hand, was still as curious and trustful as ever and, if more timid at first, he soon realized that far more attention could be his if he remained on the feeder when the window was opened. And he still owned his sweet tooth.

Coby's pregnancy did not surprise me. Female raccoons breed at ten months quite often, while the males require two years to reach breeding maturity. This, no doubt, is Creation's way of ensuring that the strain does not become weakened by in-breeding, for young raccoons of the same litter usually den together in winter time and if the males were able to breed as early as the females, brother and sister matings would result and probably harmful mutations would follow. This, at least, is how I reason it. At any rate, Coby came to us big with young and we knew that her babies were not engendered by Konk.

Four weekends after their return Konk was right back to his old form. He ignored meat and 'staples' in preference for grapes, dates, toffees, cake and raisin break (from which he carefully picked out the raisins) and began demanding his dues everytime he appeared at the window. And he still does. His habit is to turn up between nine and ten at night and stick his face against the glass. This is my cue. I must get up, find my basin of raccoon supplies and walk with it to the window. Konk backs away about two inches, shifting his position so that his nose is exactly level with the catch and there he waits until I open the window. The first time he accepted food from my hands he did it with caution, stretching his neck and head inside and being very particular, sniffing loudly and, finally, with great disdain, opening his mouth (and revealing a set of long, extremely sharp canines) and taking the cake from me. That was at nine o'clock one Saturday evening. He left with the cake, newly baked by Joan, and we did not see him again for two hours. At eleven he returned and when I opened the window in he came, walking quite casually on top of the sideboard which we have placed under the window. This time he was neither shy nor cautious, but catching sight and smell of the bowl of grapes and other good things I carried, made a lunge for me and grasped

Konk, almost full grown, on his return to us the spring after his release. At first shy after his winter of semi-hibernation, he soon remembered us and now he and Coby return nightly for food and a fuss.

my hand when I extended it with a bunch of grapes. Holding to my fingers with claws that had not lost one bit of their sharpness but which had gained in size and strength, he pulled the grapes off the bunch, one after the other, until all that was left was the little bundle of stalks. Then I gave him a piece of cake and he ate it and now those hand of this became busy feeling the palm of my hand, feeling, feeling, feeling, while his jaws were busy with the cake and he looked around the room, just like he used to do when he was a baby. Konk had come home again. He was our orphan returned, as friendly and trustful as before, and as gentle; a good-natured male raccoon who, I suspect, believe he is part human.

At about this time his sister had her litter somewhere in the bush. She missed coming to us for two weekends and when she returned she was lean and hungry and her dugs were dripping with milk. She had little time for frivolities and concentrated on the meat scraps we left for her, eating of the grapes that Joan put out, but obviously seeking the bones and meat, needing their nourishment now that she had become a mother. She has become quite accustomed to us and shows no fear, but I do not think she will ever be as intimate with us as Konk who, now that he has grown up, appears to have adopted us anew and actually seems to enjoy our society. Of course his interests are selfish to a point, but yet he takes time out for social pleasantries.

One weekend that spring we had a guest at the cabin, Gerald Nordheimer, an unofficial 'relative' of mine, and both Coby and Konk performed for his benefit Sunday morning. While Gerry was still in bed and Joan and I were just thinking of rising, we had a small visitor. Joan is always far more awake in the mornings than I am (though at sunset things began to happen to her eyelids) and she spotted our uninvited guest as he was shinning up the handle of the broom that occupies a corner beside the chimney.

"There's a mouse," said Joan in a stage-whisper.

"Mmmmm..." I replied, brightly, I thought.

"Wake up! There's a mouse!" repeated my wife, the while using her not inconsiderable strength to shake me.

"Yes, yes," I retorted. "I see it," though, of course I could not see it, but at that time of the morning who cares! Joan said that she saw a mouse; fine, I believed her, and I was quite willing to allow the entire affair to rest there.

"Well, *do* something!" Joan whispered again, rather more urgently.

So I did. I turned over and tried to get back to sleep, but this was not what she had intended and I was shaken again, with more vigour, and perforce I had to sit up and stare at the broom-handle and, of course, I could not see a mouse crawling up it, I said as much.

"Well, it's gone now. It went behind the chimney," whispered Joan, and then it occurred to me to ask her why she was whispering.

Well, it appeared that my wife did not wish our guest to know that we had a mouse in the cabin, though, for the life of me, I do not see why. I am quite sure Gerry would have reacted quite sanely to the news. However, Joan seemed to think we should keep the incident from him, so, for the sake of peace early in the morning, I agreed and promised to 'do something' about the mouse that evening. I must confess, though that my promise was quite vague and I spent little time formulating a campaign. I wanted my breakfast.

Gerry left early Sunday afternoon and Joan immediately reopened the subject of the mouse. I agreed with her that, fond as we are of the little 'critturs', we did not really want to leave this one in our cabin during the whole of the next week, for there were far too many mouse edibles in the cupboard; and it was at this point that I began to question Joan about our visitor. What kind of mouse was it? She did not know. What did it look like? Small. Well, this was not getting me very far, so I tried a new tack and eventually discovered from her description that she had seen a young white-footed mouse. This intelligence, coupled with colouring and size (eventually discovered when I held finger and thumb apart as far as they could go and asked: this big? each time I reduced the distance between my digits) informed me that our villain was a very young white-footed mouse, a little bit of a thing about one and a half inches long, dark blue-grey in colour which was certainly no more than three weeks old, this being the age at which mother mice eject their offspring so that they can rearrange the nursery for the next brood, started when their first babies were only about three days old. Thus I was dealing with a youngster seeking his way in the world for the first time and who, having found a neat hole drilled in the floor of our living-room, near the wall, by the man who came to install our gas lights, decided that our cabin would do nicely as a home.

Now the question was: what could I do about our unwanted guest? I do not own a conventional mouse trap and even if I did I would not use it on a white-foot. I pondered the problem and from some hidden recess in my mind a primitive live-trap evolved. I suppose I must have come across the idea somewhere, though I cannot remember where or when, but my mouse trap was quickly constructed. It consisted of a metal waste-container, oval in shape and about 14 inches deep, with smooth, mouse-proof sides; a piece of stiff wire cut from a clothes-hanger and a shiny-smooth shelf bracket, one that was flat.

The wire spanned the opening of the wastebasket situated at exact centre; the flat shelf bracket was in turn balanced carefully between the wire and the edge of the wastebasket; a piece of sausage was placed on the free end of the bracket. Now I had my trap, which, according to my theory, would work thus: lured by the delicious aroma of the sausage at the end of the bracket our small boarder would come out from behind the chimney (I had placed my trap close to the chimney ledge, raising the wastebasket with books). He would move out along the bracket and when his body weight passed beyond the centre of balance, bracket, sausage and mouse would tumble into the wastebasket.

That evening I set up my cunning device, but before we had turned out the lights Coby appeared on the feeding shelf. The window was open and so Joan and I lay on our cots and watched Coby, keeping quiet, so as not to disturb her. In the middle of it all my gaze was diverted to the chimney ledge and there I saw a pair of ears. Behind and under these ears was the diminutive mouse and he was aiming for the trap and the sausage. Now, as I have said, we were trying to keep quiet so as not to disturb Coby, but we wanted to watch the action at the trap, in semi-darkness, by reason that only one gas light, the one over my bed, was burning. Not wishing to lose a single detail of the drama that I felt sure was about to unfold, I aimed the beam of my flashlight at the mouse, trying to watch it while also keeping an eye on Coby, for at this point we had ringside seats in a sort of two-ring circus.

Friend mouse paused, one tiny white foot on the edge of the bracket while his ears, veritable giants on a body so small, flicked this way and that and his little pointed nose wrinkled as he sniffed sausage, his beady eyes taking in the sights of the cabin. The light did not bother him, neither did we, it seemed, and, at last, the lure of the bait was too much. Off the ledge he moved, on to the bracket, step by step walking my miniature plank and then, so it seemed, the cabin collapsed. There was an almighty crash as the bracket spanged into the bottom of the wastebasket and the wire fell to the floor and the mouse thumped against the tin. For split second silence followed the disturbance. Joan and I looked in unison at Coby, expecting to see her dashing away madly. Not a bit of it. With hardly a glance at the inside of the cabin, Coby continued munching on a piece of medium-rare sirloin steak, while the mouse, the whiles, was hopping up and down in the wastebasket, a little drummer using his own body to provide a strange percussion medley.

Still not wishing to disturb Coby I hesitated for a moment before going to retrieve my catch, but the mouse's frantic leaps made it necessary for me to move. I rose from the bed and was treated to a casual glance from Coby and when I reached the captive mouse it was crouched at the bottom of the trap, coiling its small muscles for another flying leap. I stayed this one and carried the wastebasket to my bed, the better to see my prisoner. Joan had to be coaxed a bit, but at last she craned her neck to look at Mouse. Yes, she reluctantly admitted, he was a nice little fellow.

"Now get rid of him!" she ordered.

This, however, was not quite so easy to do. These mice are nocturnal, but so are their enemies, the owls, and I just could not bring myself to set that orphan adrift in the black of night in a huge, unknown world. Besides, almost before Joan's command ended, my hand was in the wastebasket and I was scratching the little thing behind one of his big ears and he was enjoying it. I held the sausage to his nose next and he dined, so I thought he might be thirsty and I found a bottle cap and poured some milk into it and offered it to Mouse and he drank and then began to wash his face, preening his long whiskers and reaching to the back of his head and his tiny paws, bringing them forward again, right over his giant ears.

"You don't really want me to set this poor little chap adrift tonight, do you?" I asked Joan accusingly.

Reluctantly she agreed that this might not be quite right and I found some seed and put it in with the mouse and I carried him and container into the living-room and covered the container so that Mouse could not leap out. I really wanted to keep Mouse, but I decided not to make any hasty decisions until morning, so assuring Joan that our captive would be fine until daylight and since Coby had by then gone to her babies, I closed the window and put out the light and we settled down for some sleep. Mouse had other ideas. That little chap could certainly leap! You who are reading this may not have heard a baby mouse leaping through the night inside a metal container, but let me assure you that the combination of mouse, jump and metal can be quite distracting when the performance is taking place twelve feet away from your bed.

Morning came at last, though, and I inspected Mouse. He had eaten all the sausage and drunk all the milk and had made good headway with the seeds, so I judged him ready for the next stage of his adventures, for I had decided to release him. Accordingly I carried the wastebasket outside and along the path to our outhouse, that eight-by-eight building that does duty as a serviceable outdoor convenience and maternity ward for most of the white-footed mice on The Place. In one corner of the building, cunningly concealed from Joan, I knew of a nest that had but recently been vacated. Dipping into the wastebasket I produced Mouse, quite docile and evidently full, and I lowered him gently to the nest (made of kapok from my nice new yellow lifejacket that was), releasing him two inches from it. In a twinkling Mouse took possession. Making sure that he was comfortable and leaving him a supply of seed, I closed the outhouse door and went to breakfast.

The night's adventure had been just one of the many minor incidents that occur on The Place. It had been paralleled three weeks earlier by a more pungent affair, the leading figure in which had been friend Konk. This time it was Saturday night and Aut Adams (short for Austin) had paid us a visit. We sat in the living-room chatting about the wilderness, for Aut is, I am sure, second-cousin to one of the early Canadian *voyageurs,* and drinking coffee when our guest sniffed lustily and said:

"Skunk!"

Of course he was quite right. The strong aroma of skunk was invading the cabin through the closed door and windows and it was getting stronger by the instant. Hastily I rose and closed the inner door, a solid wood affair, and that helped in slight measure to keep the stink outside, but still and all the cabin became quite close with the stench. Under such circumstances it does no good to open doors or windows, for the outside smells even worse than the inside and about all that can be done is to pretend the smell is not there, and for this, man requires a great imagination.

Aut had been almost ready to leave when the smell came and then I would not let him go, for it meant opening a door. So he stayed and we chatted a while longer and the smell dwindled slightly and we speculated on the origin of the stench. Of course, we all knew *where* the smell came from, but we wondered why. Josephine was a mild-mannered lady and she had not hitherto offended us. Could it be, we wondered, that she had tangled with either Coby or Konk? This seemed a reasonable explanation, for raccoons do not appear greatly bothered by skunk oil. There we let the matter rest, for Aut had to leave. Outside the air was heavy with skunk, but still breathable as our guest drove away, lights on bright, his horn honking a warning to Josephine to stay clear.

Joan and I prepared for bed. It was past ten o'clock and it seemed that our raccoons were not coming early that night and since we were both tired I doused the lights and in no time at all we were asleep. But not for long. I was jolted out of a sound sleep by the thick, cloying stench of skunk. It was so heavy in the cabin that for a moment I thought a skunk had got in and discharged its evil shot. But moments later my flashlight showed the figure of Konk busy eating on the shelf. There was the culprit. Our guess had been right, for he had obviously fallen out with a skunk and had been well and truly sprayed. He stank so badly that the fetor of him wafted into the cabin through the closed window just as though no barrier stood between us.

Well, there was nothing to be done. We would not chase Konk away, so our alternative was endurance. Endure it we did and by about four o'clock the next morning, when I finally went to sleep, I believe I had grown quite fond of skunk smell and Joan, who can sleep through anything, hardly felt its effects at all. As for Konk, he appeared entirely impervious to the odour; certainly his appetite was not affected, though his sister kept him at arm's length (she had not had her babies then) and was careful to come to the feeders when he was nowhere to be seen, for which I do not blame her. That smell was still in the cabin next morning and outside we could quickly detect every spot at which Konk had stopped.

Shortly after the return of our orphans some of our hares returned also. Casually the first one hopped up, pausing at my feet to inspect me and continuing a little later to the feeding area, there to nibble seed. The next day two hares came, one a veritable giant, a buck I had filmed several weeks earlier, while he was courting, and that same afternoon a small doe with a raw patch on her rump padded over from the workshop I had recently completed north of the cabin.

In the meantime our first red squirrel babies of the year began to show up. Little sleek chaps, still wobbly in the trees, they showed no fear of us and quickly learned the meaning of a peanut in its shell. These were the early broods, and more were to follow as the females weaned their infants and turned them out to fend for themselves. Our black squirrels, the 'giants' of the species, had become quite tame by that spring and two of them, both females, have developed the habit of begging. One at a time they climb on to the window feeder and, if we are in the bedroom-cum-kitchen part of the cabin, peer at us; if we are in the living-room they stretch far out, staring at us through the glass door.

We feel that we have accomplished much by getting these black squirrels to accept us for, unlike their kind in the cities, they are amongst the most timid creatures of the wilderness and many of them can be in an area without man ever discovering their presence. Ours now congregate around the cabin and though not all are as tame as the two sows, still they come to us and at times there will be eight or ten of them prancing around the feeders. Visitors to The Place, accustomed to seeing the undersized city blacks, often marvel at the size and sleekness of these big fellows in our woods, though the reason for their size and condition is not difficult to see. In the city the squirrels live on garbage and whatever natural food is available; they interbreed, weakening the strain, and are subject to the attacks of bacteria and parasitic growths. Their bushland kindred are, of course, also subject to these things, but because they find plenty of natural food and do not interbreed as freely, the race is stronger. Added to this, the squirrels on The Place spice their natural diet with plentiful amounts of mixed seeds which we put out for them and the birds (and for the raccoons, flying squirrels, mice, hares, shrews, etc.) As a result, our squirrels are a healthy, handsome lot.

Now it is again summer on The Place and Joan and I are watching the forest blossom. The wild flowers are showing; the trilliums, those beautifully-simple white bells surrounded by their broad green leaves, have come and are already fading, a few of their kind, purplish, these, the 'painted' variety, still lingering under the shade of hemlock and pine. The wild irises are blooming on the marshland around the lake, and the violets are turning purple-blue on the grass down by the road. Daisies, a profusion of them, are budding, and the strawberry blooms, white little flowers hugging the ground, are dropping slowly, leaving tiny snow-like petals on the ground. Here and there a cluster of brilliantly-red wintergreen berries splash vividness under some bush or tree. Blushing in small clearings wild roses draw the bees to their hearts while in the wet places the golden marigolds shine under the sun's light.

This is the soft time of the year, the birthing time for many birds and animals, the hunting time of the dragonfly and the buzzing time of the flies and mosquitoes. The days are long and the skies blue planes dusted with the white of small cumulous clouds that scud away from atmospheric winds; the blueberries are turning, ripening, drawing to themselves the birds and insects and animals. North of our cabin the bears rise early and breakfast in some thick patch of berries; the cubs becoming purple-lipped, like human children, as they strip the ripe fruit off the stems.

Bird calls fill the air. The wood thrush bursts his magic voice upon us; the warblers trill from the shelter of a shivering poplar tree. Down in the ravine, in her nest in the aspen, the red-shouldered hawk is sitting on three eggs. I climbed the big pine that overlooks her home recently and she rose and flapped overhead, flinging her piercing, whistled challenge and threatening, but never actually harming my person; *kee-yer, kee-yer,* her call brought her mate while trying to bluff me down. I climbed higher and now I was seventy feet from the ground. Below me the narrow forest landscape became distorted, bushes became flat green shapes without perspective, rocks mere shadows. In the hawk's nest I could just see the oval outlines of the three eggs. I climbed down for I did not want to disturb the hawks further and the female immediately returned to her clutch.

Down by the road, between two rock ridges and surrounded on the west by hemlocks and on the right by pines, there is a hollow place of grass and small bushes and a few rocks. This is the family home of a tribe of woodchucks, fat fellows: a mother and her five young ones, grown now and almost her size. They are accustomed to me and I watch them play in the small natural meadow. Suddenly the gliding shadow of the male hawk darkens the grass and piercing warning whistles come from the throats of the 'chucks; in a moment they are all gone, down into their burrow, from there to watch, peeping shyly over the earthen lip, waiting for the hawk to leave.

Canada's great geese on the lake on The Place. These sturdy, beautiful birds are strong fliers, mate for life and have a complex social system.

On the old piece of road that curves inside my fence line I find the body of a weasel. The hawk has done this thing. One front leg has been torn off, there is a hole in the small killer's rib casing. He is already beginning to swell as the enzymes of death perform the chemical breakdown of his tissues. He will be gone by tonight, for her the vultures fly, and one of these great birds will see, or smell, that small decomposing body and the black bird will drop on slow wings, hop twice towards the weasel, pause, red head turning from side to side, checking for danger and then the big blunt beak will dip into the softness of rotting flesh. Quickly the weasel's carcass will disappear and the ants and other insects will come to finish the feast and by the first light of another day there will be no trace of the little killer that was himself destroyed.

χ

Evening has come and I am again down by the road, standing between a young balsam and an ageing silver birch. At my feet there is a mound of earth. A few strands of grass grow on it, a few shoots of newness are forcing their way out of the brown earth. Under the earth lies an old bitch dog, Kim, a fat, gentle duchess who came to us for a short time, won us and then was content to die. Death found her one day last spring in the garden of our city house. We put her in the car and brought her here that same night, to be buried in the land of The Place, for she had come to love this wilderness of ours during the short, short time that it was hers.

Kim belonged to a colleague of mine who was posted to England and was forced to leave her in Canada. She was too old for the quarantine of Britain, she would have died amongst strangers. So we took her and she quickly stole our affection and she quickly became another member of our growing family. She came to us in September and she learned quickly about The Place and would wait for Fridays, eager for the trip in the car and for her weekend romp in our wilderness. She was fat, as I have said, and old, and she was sick, but she was our kind of dog. She did not disturb the animals and birds, she was always obedient, patient; a great lady, that golden retriever that we inherited from the Poultons. It was natural that when she died we should want her body to come here to The Place. Now her mounded grave is a reminder of her friendship and her feeble old body has gone to put new life into our wilderness. She will live on now, in the grass, and in the soil and in the balsam and the silver birch, the matter of her being softness, lightly dusting the mind upon an evening like this.

This is my wilderness, mine and Joan's, yet we belong to it. Beside me Joan is asleep. On the window feeder Konk is eating, now and then pausing to look in, wondering if I am going to get up and offer him some new titbit. Outside the night is full; a great horned owl is calling, his voice a hoarse whisper inside the cabin, a warning in the ears of the raccoon, who stops to listen now and then, to make sure that no danger threatens.

I am propped up in bed, a pad of copy paper resting upon a board which is across my knees, the light of gas a soft yellow accompanied by the hiss of oxygen as air mixes and burns with the compressed propane. Outside the temperature has fallen to 50 degrees, a drop of almost 35 points on the thermometer, for evenings are cool here. But there is warmth in the cabin and I am content as I scribble, ending this narrative, and as I write I recall our coming here, when we were aliens in the wilderness, strangers in this quiet, fascinating wild which surrounds us. Why are we here? I wonder again what has caused us to leave the civilized comforts of a city house for the stern appointments of this backwoods cabin.

Outside the darkness. It has form and substance and I can see it, and feel it and smell it, for the dark of night carries its own aroma. Soon, I will leave my bed, put aside my writing things and go out into this friendly night, for this is my habit before seeking sleep here. I go to share the night with the hunting timber wolf, with the hoarse owls, and with Konk, and the flying squirrels, those swiftly-moving wraiths of the night who will come to me to take a peanut or two from my fingers. I take a last look at the pines and the poplars and balsams, for each species moves in its own way as the wind plucks different chords from each.

Standing quietly in the darkness of The Place the fireflies will wink their semaphore language and the whip-poor-wills will chant their dirge and I will find myself just a little nearer to the forces of Creation and my mind will become busy with new thoughts. Or perhaps I will plan a trip for the morning, possibly a visit to the lake, or a tramp through the forest, due north, towards the range of the deer and the bear and the wolf and I will wonder about the things that I shall see, the small things, perhaps a worm, or an insect, or a tiny plant, or a seed; and the big things, a giant pine, a mass of prehistoric granite that has been squatting unmoving for countless generations; and if my feet tread on pathways that are familiar to them, yet my eyes will look upon new things at every turn of the trail, for always the wilderness provides newness, reveals only a little each time to the questing eyes of man.

Again tonight I will walk upon dewed grass and hear the wild voices of the forest and the stealthy movements of things living but unseen and a taste of fear will come, for fear is the inheritance of all, and the unknown still has power over the mind. But now my fear is small and lasts but an instant, a brief moment when buried, ancient instincts rise again prompted by the wilderness night. Then I will walk, east, for this is my favourite route at this time, and I will cross the small clearing, past the rock fireplace where I heard the mouse sing and I will follow the game trail through an avenue of pines to the back clearing. Then I will return to the cabin and to Joan and I shall sleep, for this narrative is finished. Yet this is not The End; it is only the beginning...

The Place,
Uphill, Ontario,
Canada.
July, 1966.

Index